The Jerilderie Letter Part Two: Australia's Corrupt Prime Ministers

Shane Dowling

Self-Published

A book written in the Public Interest

The Jerilderie Letter Part Two: Australia's Corrupt Prime Ministers

ISBN 978-0-6488909-1-1

Self-Published – Shane Dowling - Australia
Email: shanedowling@outlook.com.au

Website: www.kangaroocourtofaustralia.com
Facebook: www.facebook.com/kangaroocourtofaustralia
Twitter: https://twitter.com/Kangaroo_Court
YouTube: www.youtube.com/c/KangarooCourtofAustralia

Send snail mail to: Po Box 1280 Coolangatta Qld 4225 Australia

NATIONAL LIBRARY OF AUSTRALIA

A catalogue record for this work is available from the National Library of Australia

Pictures on the front cover supplied by APP Images

Picture of Ned Kelly on the back cover from the State Library of Victoria: Photographer: Nettleton, C. (1900). Ned Kelly the day before he was hanged 1880.

Contents

Preface

This is my third non-fiction book about government corruption with the first being "Love Letters from the Bar Table" published in August 2009 and the second book being "Australia's Paedophile Protection Racket" published in September 2020.

I came up with the sub-title of this book "The Jerilderie Letter Part Two" a few years ago when I was thinking of a title for a book covering government corruption. I only recently settled on writing specifically about corrupt Prime Ministers.

The title comes from the famous letter, The Jerilderie Letter, written by Australian Bushranger Ned Kelly to government officials in which Kelly complains of government corruption.

The State Library of Victoria website says:

It would be easy to assume that the Kelly Gang members were tough, ignorant, uneducated men who mindlessly pursued a career in crime. But both Ned Kelly and Joe Byrne could read and write, and wrote letters to the press and others, explaining their situation and calling for justice. The most famous of these is the 'Jerilderie Letter'.

Written in 1879, the 8000-word long letter details Kelly's thoughts about being 'forced' into becoming an outlaw. It also calls for the resignation of a corrupt police force that, Kelly maintained, preyed upon Irish Catholic settlers.

To me The Jerilderie Letter is the most famous correspondence of someone complaining of government corruption in Australia. Whether Kelly was right about his complaints I do not know but if he was, little has changed since 1879.

It is also a letter where Ned Kelly didn't hold back dropping the boot into the government and its employees which is similar to how I write on my website and in my books.

When I came up with the sub-title, I wasn't a fugitive but now I am with an arrest warrant issued, in September 2021 in the NSW Supreme Court, for my arrest for what is in effect the crime of journalism. But that's another story.

As I wrote in the preface of my last book:

I started publishing the judicial corruption website Kangaroo Court of Australia in January 2011 which I was motivated to do after a failed unlawful termination case that lasted 3 years against Fairfax Media where I had worked in sales. I documented the Fairfax case in a book published in 2009 titled "Love Letters from the Bar Table".

The aim of the website was, and still is, to focus on dodgy judicial appointments, judicial bribery and the fact that Australian judges are unaccountable when it comes to corruption. While other media write about these issues from time to time, I thought it needed to be collated in one place as only then would the gravity of the problem be obvious to the public. I believe I have achieved that goal to some degree but there is a lot more work to be done.

In this book, I have reprinted numerous articles that I have published on the Kangaroo Court of Australia website over the last 11 years in relation to the former and current Prime Ministers. In those articles, there are numerous links which either show up underlined or say (Click here to read more) which I have left exactly as it is in the articles.

I have done that so you know if want more information or you want to watch the videos etc you can go to the Kangaroo Court of Australia website and find the article and click on the links and watch the video etc. To get the most out of the book you should use it in conjunction with the KCA website.

Because of a lack of financial resources, I have not had the book professionally edited. What I have done is put it through a grammar checker twice and proofread the book twice and some parts more than twice. Other parts where I have quoted have stayed as per the original article.

Becoming a fugitive on the run

I lived in Sydney from 2000 until November 2019 when I moved back to Queensland after the continual harassment by NSW judges who made it clear I will not receive justice in NSW courts and also after the Supreme Court sent NSW police to harass me again in May 2019.

I figured between Kerry Stokes, Seven West Media, the NSW Supreme Court judges and the NSW police someone was going to stitch me up for jail again in the near future, so it was time to move. The details are in the first few chapters of my second book "Australia's Paedophile Protection Racket" published in September 2020.

As you will see in the book politicians and their supporters spend a lot of time trying to control, influence and at times silence the media and they have tried to silence me and my articles many times.

Introduction

The Book

Australia is meant to be a democracy but anyone who follows politics closely knows that Australia's democracy has been hijacked by corrupt political parties. And it is the leaders of those parties that this book focuses on.

You don't have to go past the Prime Ministers to know Australia has major problems with $billions being openly funnelled out of the government's funds into the hands of the rich, powerful and people with political connections.

A lot of the content in this book you won't read anywhere else as the old media companies have a financial and political interest not to dig too deep into political corruption when it suits them.

One of the only the positives about the current Prime Minister Scott Morrison is that he doesn't try hard to hide the corruption, fraud and theft so it has become blatantly clear to many more voters how corrupt Australian politics really is.

Because the book publishes the articles from my website, Kangaroo Court of Australia, which started publishing from January 2011 the book covers the Prime Ministers since then.

The first Prime Minister I started writing about in 2011 was Julia Gillard but I start the book off with Kevin Rudd because he was Prime Minister before Julia Gillard as well as after Julia Gillard.

Kangaroo Court of Australia website is born

Because the book publishes articles from my website and readers should use the book in conjunction with the website to get the most value below is a quick overview of the website.

I set up the Kangaroo Court of Australia website at the end of 2010 and published my first article in January 2011. I set it up because I'd had a long-running unfair dismissal case against Fairfax Media which, with the help of corrupt judges, had abused the legal and court system with no media writing about it. So, I decided to become the media myself, something which anyone can do nowadays to fill the void by publishing a website focused on judicial corruption.

I also published my first book "Love Letters from the Bar Table" in 2009 about my battle with Fairfax Media.

The Prime Ministers

Kevin Rudd - 26th Prime Minister of Australia

3 December 2007 – 24 June 2010 and

27 June 2013 – 18 September 2013

Julia Gillard - 27th Prime Minister of Australia

24 June 2010 – 27 June 2013

Tony Abbott - 28th Prime Minister of Australia

18 September 2013 – 15 September 2015

Malcolm Turnbull - 29th Prime Minister of Australia

15 September 2015 – 24 August 2018

Scott Morrison - 30th Prime Minister of Australia

Incumbent - Assumed office 24 August 2018

Chapter 1

Kevin Rudd, Therese Rein and their company Ingeus Ltd. The Obeids of the federal government.

This is the first article I wrote about how Kevin Rudd and his wife Therese Rein became so rich.

Kevin Rudd, Therese Rein and their company Ingeus Ltd. The Obeids of the federal government.

BY SHANE DOWLING ON AUGUST 4, 2013 • (59 COMMENTS)

Australian Prime Minister Kevin Rudd's wife, Therese Rein, is estimated to be worth over $200 million via her company Ingeus Limited which she started in 1989 with Labor Party government contracts.

The evidence suggests that it was no rags-to-riches fairy tale and that Kevin Rudd had a huge hand in backroom government deals to help their company get rolling. As we know if it's seems too good to be true then it probably is and some of the evidence leaves one very disturbed.

Introduction

It says on Wikipedia: *"Rudd joined the Department of Foreign Affairs in 1981, serving there until 1988. He and his wife spent most of the 1980s overseas at various Australian embassies, including in Stockholm and in Beijing."*

"Returning to Australia in 1988, he was appointed Chief of Staff to the Opposition Leader in Queensland, Wayne Goss. He remained in that role when Goss was elected Premier in 1989, a position he held until 1992 when Goss appointed him Director-General of the Office of Cabinet." (Click here to read more)

What does Ingeus do? This is what it says on their website:

"The Ingeus group evolved from a small rehabilitation company that commenced operations in Australia in 1989."

"Work Directions Australia quickly established a reputation for inspiring people who were cut off from work due to disability, illness or injury, by assisting them to address the physical and psychological aspects of their condition and helping them back to work."

"In the 1990s, this expertise was adapted to provide individually tailored and enabling services to assist people who were on unemployment benefits back into work. Services were subsequently expanded to include nationally accredited training, labour hire and recruitment services."

"In 2002, we re-branded as Ingeus and took our unique approach to assisting those people most isolated from the labour market to the United Kingdom."

In 2007 the Australian business was sold off as it was seen as a conflict of interest for Kevin Rudd.

It is now operating in numerous countries and *"In 2011, we re-entered Australia with the acquisition of Assure Programs, a business psychology organisation specialising in organisational development and employee assistance programs throughout*

Australia and New Zealand." (Click here to read more on their site)

Background: Historical timeline of Therese Rein's company now known as Ingeus Limited and relevant political events. (Click here for the abstract of the company details)

1989 – 21st June – Lake Metcalfe Pty Ltd registered. I assume by Therese Rein – ACN: 010948731 – 4 directors – Therese Rein, Frances Edwards, Julie Graham and Rodney Graham. Registered office is 145 Flockton St Everton Park which is the home address of Julie and Rodney Graham

1989 – 20th July – Julie and Rodney Graham cease to be directors and the registered office changes the day before on the 19th July to 549 Stanley St South Brisbane. They were directors for only one month, so what happened? Maybe they decided they did not want their names on any of the paperwork.

1989 – 31st July – Registers business name Work Directions Australia – BN3745685 – I assume uses this as the trading name.

1989 – 2nd August – Company name changed from Lake Metcalfe Pty Ltd to Therese Rein & Associates Pty Ltd. Lake Metcalfe Pty Ltd lasted just over one month, why is that?

August 1989 – Government report published titled "The Workers' Compensation Board of Queensland report on future rehabilitation services throughout Queensland" for the then Minister for Employment, Training and Industrial Affairs, Vince Lester. I cannot get a copy of the report, but one assumes that it recommends the outsourcing of rehabilitation services. I make this assumption given the 1990 Act that follows. It is listed on the National Library of Australia Trove website which gives the August publication date. (Click here to see) I wonder when Kevin Rudd had a copy.

1989 – 2nd December – The Labor Party win government in Queensland in a landslide with Wayne Goss as Premier and

Kevin Rudd as his Chief of Staff. It was obvious to all that they would win government as the Fitzgerald Enquiry report was submitted on 3 July 1989. *"Based on the inquiry's final report, a number of high-profile politicians were charged with crimes; notably Queensland Police Commissioner (Sir) Terry Lewis was charged with corruption."* I think the Fitzgerald Enquiry report is important to the degree that the then National/Liberal state government were basically finished and Kevin Rudd knew he would have power after the election to help his wife's business.

1990 – The Queensland government legislate the Workers Compensation Act 1990 which has provisions for the outsourcing of the rehabilitation of injured workers to companies such as Therese Rein's. What month in 1990 I do not know, but one would suspect Therese Rein and Kevin Rudd would have been very keen for it to pass through parliament and legislated as it meant big dollars for them and their business. What was Mr Rudd's involvement in having the Act legislated? Did Mr Rudd tell his boss Wayne Goss he had a conflict of interest? (Click here to read the Act) The key relevant part of the Act is section 152 which says:

Board's liability for cost

152. If a rehabilitation program is accepted by the general manager as necessary for a worker in respect of whose injury the board has accepted a liability under this Act, the board is to pay such cost of the program as the general manager accepts to be reasonable, having regard to the injury, in addition to compensation under this Act otherwise payable.

Bingo. Therese Rein is up and running with her company and Kevin Rudd is in a position to influence who gets the business/contracts. Would Kevin Rudd and Therese Rein do something like that? We will have a look at some of the things that they have done later in the post.

Is this the Smoking Gun?

Interview with The Australian 15th March 2013:

"In 1989, the then 30-year-old mother of two resigned from her job over a difference of opinion about the way the business was being run. She talked to Jane Edwards, a physiotherapist and former Catholic nun who had a practice in the same building. "She asked me if I had ever thought of starting my own company," Rein recalls. "She said: 'Southeast Queensland needs a high-quality, ethical, rehabilitation provider and I think you could do that. And if you were prepared to do it, I would be prepared to invest in it.'" A stunned Rein returned to her office and took out some paper."

"I landscaped it," she says, taking paper and a blue pen and redrawing the diagram she did more than two decades ago. "I went: OK, if you have a psychologist and an occupational therapist with access to a physiotherapist, what are the services that each of them can provide and what services can they provide together? Who would benefit from those services and who would pay for them?"

"Rein scribbles furiously, recreating the conceptual map (or "meme", as she calls it), with three people in the middle and lots of squiggly lines stretching out to thought bubbles. The most likely client, she decided, would be the Workers' Compensation Board of Queensland, but she could envisage other clients down the track." (Click here to read more)

"The most likely client, she decided, would be the Workers' Compensation Board of Queensland" How did she know they would be looking to outsource the rehabilitation of injured employees when she registered her company in June 1989? Kevin Rudd would have known as "The Workers' Compensation Board of Queensland report on future rehabilitation services throughout Queensland" report was published less than two months later in August 1989 and he quite possibly had a draft copy at the time Therese Rein registered the company. At the very least Mr Rudd would have known what was coming in the report as he was Chief of Staff to Wayne Goss and it was his job to know these things. Are we to believe he never discussed it with his wife when she says she decided to set up the business? And what about the Workers Compensation Act 1990, did he discuss that with his wife? Of course he did.

Goss Government Contracts?

What contracts Therese Rein did or didn't get from the Goss Labor government is unknown. But the above quote *"The most likely client, she decided, would be the Workers' Compensation Board of Queensland"* seems to suggest that she did win contracts. Did she declare that Kevin Rudd was her husband when she tendered for business? Did she have to tender or were contracts given to her?

An article on crikey.com on the 8th July 2013 says; *"Therese Rein's significant wealth comes from her multinational business Ingeus, which she founded with her late business partner Frances Jane Edwards in 1989 (it was then known as WorkDirections Australia). The company's main business was helping those with injuries or disabilities enter or re-enter the workforce — a business built on Rein's earlier career as a psychologist counselling injured workers."*

"It was a good time to kick off — governments were outsourcing programs to private providers. Rein won her first government contract from the Hawke government and went on to execute major contracts for the Howard government's Job Network agency." (Click here to read more)

If that is correct and Therese Rein won her first government contract from the Hawke Labor government then that is not much better as we have a Labor girl getting business from a Labor government.

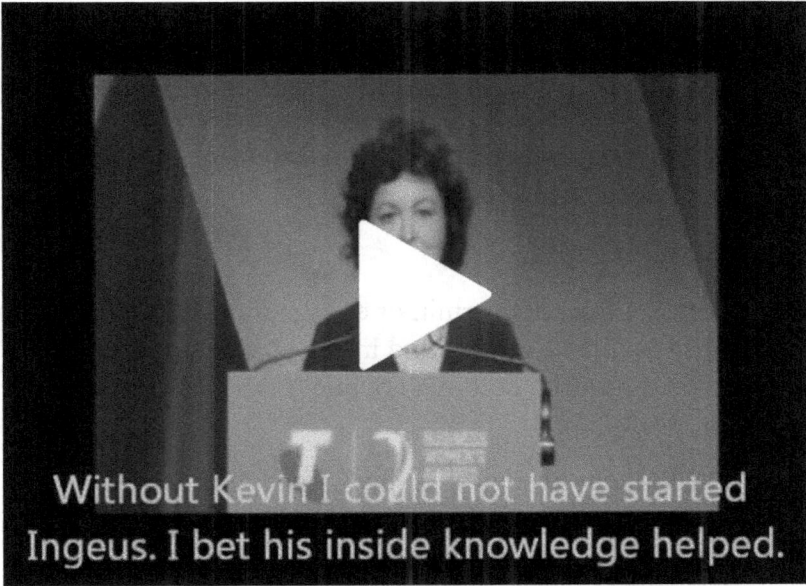

Without Kevin I could not have started Ingeus. I bet his inside knowledge helped.

(Click anywhere on the above video to watch)

The key thing that I find odd in the video is when Therese Rein says that the Commonwealth Bank lent her money to buy shares in the company that she started. If she owned the company then why is she buying shares in it? Were there hidden shareholders such as Julie Graham and Rodney Graham?

Kevin Rudd and Therese Rein's form guide

Ingeus Limited expanded to the UK in 2002. In 2011 in partnership with the accounting firm Deloitte it won a massive contract with the David Cameron led UK Government valued at $1.4 Billion in controversial circumstances.

"David Cameron has been accused of cronyism after a City firm which bankrolled the Tories was handed contracts worth £773.5million."

"Deloitte won the deals as part of the Government's work programme. The firm has given the party £700,000 since Mr Cameron became leader in 2005 including a £28,000 donation in kind to Welfare Minister Chris Grayling."

"It has a 50% stake in Ingeus Deloitte, which will pocket the £773.5million if it meets targets on cutting jobless figures." (Click here to read more)

Ingeus is clearly in breach of their own statement of ethics. It says on the Ingeus website:

Statement of Ethics

Ingeus does not tolerate, permit, or engage in bribery, corruption, or improper payments of any kind in our business dealings, anywhere in the world, both with public officials and people in the private sector.

- We will not give or offer any money, gift, hospitality or other advantages to any foreign public official with the intention of influencing them to our business advantage.

- We will not use intermediaries or contractors for the purpose of committing acts of bribery. (Click here to read more) But Therese Rein will go into partnership with them.

Ingeus has hit a few hurdles with their business in the UK lately as it failed to deliver on promises and there are some questions about the level of taxes it pays.

Wayne Goss, Ingeus and Deloitte

It is worth noting that Kevin Rudd's former boss Wayne Goss was a director of Ingeus from 2003 until 2007. Was it payback for helping the company get started? Mr Goss was also Chairman of the Australian firm of Deloitte Touche Tohmatsu (commonly known as Deloitte) for 8 years until his retirement in May 2013. Did Mr Goss help and/or benefit from the partnership between Therese Rein and Deloitte?

During Kevin Rudd's last tenure as Prime Minister he had a long history of looking after Labor Party boys and girls. So would he look after his wife's company which in reality is his as well. Of course he would.

There is no doubt that Therese Rein went on to grow the business way beyond anything Kevin Rudd did to help and she did win business from the Liberal Howard government. But that is quite often the case. People rip off others then make money in legitimate businesses like the Mafia do. Just ask the former NSW politician Eddie Obeid who was a master of using government inside information to make a fortune and he was not the first.

If the wife of the Chief of Staff of any Premier or Prime Minister was to set up a business and win government contracts today there would be a call for a Royal Commission and rightly so. Unfortunately, it is so far back the document trail is hard to find but I will keep on the job and see what I can find. In saying that the above alone raises many questions that could and should be answered by Kevin Rudd as he is the Prime Minister of Australia and the public have a right to know.

Chapter 2

Kevin Rudd, Therese Rein and Ingeus. How did they really make the $210 Million?

I jumped on a plane from Sydney to Brisbane to investigate further and published the below follow-up article.

Kevin Rudd, Therese Rein and Ingeus. How did they really make the $210 Million?

BY SHANE DOWLING ON AUGUST 11, 2013 • (14 COMMENTS)

Kevin Rudd's wife Therese Rein started and built their $210 million company Ingeus (then known as Work Directions) on the back of government business in 1989. Therese Rein herself has stated her initial targeted customer when she set up the company was a Queensland government department.

Kevin Rudd, as Chief of Staff to the then Premier Wayne Goss, was in a position to influence the government to give Work Directions government business. Did he do that? As you will see in the video interview in this post a witness has come forward.

This is important because if the same situation arose today the Chief of Staff would be sacked and there would be at the very least a police investigation. Why no one has investigated at all to date is very disturbing and a failure of democracy given Kevin Rudd is the Prime Minister of Australia.

I went to Brisbane on Saturday the 10th of August and interviewed Des O'Neill who is a former Executive Member of the State Public Services Federation in Queensland. He was able to shed further light on how Kevin Rudd, Therese Rein and their company Ingeus (then known as Work Directions) was able to get its start to mega riches which now stands at an estimated $210 million.

Background to the video

This is a follow-up post to the last post which is more detailed and worth reading as it ties into the content of the video. (Click here to read the post) Broadly though, Therese Rein set up business helping injured workers with rehabilitation in July/August 1989 when Kevin Rudd was then the Chief of Staff to the Queensland Opposition Leader Wayne Goss.

A few months later on the 2nd December 1989 the Labor Party won the election and then Kevin Rudd was Chief of Staff to Queensland Premier Wayne Goss. In 1990 the Queensland government legislated the Workers Compensation Act 1990 which has provisions for the outsourcing of the rehabilitation of injured workers to companies such as Therese Rein's.

The question is if Kevin Rudd used his power and position to help Work Directions get business from the state government and if so to what degree?

The below video interview was filmed outside Kevin Rudd's electoral office in Brisbane. It is direct and to the point and goes for 2 1/2 minutes.

Kevin Rudd, Therese Rein and Ingeus. H...

Watch later   Share

Watch on ▶ YouTube

(Click anywhere on the video to watch)

I will continue to follow-up with this and have more leads. Hopefully others will start to come forward as well. When investigating something like this, which is going back over 20 years, it is a piece by piece game. But if I keep at it and with the help of others I am sure the true story will come out. And thank you to Des O'Neill for coming forward.

The main purpose of going to Brisbane was to interview Des O'Neill but I also recorded two other videos which are on the new KCA 2013 Federal Election page which is in the second menu bar above or click here to go to the page. Both are short and worth a watch.

Chapter 3

Kevin Rudd and Therese Rein made millions from their contract with a Nun

Kevin Rudd and Therese Rein made millions from their contract with a Nun

BY SHANE DOWLING ON SEPTEMBER 4, 2013 • (34 COMMENTS)

Therese Rein instituted Queensland Supreme Court proceedings to legally enforce a contract with the estate of deceased nun Frances Jane Edwards in 2006. By doing so it is estimated that Ms Rein saved herself $4.5 million.

Frances Edwards was Therese Rein's original business partner when she set up the rehabilitation business Work Directions in 1988 (now Ingeus) and Ms Edwards had 5200 shares in the business when she died in 2006. It was estimated the true value of the shares was over $5 million at the time.

"Ms Rein and Edwards – the founding shareholders in the company – signed an agreement on or about May 22, 1988, declaring that their shares would be sold to the other, for a predetermined price of $100 a share, if either of them died."

"Within weeks of the Supreme Court granting probate to three executors, Ms Rein gave notice, on June 21, of her intention to

buy the Ingeus shares in accordance with the agreement and sent a cheque for $520,000 and a share transfer form the following day."

"When the executors of the estate tried to stop the sale, Ms Rein took them to the Queensland Supreme Court until they relented" (Click here to read more)

This raises two key questions:

1. While on the face of it some might think that it is standard practice to have a clause if one partner dies the other can buy their shares. But in 1988 when the contract was signed Therese Rein was about 30 years old and her partner Frances Edwards was 56 years old. So, the chance that Ms Rein would die before Ms Edwards was almost zero. Which means the deal was really just an option for Therese Rein to buy the shares later down the track at a fixed price. And a very low price it turned out to be to the benefit of Ms Rein and Kevin.

2. $520,000 is a lot of money especially back in 1988 for a rehabilitation business that has not even started trading. But it is not a big amount if you know the business is about to start getting millions of dollars of government business. Which is exactly what happened via Kevin Rudd, when he was Chief of Staff to Premier Wayne Goss, making sure plenty of business went Work Directions way.

Do you think Kevin Rudd had anything to do with the drafting of the contract? Of course he did!

The house deal windfall

It is worth looking at the house deal that Kevin Rudd did in 1994 where he had amazing luck. Where did the luck come from? Two Labor Party boys.

Kevin Rudd bought his current house in Brisbane for $384,000 in 1994. Seven months earlier the house had been bought for $500,000 by Larry Moses and Nick Kassos who were also directors of the Labor Party company Texberg. Housing prices were rising at the time yet Kevin Rudd managed to buy a property $116,000 cheaper than it had been valued seven months earlier.

"The businessmen were directors of Texberg with Labor luminaries and union bosses. They included Mr Brusasco, the then chairman of Labor Holdings, the major fundraising entity for the ALP in Queensland; and Harry Hauenschild, former president of the Trades and Labour Council in Queensland."

"Subsequent directors of Texberg after Mr Kassos and Mr Moses resigned from the company in 1992 include Wayne Swan, now the Opposition Treasury spokesman; Australian Workers Union head Bill Ludwig; ALP state secretary Milton Dick and his predecessors Mike Kaiser and Cameron Milner; and Queensland Teachers Union general-secretary John Battams."

"Texberg, which has been named in federal and state parliament because of its connections to the Labor Party, was deregistered last year."

Mr Moses said *"I did not even know that Kevin Rudd had bought it."*

*A spokesman for Mr Rudd said yesterday: "Mr Rudd and Ms Rein put a bid on a house in December 1994. They understood that the house had been vacant and on the market for a long period of time. **After a normal commercial negotiation through the real estate agent, they bought the property.**"* (Click here to read more)

Yep, just a stroke of good luck there by Kevin and Therese. Kevin at the time was Director-General of the Cabinet Office in the Wayne Goss state government. Would he have known Mr Moses and Mr Kassos? Of course he would have. And why the discount? Maybe a bribe, a payback or just looking after a good Labor boy.

The house deal shows the corrupt environment Kevin Rudd was operating in during the 1990's when Work Directions (Ingeus) was taking off like a rocket receiving government business and contracts which Kevin was in a position to influence.

This is a follow-up post to the two recent posts that I have written in relation to Kevin Rudd and Therese Reins and their millions. (Click here for the first post and click here for the second post)

I will keep following up on this even after the election because not enough questions have been asked and they should have been asked a long time ago. Therese Rein has popped her head up and has been doing plenty of media interviews, yet no one bothers to ask her any tough questions. A comment from a previous post rings true which said:

"Aussies are so gullible. If some African dictator's wife becomes independently rich we would not believe it, but if it's an Aussie prime minister's wife we think it is all above-board."

Chapter 4

Kevin Rudd and Love Letters from the Bar Table. The unanswered questions.

I sent Kevin Rudd a copy of my book Love Letters from the Bar Table in 2009 when he was Prime Minister. It has documented evidence of judicial and political corruption, but Kevin Rudd never responded.

Politicians almost always refuse to take any action when the public raise corruption allegations. But by at least writing to the politicians with the evidence and then publishing the evidence it does to some degree expose the politicians themselves.

Love Letters from the Bar Table

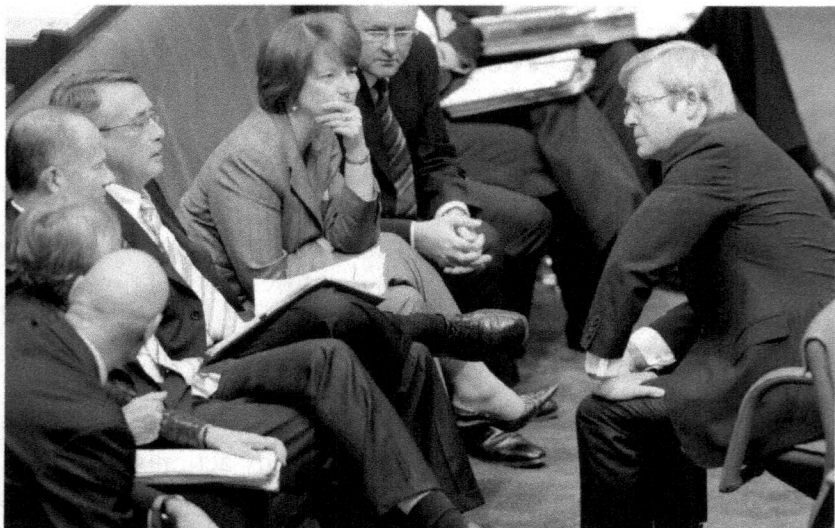

Australian Prime Minister Kevin Rudd (on right)

Who lied and who knew? Kevin!!!

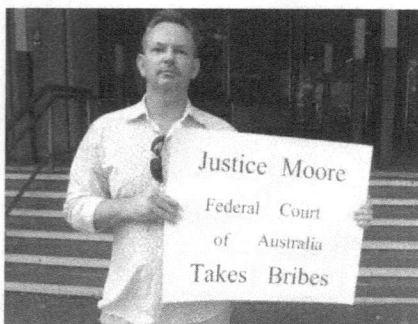

Justice Moore

Federal Court
of Australia

Takes Bribes

Sydney – Federal Court of Australia

A book that lifts the lid on corruption in the Australian Judicial System.

By: Shane Dowling
A "Crimes of the Law" book.
Book One

A true story about the systematic scandalisation of the Australian Federal Judicial System. Who by? By the Australian Federal Government, Australian Federal Police and various Judges and Magistrates.

Justice Ipp of the Supreme Court of Western Australia (now Supreme Court of New South Wales) said in a speech on Judicial Bias in 2004 that:

"The most obvious example of a judge with a direct interest in the case is the judge who accepts a bribe to decide in favour of one of the parties. There can be nothing more inimical to the idea of justice."

In relation to allegations that the respondents bribed a Judicial Officer their lawyers said in their written submissions:

"the Respondents submit that it is for the Appellant to prove his serious allegations of bribery. Unless the Appellant can make out a prima facie case, the Respondents (through their legal representatives) are not required to refute baseless allegations".

Notice how they will only talk through their legal representatives and they want to see all the evidence first. In my mind that is hardly the words of an innocent party. Just for the record the prima facie case had well and truly been made out and the respondents knew it.

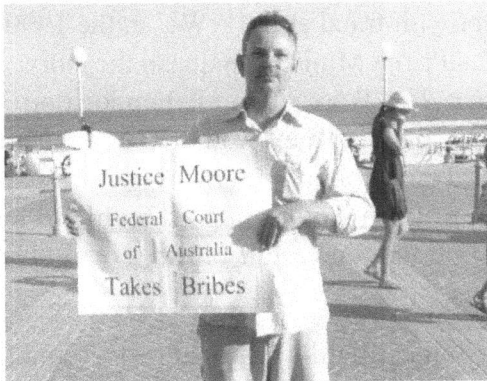

Shane Dowling at Bondi Beach
Sydney, Australia.

Shane Dowling was and still is at the time of writing this book (August 2009) a self represented litigant in an Unlawful Termination proceeding against Fairfax Media which has set an Australian record of 23 months to get a court decision. And a dodgy one at that. He can best be described as a Bush Lawyer. With his first book, in a series on corruption, he can now also be considered an investigative journalist

ISBN 978 0 646 51736 0

Chapter 5

Australian Prime Minister Julia Gillard's criminal history and her hypocrisy with WikiLeaks and Julian Assange.

This is the article that sparked the fire that led to the Trade Union Royal Commission which ran from 2014 to 2015.

After I published the article other media picked up on the story of Julia Gillard's involvement with fraud at the AWU in the 1990's. Gillard used her position as Prime Minister to quash the story, but it gained traction again later. The Tony Abbott led opposition promised an inquiry into the matter if they won the 2013 federal election. They did win and Tony Abbott became Prime Minister and expanded his promise, from an inquiry into Julia Gillard's involvement with the AWU fraud, into a full-blown Royal Commission into the unions.

Australian Prime Minister Julia Gillard's criminal history and her hypocrisy with WikiLeaks and Julian Assange.

BY SHANE DOWLING ON AUGUST 7, 2011 • (62 COMMENTS)

Julia Gillard had criminal allegations made against her in 1995 when she was accused of helping her boyfriend steal over

$1,000,000 from the Australian Workers Union (AWU) and helping him spend the money on such things as her personal home renovations and dresses.

Julia Gillard has never denied helping him rip off the $1,000,000 plus dollars, what she has done is denied doing it knowingly. Her part was helping set up an account called the "Australian Workers Union Workplace Reform Association" and possibly other accounts that the money was laundered through when she was a lawyer working for Slater and Gordon who were the solicitors representing the Australian Workers Union.

The allegations against Julia Gillard were initially raised in the Victorian Parliament in 1995.

In an interview with Glenn Milne of the Sydney Sunday Telegraph in 2007 Julia Gillard said:

"These matters happened between 12 and 15 years ago," Ms Gillard told The Sunday Telegraph. "I was young and naive."

"I was in a relationship, which I ended, and obviously it was all very distressing. I am by no means the first person to find out that someone close turns out to be different to what you had believed them to be. It's an ordinary human error.

"I was obviously hurt when I was later falsely accused publicly of wrong-doing. I didn't do anything wrong and to have false allegations in the media was distressing."

The article also says "But she has strenuously denied ever knowing what the association's bank accounts were used for." (Click here to read the full article)

I will dissect Julia Gillard's above comments later in the post because they beggar belief and raise more questions than they answer. But the part that would stand out at this point for anyone who has been following the Julian Assange and WikiLeaks matters over the past 10 months or so is the part where Julia Gillard whinges *"to have false allegations in the media was distressing"* which is exactly what Julia Gillard did to WikiLeaks and Julian Assange at the end of last year when she falsely said their actions were illegal.

In this post I will cover:

1. Julia Gillard's part in ripping off the AWU for over $1,000,000

2. Julia Gillard's hypocrisy in relation to her allegations of illegal conduct by Julian Assange and WikiLeaks.

3. Prima Facie Case to have Julia Gillard charged for breaching section 41 of the 1914 Crimes Act "Conspiracy to bring false accusation" and section 137 of the 1995 Criminal Code "False or misleading information or documents".

To appreciate how Julia Gillard's answers she gave in the 2007 interview beggar belief it is important to have some knowledge of what happened when she helped Bruce Wilson steal from the AWU. A brief outline is below.

The way the scam worked is best set out in another article by Glenn Milne where it starts off:

"THE con used by Julia Gillard's former lover to cream off possibly more than $1 million was simple and backed by standover tactics.

As union secretary, Bruce Morton Wilson would go on to construction sites and tell bosses they "needed" an industrial agreement which he would negotiate.

But there was a price – they would have to purchase hundreds of AWU membership tickets in exchange for the industrial peace guaranteed by the "agreement".

However, when the employers made out the cheques – sometimes for more than $50,000 at a time – the money for memberships that never existed would go into phony AWU accounts that actually belonged to Wilson." (Click here to read the full article)

The scam seems to have first started in Western Australia when Bruce Wilson was State Secretary of the AWU and he had already set up two bogus accounts to funnel the money through. He later moved to Victoria to become State Secretary for both Victoria and Western Australia.

By this time Julia Gillard and Bruce Wilson were in a sexual relationship and Julia Gillard should have stopped representing the AWU as there was a clear conflict of interest.

Bruce Wilson had Julia Gillard set up the account named "AWU Members Welfare Association No 1 Account".

The AWU management claimed they knew nothing about the accounts and when they found out the joint national secretary Ian Cambridge put a freeze on the accounts. Somehow money kept on going in and out of the accounts.

Some of the money was also used to buy a house and Ian Cambridge put a caveat on the house so it could not be sold. Again, the house was sold and the money disappeared.

From here we will go to the transcript from the Victorian Government Hansard where it says on the 12th of October 1995:

Mr GUDE (Minister for Industry and Employment)

"I understand the AWU is still receiving bills for strange items ordered by Mr Wilson. All attempts thus far to find him have come to nothing. What did Mr Wilson do when he found out that his actions had been discovered? The first thing he did was to seek legal advice from the union's solicitors, none other than Slater and Gordon. From whom did he receive that advice? One Julia Gillard.

I am informed that Ms Gillard is no longer with Slater and Gordon due to commitments as an ALP Senate candidate. That may not be the only reason she is no longer working at Slater and Gordon."

"Mr Gude — Consistent with the provisions of the legislation I am informed that the first thing Ms Gillard did, when asked what she would be doing and why she was getting out of Slater and Gordon, was to pay back moneys to the AWU for work" (Click here to read the rest)

Julia Gillard is alleged to have ripped off $57,500 for herself. Of which $17,500 was spent on clothing at Town Mode, which was a women's fashion house in Melbourne. Mr Cambridge has given evidence about the likely proceeds of this. And $40,000 was spent on renovations to her house in Melbourne. This shows up in the Victorian Parliament Hansard on the 28th February 2001 and the 2nd May 2001.

In January 1996 "Mr Cambridge wrote to the then Federal Minister for Industrial Relations, Mr Laurie Brereton, seeking a Royal Commission into the AWU – just as the Prime Minister, Mr Paul Keating, called an election." (Click here to read the full article)

Not long after Robert F. Smith, branch secretary at the AWU wrote a letter to Steve Harrison who along with Ian Cambridge was joint national secretary of the AWU.

The letter is in the Victorian Government Hansard and starts off:

Dear Steve,

Further to our telephone discussion this morning, I propose the following resolution to be put to national executive next month.

As we have discussed, you know as well as I do that if Cambridge is not stopped we are all history. I have spoken to Bill Kelty and Jennie George, and they are supportive of this course of action. Both you and I can work the phones before the national executive meeting to make sure we have the numbers before this motion is put. I have already spoken to a number of national executive and they are very nervous to say the least. Please ring when you have considered my proposal.

The Hansard goes on to say: By the way, there was neither a judicial inquiry nor a royal commission. Cambridge was appointed to the New South Wales Industrial Relations Court. I call for a full, open judicial inquiry. The other addressees on the letter were Bill Shorten, Terry Muscat, Graham Ray and Frank Leo. (Click here to read the full letter).

The above shows Julia Gillard being party to fraud, blackmail, money laundering and extortion etc. She claims to have not done it knowingly.

Now back to the 2007 Julia Gillard interview with Glenn Milne.

Julia Gillard *"strenuously denied ever knowing what the association's bank accounts were used for"*. For Julia Gillard to say that is a breach of lawyer-client confidentiality, but since she is prepared to say that she should also be prepared to answer other questions on the matter. It also is not believable as the first thing a lawyer would do when a client wants to set up a new association is ask what it going to used for so the lawyer makes sure they are giving the right advice and setting it up correctly. Is Julia Gillard saying she was also derelict in her duty and did not ask?

Julia Gillard said: *"These matters happened between 12 and 15 years ago,"* *"I was young and naive."* Well Julia Gillard was a partner at the law firm Slater and Gordon and in her mid-thirties. Slater and Gordon are not in the habit of appointing young and naive people as partners and being in her mid-thirties hardly made her young.

Julia Gillard said: *"I was in a relationship, which I ended, and obviously it was all very distressing. I am by no means the first person to find out that someone close turns out to be different to what you had believed them to be. It's an ordinary human error."* This is crap. Once Julia Gillard started having a sexual relationship with Bruce Wilson she should have stopped representing the AWU as they were the client not Bruce Wilson. It is a huge conflict of interest.

Julia Gillard said *"I was obviously hurt when I was later falsely accused publicly of wrong-doing. I didn't do anything wrong and to have false allegations in the media was distressing."* Well Julia Gillard was more than happy to falsely accuse Julian Assange and WikiLeaks of breaking Australian laws. It does not get much more hypocritical than that.

Both Bill Shorten and Jennie George who are mentioned above, and went on to become Federal Politicians, helped Julia Gillard become Prime Minister while they both were well aware of her history and helped cover it up.

Ian Cambridge as mentioned above became a Commissioner at the NSW Industrial Relations Commission in 1997. In 2009 Julia Gillard as Minister for Industrial Relations personally appointed Ian Cambridge as dual appointee to Fair Work Australia. I find this disturbing. While it could be argued that other Commissioners of the NSW Industrial Relations Commission were also given dual appointments at the same time they had not previously called for a Royal Commission into criminal conduct by Julia Gillard and her boyfriend Bruce Wilson.

Julia Gillard should never have appointed him and if Ian Cambridge had any self-respect he should not have accepted the position. It could be construed by some that Ian Cambridge has taken a bribe to keep his mouth shut about her criminal past.

I also notice that the Australian Mines and Metals Association has documented Julia Gillard stacking the bench at Fair Work Australia with her union mates. (Click here to read).

WikiLeaks and Julian Assange

On December 2, 2010, Julia Gillard said in relation to the United States diplomatic cables leak (Cablegate): *"I absolutely condemn the placement of this information on the WikiLeaks website – it's a grossly irresponsible thing to do and an illegal thing to do.*" Yet when she was asked what laws had been breached, she could not name any. Even so she still referred the matter to the Australian Federal Police for investigation. The Australian Attorney-General Robert McClelland supported Julia Gillard although he was not as stupid to go as far and he said that they had likely broken the law "The unauthorised obtaining of the information may well be an offence" but he also failed to name what laws had been breached.

When Julia Gillard and Robert McClelland referred the complaint to the Australian Federal Police it should have been fully documented. They should tender those documents to parliament or the media so we can see what laws they believed that WikiLeaks and Julian Assange breached.

If they cannot name the particular law or laws and what evidence they had that supported the crime than there is a very powerful prima facie case to have both Julia Gillard and Robert McClelland charged for conspiring to have someone falsely charged and making a false complaint to the police.

These are covered by section 41 of the 1914 Crimes Act and section 137.1 of the 1995 Criminal Code which are set out below. Even though WikiLeaks and Julian Assange were not charged section 41 of the 1914 crimes act still applies as even if "charging a person falsely pursuant to the agreement is impossible" they can still be found guilty which is covered by section 41(3)(a).

Crimes Act 1914

41 Conspiracy to bring false accusation

(1) Any person who conspires with another to charge any person falsely or cause any person to be falsely charged with any offence against the law of the Commonwealth or of a Territory, shall be guilty of an indictable offence.

Penalty: Imprisonment for 10 years.

(3) A person may be found guilty of an offence against subsection (1) even if:

(a) charging a person falsely pursuant to the agreement is impossible; or

Criminal Code Act 1995

Division 137—False or misleading information or documents

137.1 False or misleading information

(1) A person is guilty of an offence if:

(a) the person gives information to another person; and

(b) the person does so knowing that the information:

(i) is false or misleading; or

(ii) omits any matter or thing without which the information is misleading; and

(c) any of the following subparagraphs applies:

(i) the information is given to a Commonwealth entity;

(ii) the information is given to a person who is exercising powers or performing functions under, or in connection with, a law of the Commonwealth;

Penalty: Imprisonment for 12 months.

Julian Assange was quoted as saying that the Australian public should consider charging Julia Gillard with treason when he was on the ABC Q&A program on the 14th of March 2011. Whether that could be justified I do not know. But certainly having Julia Gillard and Robert McClelland charged with the two laws I mention above could be sustained.

It is worth noting that section 13 of the 1914 Crimes Act empowers every Australian to institute criminal proceeding so there is no need to wait for the police who of course would never do it.

When Robert McClelland was asked about the Federal Police investigation on the 10th of December 2010 he alluded that the police investigation could take a long time and he referred to the Godwin Grech investigation as an example. This is fairly standard for the Australian Federal Police to drag it out for as long as possible than quietly sweep it under the carpet when the media attention has gone.

But the Federal Police announced only one week later that WikiLeaks and Julian Assange had breached no Australian laws. Lo and behold that was the same day Dr Muhamed Haneef flew into town.

Who is Dr Haneef and what was he doing in Australia? He was here for a mediation meeting with the Federal Government on the 20th of December 2010 to settle a multi-million dollar claim for wrongful arrest and detention in 2007.

This is what it says on Wikipedia: *"During the 2008 inquiry into the Haneef affair, documents have revealed that former Prime Minister John Howard became involved in the case within 48 hours of Haneef's arrest. Lawyers in the case have suggested that the early involvement of the Prime Minister mean that John Howard colluded with Immigration Minister Kevin Andrews to politicise the issue." (Click here to read more)*

"Police officers Neil Thompson and Adam Simms who interrogated Haneef refused to charge him." Adam Simms is a Queensland Police Officer and Neil Thompson is a Federal Police Officer.

So, they had a senior Federal Police Officer, Commander Ramzi Jabbour, come over the top and charge him which is basically unheard of that leads one to believe it was being driven from the top. This is what it says on Wikipedia: "The Manager Counter Terrorism Domestic, Commander Ramzi Jabbour, had lost objectivity and was "unable to see that the evidence he regarded as highly incriminating in fact amounted to very little".

Given the Dr Haneef scandal Julia Gillard should have known better than to level the claims she did against Julian Assange and WikiLeaks and then refer it to the Federal Police. It is worth noting that she has never apologised to Julian Assange or WikiLeaks for making false allegations against them.

In summary Julia Gillard is not up to being Prime Minister of Australia. Julia Gillard is a qualified lawyer and you only have to read the above to realise that she is not much of lawyer let alone a Prime Minister.

It would be greatly appreciated if you spend a minute using Twitter, Facebook and email etc and promote this post. Just click on the icons below.

And make sure you follow this site by email which is on the top right of this page and about once a week you will get an email when there is a new post/story on this site.

Update 5/9/11: Julia Gillard over the last week has been threatening the Australian media to not report on her past which I raise above. I have done a follow-up post which is at: "Has Julia Gillard blackmailed the Media to cover-up her corrupt past? The Fairfax Media and News Corp scandal."

Chapter 6

Has Julia Gillard blackmailed the Media to cover-up her corrupt past? The Fairfax Media and News Corp scandal.

Has Julia Gillard blackmailed the Media to cover-up her corrupt past? The Fairfax Media and News Corp scandal.

BY SHANE DOWLING ON SEPTEMBER 5, 2011 • (78 COMMENTS)

Prime Minister Julia Gillard over the last few days has gone on a full-frontal attack on the Australian media which undermines free speech in this country. Her motive is to cover-up her own corrupt past. Julie Gillard has personally phoned executives and editors at News Ltd and highly likely Fairfax Media to stop reporting on her past of helping her former boyfriend Bruce Wilson rip off the AWU of over $1,000,000. It makes one wonder if she has also phoned other media as well in her cover-up attempt.

She has done this while she has had a massive conflict on interest in that the Australian government is currently considering conducting an enquiry into the Australian media. One of her press secretaries told me on Friday (2/9/11) that Julia Gillard had no intentions of standing down from the decision-making process of whether or not the government will hold an enquiry.

Over the last week two pieces of evidence have come to light to say that it is highly likely that Julia Gillard knowingly helped Bruce Wilson rip off the AWU.

Background

The focus of her public attack has been on Glenn Milne and a story he wrote that was published on Monday the 29th of August 2011 in The Australian which is a News Corp owned paper. The reporting and coverage of her attack in general by other news organisations has been scandalous and they have used it to go on an unjustified attack of News Corp's Australian subsidiary News Ltd. Fairfax Media who are also involved in the cover-up have tried to point the finger squarely at News Ltd while trying to conceal their own involvement in the cover-up.

The current outbreak started right here on this site with a post I did on the 7th August 2011 (click here to read) which was subsequently picked up by Michael Smith at radio station 2ue which is owned by Fairfax Media and Andrew Bolt of News Ltd.

Time Line:

1. I did a post on the 7th August 2011 titled "Australian Prime Minister Julia Gillard's criminal history and her hypocrisy with WikiLeaks and Julian Assange." The post had its good days and average days. It started to pick up pace in a big way and started going viral in the week beginning Monday the 22nd August.

2. On Friday the 26th August 2011 Michael Smith at 2ue and Andrew Bolt starting running with two of the key elements of my post. That being an interview Glenn Milne did with Julia Gillard in 2007 and the answers that she gave. They also were pushing an affidavit and its contents by Robert Kernohan which was mentioned in one of my links to the Hansard on the Victorian Parliament website. Michael Smith read out some of the affidavit

on air and Andrew Bolt published some on the content on his blog site. (Click here to read the Bob Kernohan affidavit) I have also put a link in the comment section as this one does not work sometimes.

3. They took the story further than me and Michael Smith pre-recorded an interview with Robert Kernohan who is a former president of the Victorian branch of the AWU on the weekend (27th and 28th August) which was meant to go to air on Monday the 29th of August. Andrew Bolt also put on his blog that he would be following up on his site on the Monday.

4. On the weekend of the 27th and 28th August Julia Gillard started calling John Hartigan who is CEO of News Ltd which is News Corp's Australian subsidiary. She wanted assurances that Andrew Bolt would not follow-up which John Hartigan gave her.

5. Monday 29th of August. The Australian ran Glenn Milne's story in The Australian and on their website. Julia Gillard called John Hartigan again and demanded it be taken down from the website and demanded a retraction. There was only one key bit that she apparently complained about, but she wanted the whole article to be taken down. Julia Gillard apparently made numerous calls and sent emails and texts. (Click here to read the Glenn Milne story ("PM A Lost Cause For Warring Unions"). I have also put a link in the comment section as this one does not work sometimes.

6. Monday 29th of August: Fairfax Media pulls the Michael Smith interview with Robert Kernohan on their radio station 2ue. There was a 7 or 8 minute recording on the 2ue website from the Friday the 26th program of Michael Smith reading from Robert Kernohan affidavit. This was also pulled from their website and the previous days recording (Thursday 25th) put in its place.

7. Monday 29th of August to date: Other media start running with the story of how News Ltd were forced to pull the story. Fairfax Media pulling the Radio interview gets very little mention or no

mention at all. No one asks the question: If Julia Gillard rang John Hartigan at News Ltd to pull the story who did she ring at Fairfax Media to pull the radio interview?

8. Michael Smith has tried a couple of more times to run the interview with Robert Kernohan but has so far been stopped by Fairfax Media management.

9. On Friday 2nd September I spoke to one of Julia Gillard's press secretaries and I asked in words to the effect: "given that Julia Gillard had called John Hartigan to have the story pulled at News Ltd who at Fairfax Media had Julia Gillard called to have the Robert Kernohan interview pulled from 2UE." The response I got from the press secretary was that he was confident that Julia Gillard would not have called Fairfax Media. He obviously has a lot more confidence than me.

10. News Ltd have since gone on the offensive and fought back to some degree. There are a few links under the Andrew Bolt heading below which show the fight-back.

As mentioned above in the second paragraph of this post Julia Gillard's press secretary also told me that she would not be standing down from the decision-making process of whether or not the government will hold a media enquiry even though I had pointed out the massive conflict of interest given that she had threatened News Ltd to pull the story. He said words to the effect: "she would not be standing down because if every politician who had interaction with the media stood down there would be no one left." and that "she would not have threatened Hartigan with legal action but just pointed out the errors in the story".

Julia Gillard helped her then boyfriend rip of the AWU in the period of approximately 1993 – 1995. The Prime Minister says it is old and no longer relevant and she has addressed the issue many times before.

Well, it is relevant now for many reasons and she has never addressed it in full or to any real degree.

The reasons it is relevant now:

1. In the interview in 2007 with Glenn Milne she complained about how distressing it was to be falsely accused of wrongdoing in the media. As I pointed out in my post on the topic that is what she did to Julian Assange and WikiLeaks at the end of 2010.

2. That the Prime Minister has clearly been trying to cover up the current scandal of the federal politician Craig Thomson ripping off the Health Services Union. Given that the AWU clearly covered up her former boyfriend of ripping off the AWU and her involvement it is clearly in the public interest to look at that as it shows a history in the Union movement of ripping off their members. How many more people in the Union movement are ripping off their members that no one knows about? There should be a broad enquiry.

3. Given that Julia Gillard has tried to close down media coverage of her involvement in ripping off the AWU it is in the public interest to have a good look at it to clear the air so the public can have confidence in the Prime Minister. Which the Prime Minister does not want to do.

Julia Gillard has never fully addressed the issue:

I have been aware of her history in this matter since 2005/2006. I have never come across anywhere in media reports where she has fully addressed the matter in any detail. Just vague palm offs, she generally says that it happened a long time ago and that she had already addressed the matter. Even the 2007 interview is only brief and as I have already pointed out in a previous post what she says beggar's belief.

Michael Smith on 2ue has also been following up this week with questions to the PM which she has avoided answering. On the

2ue site it shows the email correspondence to and from the PM's office this week:

He asks her a number of questions like:

30/8/11

Did you ever create or cause any legal entity(ies) to be created with the letters AWU or words Australian Workers Union in its/their title(s)?

Did you establish or in any way instruct any person to establish any bank accounts for the Australian Worker's Union?

Have you ever paid back any money to the Australian Workers' Union?

The response from the PM's office the next day "These are matters that have been dealt with on the public record over a period of fifteen years." and after another email from Michael Smith the PM's office replies "The Prime Minister, as you note, has made comments about these matters in the past. I'd refer you to her comments."

Michael Smith sends another email on Wednesday the 31st of August: May I ask that you make good on the offer you made below to refer me to her comments? Where are they, what are the comments that you are happy for me to use?

And the PM's office responds with: Well actually Julia Gillard's office did not respond even though Michael Smith had staff following it up. She is ducking for cover. Very similar to the Craig Thomson affair as he has gone all silent as well. I would put a link to the Michael Smith emails but they will probably go down in a day or so based on current form. He does seem to be the only one following it up so if you have the time his show is on 2ue M-F from midday to 3pm.

Fairfax Media and Michael Smith

Fairfax Media have at this point acted disgracefully and have buckled to Julia Gillard's pressure. While they have not closed down Michael Smith totally, they have stopped his interview with Robert Kernohan going to air. Maybe they will never let it be broadcast or maybe they think if they hold it back long enough even if it does go to air, it will have no impact.

I called Fairfax Media on Friday to ask who there had spoken to Julia Gillard and who had stopped the Kernohan interview going to air. A person at their PR company Access PR told me Peter Fray was probably the person to speak to and she would call me back. She never got back to me.

I spoke to Michael Smith on Friday as well and he said he had "no comment" to make as why the story had been pulled. I had spoken to an assistant at 2ue prior to that and she said that because it had not been approved yet. Well, it was meant to go to air on the Monday, Tuesday and Wednesday but kept getting pulled. Andrew Bolt I recall said on his blog that it had already been legally approved.

In reporting in their papers Fairfax Media have not said why the 2ue interview has not gone to air. In one report at least which is titled "Bombshell for Gillard explodes under Murdoch press" which was printed on Tuesday the 30th of August they point the finger at News Ltd but make no mention of the fact that they are involved in the cover-up. (Click here to read) It says in another article in the Fairfax Press where they put the boot into News Ltd "Michael Smith of Fairfax Media's 2UE, who decided yesterday not to discuss Milne's column or read the promised statutory declaration" Well that is a lie and there is no mention of the Kernohan interview, Fairfax Media management pulled the interview and shut it down. (Click here to read)

Who pulled the pin at Fairfax Media? Well, the likely suspects are the directors who are:

- Roger Corbett AO, Chairman

- Michael Anderson

- Nicholas Fairfax

- Greg Hywood, Chief Executive Officer and Managing Director

- Sandra McPhee

- Sam Morgan

- Linda Nicholls AO

- Robert Savage AM

- Peter Young AM

Or maybe it was Gail Hambly who is the Group General Counsel for Fairfax Media. I thought that given that the likes of John Hartigan get mentioned in this story it would not be right for me not to name and shame the directors of Fairfax Media who are overseeing a cover-up and aiding in the denial of free speech.

Andrew Bolt

Andrew Bolt had a lot of what was on his site pulled down but has written two posts on what happened since that are well worth a read.

Prime Minister Julia Gillard's hand overplayed

Protecting Gillard: ABC sacks Milne

There is also a good story in The Australian which details the phone calls between the Prime Minister Julia Gillard and John Hartigan and Chris Mitchell who is the editor of The Australian.

8am call that put Julia Gillard's old news on front page

Other Media Reports

As I have stated above, reports in other media of what has actually transpired have been disgraceful, full of errors and sometimes out-right defamatory in an attempt to bag News Ltd, Glenn Milne and Andrew Bolt. Amazingly Michael Smith and Fairfax Media rarely get mentioned.

ABC – Jeremy Thompson

The ABC on Thursday sacked Glenn Milne from appearing further on their Insiders program for not meeting its editorial standards. That is a joke as Julia Gillard was clearly trying to shut down any reporting of her past before the Glenn Milne story was published. The timeline above shows that Julia Gillard was calling John Hartigan at News Ltd on the Saturday and Sunday to stop Andrew Bolt from reporting on it anymore. It does not really matter what Glenn Milne said in his story because as long as it mentioned Julia Gillard's corrupt past it was going to be pulled.

Jeremy Thomson did a report on the ABC website on the Tuesday the 30th of August which was updated on the 31st which is nothing more than a joke. There are solid grounds for News Ltd and Andrew Bolt to sue for defamation.

He says in relation to a section Andrew Bolts blog which began: "On Monday, I'm tipping, a witness with a statutory declaration will come forward and implicate Julia Gillard directly in another scandal involving the misuse of union funds."

"No such witness has come forward."

Well Jeremy Thomson is either a very sloppy and lazy reporter or he is straight out lying. A person has come forward, Robert Kernohan, and the interview was meant to go to air on Michael Smith program on 2UE. Why did Jeremy Smith not know that? Why did he not report anything about Fairfax Media pulling the story? Why did he not ask who Julia Gillard had spoken to at Fairfax Media?

He also says: "The article, written by journalist Glenn Milne – but later repudiated by the newspaper – claimed Ms Gillard had been unknowingly implicated in a "major union fraud" while she was working as a lawyer in Melbourne before she entered parliament."

Well, they did not repudiate the whole story just a small part. Which even says it at the end of the story. (Click here to read the full story)

Given that the ABC sacked Glenn Milne (they say he was not sacked because he was not actually an employee) from the Insiders program for "not meeting its editorial standards" what will they do to Jeremy Thomson?

Crickey.com.au

I am a fan of the Crikey news website. A democracy needs a diverse media, and they have some good articles on there. But a posting by Andrew Cook is a disgrace which is titled "Milne debacle: how a 16-year-old story was spiked by The Oz". It starts off "Glenn Milne has egg all over his face after the re-hired columnist filed an error-filled op-ed reviving discredited allegations that Prime Minister Julia Gillard had somehow been an accomplice to her one-time partner Bruce Wilson's alleged fraud."

The claims are not discredited at all. What because Julia Gillard denies them? How many criminals admit their crime?

Andrew Cook goes on to say, "While a popular topic in the right-wing blogosphere, the allegations are rarely taken seriously by professional journalists." Really, has Andrew Cook done a survey has he? I wouldn't mind a look. When people write dribble like that it is because they cannot attack the content, so they attack the messenger.

In relation to current media attention on Gillard's past in helping rip off the AWU he says, "The fresh outbreak was three days in the making." Well, it actually started with my post on the 7th of August. Mr Cook obviously cannot use the internet.

He goes on to say, "In fact, the PM has consistently shot down the suggestions with supreme force each time they get trotted out." Well, where is her detailed side of the story Mr Cook? You obviously have a copy, can I see it?

Andrew Cook goes on to try to discredit Robert Kernohan. He might be right, but he makes no mention of the response that Julia Gillard gave to the Glenn Milne interview in 2007 that beggars belief. Maybe Andrew Cook believes her answers. The reality is that Julia Gillard openly admits helping rip off the AWU so even though she says she did not do it knowingly, it should still be scrutinised even more so, when she has never given a detailed account of what happened. But a simple denial is good enough for Mr Cook. (Click here to read the full article)

The question that is going through my mind is how many media organisations has Julia Gillard called to close down the reporting of her grubby history?

We know she called News Ltd many times over three-days, firstly to close down Andrew Bolt and then Glenn Milne. Given that and the conduct of Fairfax Media logic says that she also called them. The ABC sacking Milne seems very odd to me given what I have already written above. And what have the TV stations Channel 7, Channel 10, Channel 9 and SBS been saying? Not much to my knowledge or maybe that has something to do with the $250 million election year bribe Tony Abbott has previously spoken about.

Given that a lot of the material has been taken down from the net has Julia Gillard also contacted Google, Yahoo and Bing to make sure that negative articles do not show up in a search or at least far back in the search results. It does happen, so why wouldn't Julia Gillard try it given her current form.

The Media Enquiry

The Federal Government is currently evaluating whether or not we should have a Media Enquiry. I have no doubt we should and the first port of call should be Julia Gillard and her intimidation of the Australian media. She should have never called Hartigan and once she did she had an obligation to put out a press release stating, given her fight with News Ltd and Fairfax Media, she would no longer be part of the decision-making process on whether or not to have an enquiry or its potential terms of reference.

In 2007 Julia Gillard said she was young and naive when she had a huge conflict of interest of having a sexual relationship with Bruce Wilson and taking instructions off him for her client the AWU. As I have previously said, when she started having a relationship with Wilson she should have handed the AWU account to someone else at the law firm Slater and Gordon. But her excuse was she was young and naive. What is her excuse now she has a massive conflict of interest but is still the main decision maker of whether or not to have the media enquiry? Is Julia Gillard still claiming to be young and naive?

The two pieces of evidence that I spoke of at the start to say that it is highly likely that Julia Gillard knowingly helped Bruce Wilson rip off the AWU. 1. Her personal jihad to close down the reporting on the story and 2. Her lie about previously addressing the issue. If she had she would have responded to Michael Smith's emails and said where she had previously addressed them.

One of the key reasons that I point out that the above started with my post on the 7th of August is so all the people who have promoted the post on Facebook, Twitter and emailed their friends etc know they have made a difference. Without your support not much would have happened. Even if the so-called mainstream media do not pick up issues of public importance you can make a difference.

Chapter 7

The Michael Smith 2ue emails to Julia Gillard and the Bob Kernohan Statutory Declaration.

The Michael Smith 2ue emails to Julia Gillard and the Bob Kernohan Statutory Declaration.

BY SHANE DOWLING ON SEPTEMBER 11, 2011 • (63 COMMENTS)

This is the next instalment in the series of posts that I have been doing on Julia Gillard and her history of helping rip off the AWU and closing down the Australian media from reporting on it. It is also a lead up post to my next one which will dissect a story that was on the ABC program Media Watch which is hosted by Jonathan Holmes.

It is important that you have read at least a couple of my previous posts to fully understand this post. The links are:

7th August 2011: Australian Prime Minister Julia Gillard's criminal history and her hypocrisy with WikiLeaks and Julian Assange.

28th August 2011: Julia Gillard who admitted helping rip off the AWU of over $1million stands by and supports Craig Thomson who is accused of ripping off the Health Services Union. The Australian Labor Party, beautiful one day, perfect the next.

5th September 2011: Has Julia Gillard blackmailed the Media to cover-up her corrupt past? The Fairfax Media and News Corp scandal.

I will not write too much as I do not want to take focus off the email correspondence between Michael Smith at 2ue and the Prime Minister's office which tells a story by itself. I put part of the correspondence in my previous post which was on the 2ue website. When Michael Smith was suspended from 2ue last Tuesday it was taken down, but luckily I had saved a copy.

Below is the correspondence where Michael Smith was asking valid questions of Julia Gillard and the palm off that the Prime Minister's office gave him. Below that is the Bob Kernohan statutory declaration that has been doing the rounds.

The statutory declaration by itself only has a certain amount of credibility, but when put together with the Michael Smith emails and other evidence the statutory declaration grows in power. If Bob Kernohan lied in the statutory declaration that is a criminal offence which I personally doubt very much that he would have done so. It must be remembered that Commissioner Ian Cambridge and current AWU boss Bill Ludwig also signed off on affidavits asking some serious questions about Julia Gillard's time at the law firm Slater and Gordon.

This shows up in an article by Glenn Milne in The Australian in November 2007 where it says:

"In an affidavit the AWU's then joint national secretary, Ian Cambridge, raised specific questions about the role of Ms Gillard's law firm, Slater & Gordon, in the purchase of a Melbourne property by Wilson. "I am unable to understand how Slater & Gordon, who were then acting for the Victorian branch of the union, could have permitted the use of funds which were obviously taken from the union, in the purchase of private property of this nature, without seeking and obtaining proper authority from the union for such use of its funds," Mr Cambridge said."

"Current AWU boss, "Big Bill" Ludwig, a major Labor powerbroker on the Right, also provided an affidavit to the court outlining corruption involving Ms Gillard's former lover." (Click here to read the full article)

It must be noted that Bill Ludwig has in the last few days been caught with his hand in the AWU till to pay for his personal legal costs. (Click here for The Courier Mail report) (Click here for the ABC report).

The Australian has started reporting on Julia Gillard's past again at least to some degree. Michael Stutchbury did a story on the 9th September where it gets mentioned. (Click here to read the article)

Like I said at the start the key focus of this post is the email correspondence. Read it and then read the statutory declaration and then read the emails again. It is important to have this knowledge for my next post.

I will do a follow post in the next week or so on the Media Watch program and Jonathan Holmes where they did, what I regard, as nothing more than a disgraceful hatchet job. (Click here to watch the program).

Remember that Julia Gillard who admits having knowledge of and involvement in ripping off the AWU has never signed an affidavit or statutory declaration outlining her knowledge and involvement in the fraud and theft. She has also never given any detailed account of what she knows. When she has been asked in the past she just gives blanket denials and vague answers or answers that beggar belief as I have shown in previous posts. For 16 years she has refused to answer any detailed questions as the below emails reinforce.

Michael Smith emails to Julia Gillard:

It's On the Public Record:

I write to the Prime Minister's office on your behalf quite a lot. They're normally very professional and speedy in getting back with responses.

The PM has a large staff, as you would expect.

I have set out my correspondence with the PM's office below, starting with my first note and ending with my last, unanswered note.

During my program today my producer sent a further chaser, she received a brief response that said "Maryann, I provided a response, regards, Sean."

Are you satisfied with the PM's response to my questions? Are they reasonable questions? Can you show me where the answers are?

30/08/2011, at 8:44 AM, "Michael Smith \(2ue\)" wrote:

Dear Prime Minister,

Did you ever create or cause any legal entity(ies) to be created with the letters AWU or words Australian Workers Union in its/their title(s)?

Did you create an Association known as "AWU Members Welfare Association"?

Did you establish or in any way instruct any person to establish any bank accounts associated with the "AWU Members Welfare Association" or "AWU Workplace Reform Association Inc"?

Did you establish or in any way instruct any person to establish any bank accounts for the Australian Worker's Union?

Did you receive any monies from any of the following bank accounts "AWU Workplace Reform Association" or "Australian Workers Union Members Welfare Association"?

Did you receive any clothes paid for by any other person or entity from the business known as Town Mode of Melbourne Fashion House?

Have you ever paid back any money to the Australian Workers' Union?

Thanks,

Michael

From: Michael Smith (2ue)

Sent: Tuesday, 30 August 2011 9:55 PM

To: Michael Smith (2ue)

Cc: Kelly, Sean

Subject: Re: For the PM Please

Dear Sean,

I am looking at my file of correspondence with your office.

You have always impressed me with your speed in reversion.

What's gone wrong? Why is this enquiry different? Did my message go missing?

Michael

From: Kelly, Sean

Sent: Wednesday, 31 August 2011 8:20 AM

To: Michael Smith (2ue)

Subject: RE: For the PM Please [SEC=UNOFFICIAL]

Hi Michael,

These are matters that have been dealt with on the public record over a period of fifteen years.

Sean

From: Michael Smith (2ue)

Sent: Wednesday, 31 August 2011 9:38 AM

To: Kelly, Sean

Subject: RE: For the PM Please [SEC=UNOFFICIAL]

Thanks Sean,

Just for clarity, the only public record I can find that goes close to answering those questions can best be summarised thus.

The PM was a partner at Slater and Gordon. She took instructions from Bruce Wilson, an official with the AWU.

On Mr Wilson's instructions she set up legal structures styled in a similar fashion to "AWU Welfare Association".

The public record (i.e. media reports, including Glen Milne's) says she set up the accounts, I infer from that bank accounts.

The PM is explicit in saying that she had no idea what the accounts were being used for. She specifically and emphatically denies any prior knowledge of improper conduct or fraud.

She vigorously denies being involved in any way in any improper or illegal conduct.

The public record includes the Hansard reports in the Victorian Parliament. The statements in the parliament include specific commentary about the renovation of a house and the acquisition of certain clothing from the Melbourne fashion house. Just for clarity, is that public record accurate?

Michael

From: Kelly, Sean

Sent: Wednesday, 31 August 2011 9:41 AM

To: Michael Smith (2ue)

Subject: RE: For the PM Please [SEC=UNOFFICIAL]

Michael,

The Prime Minister, as you note, has made comments about these matters in the past. I'd refer you to her comments.

Sean

From: Michael Smith (2ue)

Sent: Wednesday, 31 August 2011 9:44 AM

To: Kelly, Sean

Subject: RE: For the PM Please [SEC=UNOFFICIAL]

Thanks Sean, clearly we would love an interview about them, are there any circumstances in which the PM will speak with me?

Michael

From: Kelly, Sean

Sent: Wednesday, 31 August 2011 9:52 AM

To: Michael Smith (2ue)

Subject: RE: For the PM Please [SEC=UNOFFICIAL]

Michael, the Prime Minister has made comments about these matters, and has nothing to add to those comments.

From: Michael Smith (2ue)

Sent: Wednesday, 31 August 2011 9:56 AM

To: 'Kelly, Sean'

Subject: RE: For the PM Please [SEC=UNOFFICIAL]

Sean,

I'll wait to hear from you about the circumstances in which the PM might be available for an interview.

Separately, I would like to take you up on the offer in your last sentence to refer me to the PM's comments. You have a considerable taxpayer funded media unit with publicly funded access to the Media Monitors organisation and its resources in collating and analysing media commentary.

May I ask that you make good on the offer you made below to refer me to her comments? Where are they, what are the comments that you are happy for me to use?

Michael

State of Victoria

Statutory Declaration

I, Robert John Kernohan

Of 33 View Street, Castlemaine, Victoria 3450

Workcover recipient, do solemnly and sincerely declare that:-

Between approximately 1992 and 1995, financial fraud was rampant within the Victorian Branch of the AWU. Bruce Wilson was Victorian Branch Secretary, then National Construction Branch Secretary, based in Victoria between 1992 and 1995. By this time the unauthorised accounts had been in operation for at least 4 years.

The extent of this fraud is set out in sworn affidavits made in 1995 by then AWU National General Secretary, Ian Cambridge and present AWU Queensland Secretary and National President Bill Ludwig.

I was President of the Victorian General Branch of the AWU during the time a number of these frauds were occurring. In 1995 I was made aware of a

1

Bob Kernohan — Statutory Declaration — P1

number of unauthorised bank accounts/trusts that had been established in the name of the AWU by Bruce Wilson and his colleagues. Wilson was not authorised to establish these accounts and I became aware that money that should have rightfully gone into legitimate AWU accounts was being directed into the unauthorised accounts. These accounts were controlled by Wilson and not the AWU. Wilson was secretary of the AWU construction branch at the time. Wilson and Julia Gillard were in a relationship for an extended period, I believe including the time when the fraud was uncovered.

Julia Gillard was a partner of Slater & Gordon at the time and had done a great deal of legal/industrial work for Wilson's AWU branch over several years. This included work relating to the union's rules and internal union disputes. It has previously been reported that Julia Gillard, acting on instructions from Wilson set up these accounts.

There is evidence in the Ludwig and Cambridge affidavits that many hundreds of thousands of dollars of AWU member's money from these unauthorised accounts was used by Wilson for his own purposes, without the legal authority of the AWU. Ludwig's lawyers told the Federal Industrial Relations Court in 1996 that the full extent of the fraud exceeded well over one million dollars. A property was purchased in 1993 by

2

Bob Kernohan

Wilson and Ralph Blewitt with some of this money. Slater & Gordon did the legal work related to the purchase of this property. Wilson lived in the house after it was renovated. The house was sold just after Wilson left the union as part of a deal that was designed to 'hush the fraud up'. None of the proceeds of the house sale came back to AWU members. Bruce Wilson was clearly a beneficiary of the unauthorised accounts, as he had established the funds. He and Ralph Blewitt(Secretary of the WA branch of the AWU) were signatories for the accounts. A number of Wilson's AWU colleagues also benefitted financially from these arrangements.

I became aware of the fraud in 1995. By this time the unauthorised accounts had been in operation for 4 years. During 1995, the then State Secretary of the AWU Victoria General Branch was approached by building contractors demanding payment for work carried out on two houses during Wilson's tenure as State Secretary that was purportedly authorised by the AWU. One of these houses was the property purchased by Wilson, in Kerr Street, Fitzroy with funds from the unauthorised accounts. AWU Secretary Bob Smith, AWU official Bill Shorten and myself believed that the other property was owned by Bruce Wilson's then partner, Julia Gillard.

3

Bob Kernohan

Following the revelation of the frauds, the AWU's National Office took over responsibility for cleaning up the mess. I was not personally involved in this process, nor was I involved in the deal that resulted in Wilson and his colleagues leaving the AWU. I personally made a statement about the Wilson fraudulent accounts to the Fedpol Fraud Squad. I had a significant falling out with other AWU officials in relation to the handling of the matter. I believe other AWU officials were determined to cover up the affair and not pursue the vast sums of money that had been defrauded.

I was informed by Bob Smith, with Bill Shorten present, that some thousands of dollars were paid illegally from union funds, by Wilson, for house renovations to Julia Gillard's property. These payments were made from AWU funds out of one of the fraudulent accounts. In 1996, the AWU still had contractors chasing money for work they had carried out on other properties and were yet to be paid.

A number of high profile AWU officials who have moved into state and federal parliaments knew that Wilson and Julia Gillard were in a relationship at the time and that she was doing industrial legal work for Wilson during this period. They were also involved   and/or aware of negotiations

4

Rob Kernohan

regarding the deal that resulted in Wilson and others leaving the AWU.

Wilson has never been held to account for these frauds notwithstanding a court order granted to Ludwig to recover over $40,000 paid to Wilson as a redundancy payment. Wilson resigned from the AWU as a result of the deal reached. This deal was signed by then Victorian AWU Secretary Bob Smith, now a Victorian MP. This deal included various measures to keep details of the fraud quiet. As part of the negotiations surrounding this deal, I was personally offered preselection for a safe Victorian Labor seat if I kept my mouth shut. I declined the offer.

To my knowledge, well over one million dollars in funds that rightly belonged to AWU members has never been recovered. In the interest of AWU members I continue to hold the view that these matters require a full and open investigation, as also advocated at the time by Ian Cambridge, Joint National Secretary and supported by Bill Ludwig, Queensland AWU Secretary and National President, to ensure that justice is done.

I acknowledge that this declaration is true and correct, and I make it with the understanding and belief that a person who makes a false declaration is liable to the penalties of perjury.

5

Declared at ...Castlemaine...

This....11....day of....August....2010

....Bob Kernohan....

signature of person making this declaration(to be signed in front of an authorised witness)

Before me,

....M. CRANE.... ....Sig. 7191....CASTLEMAINE POLICE STATION
50 LYTTLETON STREET
CASTLEMAINE 3450

Signature of Authorised Witness

The authorised witness must print or stamp his or her name, address and title under section 107A of the Evidence(Miscellaneous Provisions) Act 1958(as of 1 January 2010), (previously Evidence Act 1958)

6

Bob Kernohan – Statutory Declaration – P6

Chapter 8

Julia Gillard appoints Bernard Murphy, her partner in crime from Slater and Gordon Lawyers, as a Federal Court of Australia judge.

Julia Gillard appoints Bernard Murphy, her partner in crime from Slater and Gordon Lawyers, as a Federal Court of Australia judge.

BY SHANE DOWLING ON OCTOBER 17, 2011 • (39 COMMENTS)

Julia Gillard has appointed Bernard Murphy as a judge of the Federal Court of Australia. When the $1 million fraud and theft of the AWU hit the fan in 1995 Ms Gillard and Mr Murphy both left Slater and Gordon lawyers around the same time as Ms Gillard's boyfriend Bruce Wilson left the AWU for his part in the fraud and theft. (Click here to read previous postings for the background – 7th August, 28th August, 5th September, 11th September and 19th September)

This post ties in a lot with what I have previously written and for that reason I will make substantial reference to it.

Before we get started, in all fairness to Julia Gillard, she is not the first Prime Minister to corrupt the judiciary by appointing her mates as judicial officers. For example, Kevin Rudd appointed his mate Chief Justice Patrick Keane and John Howard appointed his mate Chief Federal Magistrate John Pascoe as did others which I have written about on this website previously and will continue to do so. But to my knowledge none have ever appointed their former boss and mentor as a judge.

Background

Julia Gillard graduated law school in 1986 followed by a further year of study doing the Leo Cussen's workshop which is a legal practice course in Melbourne. During this time she also did work experience at Slater and Gordon.

Bernard Murphy is the one who recruited Julia Gillard to work full-time at Slater and Gordon in 1987. She became a partner in 1990 until 1995 when she left in a hurry and became Chief of staff to Victorian Opposition Leader John Brumby from 1995 to 1998. In 1998 she was elected to the Federal seat of Lalor.

This is what Julia Gillard had to say in an interview with the Young Lawyers Journal when she was still the Deputy Prime Minister in relation to her time at Slater and Gordon:

"Did you have a great mentor in practice? What did they say to you? I worked side by side with Bernard Murphy who today is a partner at Maurice Blackburn. He taught me how to organise competing workloads, how to deal with clients, how to create the right expectations about what's going to happen next to them in their legal case." (Click here to read the full article)

Bernard Murphy's father, Joe Murphy, "was a Wodonga solicitor in the 1970s and 1980s and a one-time Labor Party parliamentary candidate." (Click here to read) So I wonder if Bernard Murphy is or was a member of the Labor Party?

Appointment Process

Bernard Murphy's appointment raises serious questions in relation to the separation of powers. That being the judiciary is meant to independent of the government. Mr Murphy would be well aware of this and if he had any self-respect, he would not have applied for the position in the first place, at least not while Julia Gillard is the Prime Minister.

This is what it says on the Maurice Blackburn Lawyers website:

"If you had asked Maurice Blackburn chairman Bernard Murphy this time last year whether he hoped to be a judge, he would have said no. "It hasn't really been on my radar," he admits. "It isn't something that I had thought about until I applied in about October last year." (So, what happened between the beginning of 2010 when he had no intention of applying to be a judge and October 2010 when he applied. Well, his mate Julia Gillard became Prime Minister).

"A former solicitor is rare enough on the bench; a former plaintiff lawyer is rarer still."

"The man who once recruited Prime Minister Julia Gillard to his previous firm Slater & Gordon has spent 30 years defending the "victim" in court, as he has described clients in the past. More recently, it has been a sophisticated, shareholder victim, in the multimillion- dollar shareholder class actions Murphy has become known for."

"Murphy built Maurice Blackburn's class action practice – the largest in Australia – from a one-man show, winning more than $700 million in damages along the way. And he still holds the record for the largest shareholder class action settlement – $144.5 million in the 2008 Aristocrat case." (This was not only against Aristocrat but also the directors at the time one of which was none other than Chief Federal Magistrate John Pascoe) – (Click here to read my posting on John Pascoe's corrupt past)

"He applied to the bench on the recommendation of several legal practitioners and two judges, although Murphy will not say who."

Of course he will not say who. It was just one Prime Minister that's who. (Click here to read the full article)

In my first posting on this website, I covered dodgy judicial appointments by the Federal Government and the Attorney-General Robert McClelland and I said this: "One thing that Robert McClelland did when he was made Attorney-General was to set up two so-called independent panels to advise on appointments. One for Federal Court of Australia judges and another for Federal Magistrates Court of Australia magistrates. (click here for more) This was for the purpose as he put it "the Government has implemented more transparent processes to ensure that appointments are clearly based on merit, so that the public can have confidence that the Government is making the best possible judicial appointments." (Click here to read the full posting)

When Bernard Murphy was appointed a judge in April 2011 this is what Robert McClelland had to say: "In 2008, the Attorney-General introduced new processes for appointing judges and magistrates to federal courts to ensure greater transparency and public confidence in the judicial appointments process."

"The advisory panel comprised Chief Justice Patrick Keane, Sir Gerard Brennan AC KBE, the Hon Acting Justice Jane Mathews AO and a senior official of the Attorney-General's Department." (Click here to read the press release) Obviously the three mentioned had no say in the appointment of Bernard Murphy but are happy to get paid and have their name used to give the appointment some credibility. All it really shows is how deceitful they are and that they have sold their soul for a dollar. Real classy people.

The AWU fraud

Mr Murphy's appoint also reignites the $1 million AWU fraud that has been in the media recently. One of the things that the Julia Gillard's supporters have been arguing is that it happened

16 years ago and is old news. Well Mr Murphy's appointment was just over 7 months ago in April 2011 and he started as a judge in June which is five months ago.

What was Mr Murphy's knowledge of and/or involvement in the fraud? Did he benefit financially in any way? Why has he never given a public statement of his knowledge or involvement in the fraud?

This what I said in a previous post on the 11th of September: *It must be remembered that Commissioner Ian Cambridge and current AWU boss Bill Ludwig also signed off on affidavits asking some serious questions about Julia Gillard's time at the law firm Slater and Gordon.*

This shows up in an article by Glenn Milne in The Australian in November 2007 where it says:

"In an affidavit the AWU's then joint national secretary, Ian Cambridge, raised specific questions about the role of Ms Gillard's law firm, Slater & Gordon, in the purchase of a Melbourne property by Wilson. "I am unable to understand how Slater & Gordon, who were then acting for the Victorian branch of the union, could have permitted the use of funds which were obviously taken from the union, in the purchase of private property of this nature, without seeking and obtaining proper authority from the union for such use of its funds," Mr Cambridge said." The above also relates to Bernard Murphy given he was Julia Gillard's boss at the time at Slater and Gordon.

"Current AWU boss, "Big Bill" Ludwig, a major Labor powerbroker on the Right, also provided an affidavit to the court outlining corruption involving Ms Gillard's former lover." (Click here to read the full article)

And this from another post on the 7th of August: *"Ian Cambridge as mentioned above became a Commissioner at the NSW Industrial Relations Commission in 1997. In 2009 Julia Gillard*

*as Minister for Industrial Relations personally appointed Ian
Cambridge as dual appointee to Fair Work Australia. I find this
disturbing. While it could be argued that other Commissioners of
the NSW Industrial Relations Commission were also given dual
appointments at the same time they had not previously called for
a Royal Commission into criminal conduct by Julia Gillard and
her boyfriend Bruce Wilson."*

*"Julia Gillard should never have appointed him and if Ian
Cambridge had any self-respect he should not have accepted the
position. It could be construed by some that Ian Cambridge has
taken a bribe to keep his mouth shut about her criminal past."*

*"I also do notice that the Australian Mines and Metals
Association has documented Julia Gillard stacking the bench at
Fair Work Australia with her union mates. (Click here to read)."*

Bernard Murphy is not the first person from the AWU fraud
scandal that Julia Gillard has appointed as a judicial officer, nor
is it the first time she has been accused of corrupting the
judiciary.

This is what Stephen Mayne on his website The Mayne
Report had to say in an article written on the 30th August titled
"Why it is okay to look at Gillard's AWU dealings" and
specifically the section titled "What were Gillard and her then
boss-turned-Judge doing in mid-1995?"

"One of the PM's Slater & Gordon bosses at the time was
Bernard Murphy, who the Gillard Government in April elevated
from chairman of Maurice Blackburn to the bench of the Federal
Court, a position from which he will be highly unlikely to ever
proffer an opinion on this saga.

"Frankly, in my opinion this looks like pretty ordinary cronyism,
especially given most judges have experience at the bar and
Murphy has only ever been a solicitor."

The defamation

In relation to Murphy, in a law suit when he was at Slater in Gordon against the former politician Ian Smith having an affair with Cheryl Harris, a staffer who became pregnant to him, he says this "he deployed some controversial tactics in taking the long handle to Jeff Kennett's former Finance Minister, Ian Smith."

"Slaters was acting for Smith's embittered former chief of staff Cheryl Harris and Bernard Murphy was calling the shots."

"On Tuesday evening of this week I was first made aware of the allegations against me in the Magistrates Court earlier that day. This information was conveyed to me by a Herald Sun journalist who had been given a copy of the lodged documents before they were served on me. The documents were not served on me until approximately 9.50am the next morning, Wednesday, in a blaze of media coverage. This is the first serious breach of the legal process. The second breach is in the unsubstantiated allegations being publicly aired by Slater and Gordon before the court hearing. Slater and Gordon will be called to account for these disgraceful and unethical actions. Any action by me against Slater and Gordon for redress will be commenced once the Magistrates Court allegations have been disposed of and my name is vindicated."

"This was an example of Slaters absolutely going the knuckle against a political figure in a sensational story with a sexual element. It would be interesting to know if Gillard helped her then boss in this or assisted in negotiating his subsequent exit from Slaters." (Click here to read the full article – about half way down the page)

Ian Smith won a defamation settlement against Slater and Gordon believed to be about $200,000 over a wide range of allegations, including allegations by Harris that Smith had bashed her and tried to force her to have an abortion.

So, who leaked the court documents to the media before they had even been served on Ian Smith? Slater and Gordon were running the case through the media, so it had to be Bernard Murphy or at least on his direction.

This is what it says on the website Beast Lift from the time:

"In the firm's Little Bourke Street office this week, a storyline not dissimilar to the American television show LA Law was played out. Television cameras and journalists jostled for position to record the real-life drama involving Ms Harris and Mr Smith. After the press conference, a public relations consultant with the law firm handed out photocopies of Ms Harris's employment contract. Other handouts included photographs of Ms Harris and Mr Smith enjoying champagne and dinner on the night he allegedly proposed marriage." (Click here to read the full article)

But Bernard Murphy seems to have tried to deny it was him or his firm. At the time he is quoted as saying on the Slater and Gordon website: "Mr Murphy said he warned Ms Harris that once she lodged a statement of claim it would be "like World War III". "You can't issue this type of claim without it attracting a very high level of media (attention). It never happens. Journalists are too good, clerks of court are too good. People talk too much, including lawyers." He is trying the blame everyone else for the unethical leak, but he was the one calling the press conferences. (Click here to read the full article)

At a Senate Budget estimates hearing in May 2011 the opposition did raise the question of Mr Murphy's appointment given his relationship with Julia Gillard. The Attorney-General's Department told the hearing that the process of selecting Mr Murphy complied with all requirements. Yeah right. The opposition did not take it any further probably because of the skeletons that they have in the closet in relation to their own judicial appointments.

When judicial officers are appointed, it needs to be done in open and transparent manner. Not some smoke and mirrors routine that the Attorney-General Robert McClelland has set up. All judicial officers should go before a public senate committee before appointment so their suitability can be questioned as they do for the Supreme Court in the US. This alone will not stop dodgy appointments but at least it would weed out people like Mr Murphy.

I must note that Andrew Bolt after initially being closed down on the reporting of the AWU fraud did do a post relevant to the above which said:

"Ms Gillard and her boss at the time at Slater & Gordon, Bernard Murphy, who was appointed a Federal Court judge six months ago, were overseeing much of the firm's legal work for unions including Mr Wilson's AWU national construction branch."

"As with Ms Gillard, there is no suggestion Mr Murphy was involved in any wrongdoing." (Click here to read the full article)

Well the concealment of a crime is a crime. Once again what does Mr Murphy know?

Most importantly is Bernard Murphy suitable for being appointed a judge given the above. The obvious answer is no.

Chapter 9

The day the Australian media died.

The day the Australian media died.

BY SHANE DOWLING ON NOVEMBER 15, 2011 • (32 COMMENTS)

In the last two months and especially the last few days the Australian media have been found to be so subservient to the Australian Prime Minister Julia Gillard, that their integrity is shot.

From this they will never be able to recover, at least as far as a lot of Australians are concerned. What's the saying "You can fool some of the people some of the time" …

It's a story that involves the Prime Minister Julia Gillard personally intervening to close down reporting of her involvement in a $1 Million fraud which led to the sacking of one journalist (Glenn Milne), the departure of another journalist from his job (Michael Smith) after legal proceedings, her dodgy judicial appointments of people who were involved and/or had knowledge of the fraud (Ian Cambridge and Bernard Murphy) and the public broadcaster, the ABC, running a clear propaganda piece on its show Media Watch to support the PM Julia Gillard. The above is just for starters.

The Michael Smith v 2UE / Fairfax Media have settled their court case and the best we have from the Australian media is one small report, one blog post and one tweet on twitter. The Australian media have basically not reported the settlement in any real manner.

The settlement itself is not the big story, it's what led up to it that is a story that is in the public interest and has to be told. In fact, I had no intentions in doing this post as I was saving it for a future post but given the failure and outright submission of the so-called mainstream media to do so, I will.

Keep in mind that there is a coalition of media companies that claim they are protecting free speech in Australia. It is called "Australia's Right to Know" and this is what it says on its website: "Australia's Right to Know is a coalition of 12 major media companies formed in May 2007 to address concerns about free speech. The coalition is working with the Commonwealth and State governments to establish new policy and best practice to improve Australian's relatively poor world ranking for freedom of speech." (Click here to go to their website)

After reading this post you will realise that the Australia's Right to Know coalition has probably done more to undermine free speech than promote it.

In this post I will be mainly focusing on the conduct of 2UE / Fairfax Media and Media Watch / Jonathan Holmes.

I have covered the background in-depth in other posts but will give a broad background now.

Michael Smith, who was an announcer on the Fairfax Media owned radio station 2UE was reporting on Julia Gillard's involvement in the AWU $1 Million fraud and was suspended by 2UE after a report on the ABC program Media Watch. Media Watch highly criticised Michael Smith as well as Andrew Bolt and Glenn Milne from News Ltd for reporting on Miss Gillard's involvement in the fraud.

The timeline below up to section 10 is from a previous post but obviously plenty more has happened since then.

Time Line:

1. I did a post on the 7th August 2011 titled "Australian Prime Minister Julia Gillard's criminal history and her hypocrisy with WikiLeaks and Julian Assange." The post had its good days and average days. It started to pick up pace in a big way and started going viral in the week beginning Monday the 22nd of August.

2. On Friday the 26th of August 2011 Michael Smith at 2ue and Andrew Bolt started running with two of the key elements of my post. That being an interview Glenn Milne did with Julia Gillard in 2007 and the answers that she gave. They also were pushing an affidavit and its contents by Robert Kernohan which was mentioned in one of my links to the Hansard on the Victorian Parliament website. Michael Smith read out some of the affidavit on air and Andrew Bolt published some on the content on his blog site. (Click here to read the Bob Kernohan affidavit) I have also put a link in the comment section as this one does not work sometimes.

3. They took the story further than me and Michael Smith pre-recorded an interview with Robert Kernohan who is a former president of the Victorian branch of the AWU on the week-end (27th and 28th August) which was meant to go to air on Monday the 29th August. Andrew Bolt also put on his blog that he would be following up on his site on the Monday.

4. On the weekend of the 27th and 28th August Julia Gillard started calling John Hartigan who is CEO of News Ltd which is News Corp's Australian subsidiary. She wanted assurances that Andrew Bolt would not follow-up which John Hartigan gave her.

5. Monday 29th of August. The Australian ran Glenn Milne's story in The Australian and on their website. Julia Gillard called John Hartigan again and demanded it be taken down from the website and demanded a retraction. There was only one key bit

that she apparently complained about, but she wanted the whole article to be taken down. Julia Gillard apparently made numerous calls and sent emails and texts. (Click here to read the Glenn Milne story ("PM A Lost Cause For Warring Unions").

6. Monday 29th of August: Fairfax Media pulls the Michael Smith interview with Robert Kernohan on their radio station 2ue. There was a 7 or 8 minute recording on the 2ue website from the Friday the 26th program of Michael Smith reading from Robert Kernohan affidavit. This was also pulled from their website and the previous days recording (Thursday 25th) put in its place. It is worth noting that the Channel 7 Today Tonight show also recorded the interview Michael Smith did with Robert Kernohan.

7. Monday 29th of August to date: Other media start running with the story of how News Ltd were forced to pull the story. Fairfax Media pulling the radio interview gets very little mention or no mention at all. No one asks the question: If Julia Gillard rang John Hartigan at News Ltd to pull the story who did she ring at Fairfax Media to pull the radio interview. And did she call Kerry Stokes at channel 7?

8. Michael Smith tried a couple of more times to run the interview with Robert Kernohan but was stopped by Fairfax Media management.

9. On Friday 2nd September I spoke to one of Julia Gillard's press secretaries and I asked in words to the effect: "given that Julia Gillard had called John Hartigan to have the story pulled at News Ltd who at Fairfax Media had Julia Gillard called to have the Robert Kernohan interview pulled from 2UE." The response I got from the press secretary was that he was confident that Julia Gillard would not have called Fairfax Media. He obviously has a lot more confidence than me.

10. News Ltd have since gone on the offensive and fought back to some degree. There are a few links under the Andrew Bolt heading below which show the fight-back.

11. Monday the 5th of September: Media Watch do a very damming story attacking Michael Smith, Andrew Bolt, Glenn Milne for reporting on Julia Gillard's involvement in the AWU fraud. The program also attacks a statutory declaration by Bob Kernohan. I would rate it as one of the most brutal attacks I have ever seen. And one that does not stand up to scrutiny as you will see. (Click here to watch the episode)

12. Tuesday the 6th of September: Radio Station 2UE suspend Michael Smith. This is what Fairfax Media had to say in their paper The Age "The talkback host Michael Smith has been temporarily suspended by 2UE station management after he was "slammed" by the ABC's *Media Watch* program last night." (Click here to read more)

13. Sunday the 11th of September: I send an email to Media Watch and its host Jonathan Holmes asking some questions about the failings of its show on the 5th of September and put them on notice that I am planning to do a story on it. They fail to respond.

14. Wednesday the 14th of September. I sent a follow-up email and they again fail to respond.

15. Monday the 19th of September: I publish my story on this site titled "The lies and deception of Media Watch and host Jonathan Holmes in defence of Julia Gillard." I sent an email notifying Media Watch of the post. About 12 hours later I receive a response from Media Watch in relation to the questions I asked on 11th of September. (Click here to read the post and the emails) One of the key parts in the post is where I say "I understand the appropriate body to deal with Mr Holmes is the Australian Communications and Media Authority which I will send copy of this post and we will see what happens." They were clearly put on notice.

16. Monday the 19th of September: Media Watch in their 32nd episode titled "One regulator to rule them all" put a screen grab of my website Kangaroo Court of Australia in the show. The

below video is an edited version of the show. It goes for 1 minute and 17 seconds to put it into some context and my site shows up at the 28 second mark for 2 seconds. It is my viewpoint that this is admission by Media Watch that at least some of the issues that I had raised with them in relation to their failings in the show on the 5th of September were true and correct. I will get into more detail of the reasoning for my viewpoint later.

In the full show which runs for just over 12 minutes my site shows up at the 4.08-minute mark. (Click here to watch the full episode)

17. Wednesday the 21st of September: In an article in The Australian newspaper written by Media Watch host Jonathan Holmes titled "Let no one license truth and understanding" my website is mentioned where it says ""So, by all means, let's try to find a way to beef up and properly fund the Australian Press Council. Let's grapple with the vexed issue of how the blogosphere, from Crikey to Kangaroo Court, can be persuaded to submit to its adjudications." Although he only refers to it as

"Kangaroo Court" but it is in the same sentence he mentions the website Crikey. In the video above there is a screen grab of Crikey then my site. So in the paper he was definitely referring to my site. Once again I take this as admission of their failings in the show on the 5th of September. (Click here to read the full article)

18. Wednesday the 21st of September: While still suspended and after his lawyers were told by 2UE's lawyers that he was about to be sacked, Michael Smith launches legal action in the Federal Magistrates Court of Australia. He was seeking an injunction to stop 2UE from sacking him.

19. Thursday the 22nd of September: In court the 2UE lawyers ask for more time to prepare a defence and give the court an assurance that they will not sack Michael Smith until the hearing. It is set down for hearing on the afternoon of the 12th of October.

20. Wednesday the 12th of October: After a few hours of the hearing which started at 2.15pm Federal Magistrate Barnes adjourns for further hearing on the 11th of November. On the 11th and 12th of October 2UE file a total of five Notice of Objections to the subpoenas that were filed by Michael Smith. 2UE obviously had plenty to hide and why did they leave it up the day before and the day of the hearing to file them. Clearly, they were abusing the process and system.

21. Monday the 17th of October: Fairfax Media Limited file a Notice of Appearance and join their subsidiary 2UE at the card table. Why? I do not know. Maybe they were trying to intimidate Michael Smith or trying to run up his legal bills or maybe he tried to subpoena documents from them or wanted some of their staff to give evidence.

22. Thursday the 10th of November: I checked the daily court lists for the next day at the Federal Magistrates Court of Australia and seen the Michael Smith v 2UE case was not listed. I checked the file online and it was no longer set down for hearing.

23. Friday the 11th of November: I phoned the court and they said that the hearing had been vacated. I sent a message on twitter which read "Mike Smith v 2UE and Fairfax Media hearing set down for hearing today, vacated – Maybe a settlement? #Auspol 11 Nov" That's right, it was left up to a blogger who works on his site part-time to get the ball rolling and it didn't roll too far. All we got after that was 1. A News Ltd journalist doing a tweet in the afternoon that the matter had been settled and that Michael Smith would leave 2UE. 2. A News Ltd journalist doing a short article on The Australian website and 3. News Ltd journalist Andrew Bolt doing short piece on his blog on Saturday. Where was the rest of the media?

Media Watch

The Media watch show on the 5th of September will go down in history as one of the most disgraceful pieces of journalism the country has ever seen. In fact, it was not journalism, it was propaganda on behalf of the PM Julia Gillard.

When I did my post in response to the show titled "The lies and deception of Media Watch and host Jonathan Holmes in defence of Julia Gillard." what did Media Watch and Jonathan Holmes do? Did they send me a nasty letter of complaint? No. Did they get a lawyer to send me a threatening letter to amend the post of alleged defamatory material? No.

So, what did they do? They responded to the questions they had been avoiding answering (although the response was garbage) and then they promoted my site on the Media Watch show and in Jonathan Holmes article in The Australian.

Why is this? Because they knew that I was going to the Australian Communications and Media Authority to make a formal compliant and they knew they were in a lot of trouble for the hatchet job they did. As it turns out when I checked the website of the Australian Communications and Media Authority it says I first had to make a complaint with the ABC which I have and that is still in progress, and I am waiting to hear back from them. It has been an interesting experience to say the least. I could write more but I will be doing another post on that later on so I will save it for then.

Fairfax Media

Fairfax Media are a main player in the Australia's Right to Know coalition and are meant to be protecting free speech. Just not when it comes to their own dirty laundry. As stated above they were challenging the subpoenas that Michael Smith filed for access to documents and filed five Notice of Objections to the subpoenas.

If Fairfax Media were trying to get documents off the government and they refused, Fairfax Media would be screaming and probably accuse the government of a cover-up.

Fairfax Media would have been well aware that the Media Watch program was nothing more than a hatchet job and was no justification for suspending Michael Smith.

As we know Julia Gillard personally phoned executives News Corp to stop the reporting. Given that Fairfax Media / 2UE stopped the reporting at the same time are we really to believe she did not call anyone at Fairfax Media. Off course she did. The most likely suspects would be Roger Corbett – Chairman Fairfax Media, Gail Hambly – General Council Fairfax Media or Greg Hywood – CEO Fairfax Media.

The Australian media

Where are they? People sit around bagging News Corp all day every day and some of that criticism is justified and probably a lot of it is. But at least they did report on the matter to some degree and that is while they are under extreme pressure from the government with the media enquiry that is currently afoot.

Not even a squeak from the rest of the Australian media. That is why I say may the 11th of November 2011 be remembered as the day the Australian media died.

The story is not over yet, and I will keep you posted.

Chapter 10

Julia Gillard's corrupt past raised in parliament by ALP member Robert McClelland.

Julia Gillard's corrupt past raised in parliament by ALP member Robert McClelland.

BY SHANE DOWLING ON JUNE 24, 2012 • (174 COMMENTS)

The former Attorney-General Robert McClelland has let Julia Gillard know it is game on in relation to the prime ministership. By naming Julia Gillard and the case involving her then boyfriend Bruce Wilson who was involved in fraud and theft when he worked at the AWU in parliament last Thursday Mr McClelland has put the focus and blow torch on Ms Gillard and her involvement in the fraud.

Mr McClelland's motives are fairly clear given that he is a well-known Kevin Rudd supporter and lost his position as Attorney-General because he supported Kevin Rudd in the last leadership ballot in February. It has been picked up by two senators, the Nationals Barnaby Joyce and the Liberals George Brandis, who started asking questions on Friday in parliament.

Andrew Bolt broke the story on Thursday and has done two posts on it since which I will get to in a minute. But it looks like it could explode so let's have a quick overview first.

This has been on the boil since last year when Julia Gillard moved hard and fast when it hit the mainstream media. It started right here on this site with the post I did on the 7th of August 2011 titled "Australian Prime Minister Julia Gillard's criminal history and her hypocrisy with WikiLeaks and Julian Assange." (Click here to read the post)

It was picked up a couple of weeks later by Mike Smith who was then a radio announcer at 2UE, and he ran with it but focused on Julia Gillard's involvement in the fraud. Andrew Bolt from News Ltd joined in the reporting and so did Glenn Milne from News Ltd.

Julia Gillard personally jumped on the phone to the then CEO of News Ltd John Hartigan and had the reporting by Bolt and Milne stopped. Mike Smith was also stopped from reporting on it so it is not hard to work out Gillard also phoned a director of Fairfax Media (owner of 2ue). At that stage Mike Smith had done an interview with Bob Kernohan who had signed a statutory declaration that implicated Julia Gillard and Channel Seven had also recorded the interview. The Channel Seven interview never want to air. So, one has to assume Gillard also phoned Channel Seven owner Kerry Stokes or one of his executives. This has been covered in a previous post on the 5th of September 2011 titled "Has Julia Gillard blackmailed the Media to cover-up her corrupt past? The Fairfax Media and News Corp scandal." (Click here to read the post)

Glenn Milne was sacked from a casual on-air position with the ABC and has never been heard of again at News Ltd. Mike Smith was suspended from 2ue and lawyers from 2ue told Mike Smith's lawyers they were about to sack him, so he took court action seeking an injunction to stop them. It was settled out of court and Mike Smith left 2ue.

There was nothing legally wrong with the reporting of her past or the Bob Kernohan statutory declaration. I have reported on it and posted the statutory declaration on this site and have never heard from the PM. My next post on the matter was on the 11th September 2011 titled "The Michael Smith 2ue emails to Julia Gillard and the Bob Kernohan Statutory Declaration." (Click here to read the post)

The ABC television show Media Watch came out in support of Julia Gillard with an extremely biased show which I did a post on the 19th of September 2011 titled "The lies and deception of Media Watch and host Jonathan Holmes in defence of Julia Gillard." (Click here to read the post)

My final post on the matter was on the 15th of November 2011 titled "The day the Australian media died." which covered the black out by the media under Julia Gillard's instructions and their failings. (Click here to read the post)

Now back to Bolt and his latest posts on Robert McClelland throwing a hand grenade into the Prime Minister's office.

On Thursday Bolt reported "McClelland brings back Gillard's past to haunt her"

In Parliament today, McClelland hit back – by referring obliquely to an explosive scandal in the 1990s involving her then boyfriend Bruce Wilson, an Australian Workers Union state secretary accused of ripping off union money. McClelland said it was a case in which Gillard and he were "representing opposing clients" and "that matter has coloured much of my thinking in this area (of cracking down on malfeasance by union officials).

Even more pointedly, McClelland told Parliament the Government's proposed toughening of Fair Work Australia's investigative process did not go far enough, and needed the power to force union officials "to compensate the organisation for loss arising from their misconduct".

As I mentioned, these issues also arose in those matters that I was involved with in the mid-1990s, which were filed in both the then Industrial Court of Australia and the Federal Court of Australia. There are a number of matters, generally under the name of Ludwig and Harrison and others, but probably most relevantly matter no. 1032 of 1996. (Click here to read Bolt's full post)

On Friday Bolt wrote "Gillard confronted with the scandal she almost buried"

Robert McClelland has lifted the lid on a story that many in the media have been too scared to touch – a scandal involving a then boyfriend of the Prime Minister.

The Financial Review reports on a story I broke yesterday:

Dumped attorney-general Robert McClelland says the Labor Party has not gone far enough in cracking down on corruption in the union movement, citing examples going back to the 1990s connected to Prime Minister Julia Gillard.

It is a good read as it has the transcript of the Nationals Barnaby Joyce and the Liberals George Brandis raising it in the senate. (Click here to read Bolt's full post)

Then today, Saturday, Bolt writes "McClelland twists the knife"

Robert McClelland confirms he was indeed referring to a scandal involving Julia Gillard and her former partner:

Pressure on Julia Gillard's leadership has intensified after an act of internal destabilisation by dumped attorney-general Robert McClelland that triggered a Coalition attack on the Prime Minister's integrity...

Labor MPs viewed the comments as inflammatory and an act of revenge on Ms Gillard... (Click here to read Bolt's full post)

This will obviously play out over the next few days and weeks. Why was it left to an ALP MP to bring this to a head in parliament and why have the liberals and nationals not gone after this sooner who knows.

But if the Nationals and Liberals drop off it will be very sad indeed. With Julia Gillard's past she should have never been Prime Minister in the first place.

Chapter 11

Bagman Ralph Blewitt wants to reveal all in the Bruce Wilson – Julia Gillard AWU fraud scandal.

Bagman Ralph Blewitt wants to reveal all in the Bruce Wilson – Julia Gillard AWU fraud scandal.

BY SHANE DOWLING ON AUGUST 4, 2012 • (81 COMMENTS)

Ralph Blewitt who helped Julia Gillard's partner Bruce Wilson rip off the AWU in the 1990's says he will reveal all if he is given immunity from prosecution. This was revealed in The Australian on Friday in a front-page story.

The story starts off: *THE former union official and alleged bagman for a financial scandal linked to the then boyfriend of Julia Gillard wants to give evidence for the first time to police and prosecutors about his role and the conduct of others.*

The Australian can reveal that Ralph Blewitt, a one-time branch head for the Australian Workers Union, is seeking immunity from criminal prosecution in return for breaking a 17-year silence and providing a statement to police. (Click here to read the full story)

The Australian have also run with the story again today (Saturday 4/8/12) The evidence to come out in the articles is nothing greatly new but there are a number of key points of interest the first obviously being that News Ltd have decided to go hard on the issue again with front page stories. Although it must be noted that Andrew Bolt has been continuing to run with the story since last year and some other media picked up on the story on Friday as well.

For those new to the story I did a very detailed post August last year on Julia Gillard's involvement titled "Australian Prime Minister Julia Gillard's criminal history and her hypocrisy with WikiLeaks and Julian Assange." (Click here to read the post)

The second is Ralph Blewitt being prepared to tell all. He has been living in Asia since 1997 and currently lives in Malaysia. He is back in Australia to come clean on the fraud and has a criminal lawyer to represent him. The man who seems to have made this happen is Harry Nowicki who is a retired Melbourne lawyer who has been investigating the matter for the last six months for a book on the scandal. (Click here to read the story)

The third could and would mean major problems for Julia Gillard given that she has never given a detailed account of her involvement and/or knowledge of what happened. Blewitt potentially could implicate her and if I was a betting person I would say that is exactly what would happen. Then it would be a bit late for any denials from Gillard to carry any weight as she should have given a fully detailed account a long time ago.

This is important for this site and its supporters as well. Some people write in the comment section that there is nothing we can do about corruption and others have said we should have a revolution to get rid of corrupt governments. Well, the revolution will never happen physically, but it is happening online. So even though Julia Gillard killed off the story in the mainstream media last year she never killed the story online. This website got the ball rolling last August with the post mentioned above and other blogs picked it up and ran with it as well and it has been kept going by the people using Facebook, Twitter and email etc. So, no matter what happens with this matter now we have made our presence felt.

As this website and others like it grow so will our power to drive the political agenda and real change. Give it a few years and websites like this one, and hopefully this one, will be as much the mainstream media as the major players.

Chapter 12

Prima facie case to charge Julia Gillard with concealing a serious indictable offence in the AWU Scandal

Prima facie case to charge Julia Gillard with concealing a serious indictable offence in the AWU Scandal

BY SHANE DOWLING ON AUGUST 26, 2012 • (373 COMMENTS)

There is enough evidence to charge Julia Gillard for concealing a serious indictable offence which carries a jail term of 2 years. Julia Gillard has dared anyone to make allegations against her. I have before and will again and in this post, I make out the prima facie case against Julia Gillard.

There are two key elements

1. Does Julia Gillard know about the fraud. and

2. Did she conceal the fraud.

If you are new to this story, please go to the Julia Gillard / Bruce Wilson – AWU Fraud page at the top in the menu bar for previous posts with all the history. (Click here to go to the page)

Evidence that Julia Gillard knew that there was a fraud.

Everyone knows that her former boyfriend ripped off the AWU and Julia Gillard knows this as well. Gillard helped him but says she did not do it knowingly. The evidence that Julia Gillard knew about the fraud is a mile long but let's have a look at just some of it.

1. Her excuses that she was "young and naive" and "I was in a relationship, which I ended, and obviously it was all very distressing. I am by no means the first person to find out that someone close turns out to be different to what you had believed them to be. It's an ordinary human error." (Click here to read the article)

2. She said in her press conference on Thursday that as soon as she found out what Bruce Wilson had been up to, she ended the relationship.

3. She was left Slater and Gordon not long after as a direct result of the AWU fraud. Although in the press conference on Thursday she seemed to be claiming there were other reasons as well.

4. Slater and Gordon interviewed her and taped the interview which clearly suggests wrongdoing or knowledge of it. In the press conference on Thursday Gillard tried to make out this was not unusual.

I could keep going but if Julia Gillard wants to deny knowing about the fraud it would be a bad joke.

Did Julia Gillard conceal the fraud?

All of the media attention on Julia Gillard in relation to this matter could have been cleared up by her by simply releasing the statements and/or affidavits she gave to the police in 1995/96. There does not seem to be any. Why not?

She could also have released the statements she gave to the AWU in this matter in 1995/96. As we will see she did not give them any and must have refused to. Why?

In the Ian Cambridge affidavit dated 19th September 1996 on page 19 he says in relation to the purchase of the house by Bruce Wilson in Melbourne "I am unable to understand how Slater & Gordon, who were then acting for the Victorian branch of the union, could have permitted the use of funds which were obviously taken from the union, in the purchase of private property of this nature, without seeking and obtaining proper authority from the union for such use of its funds" (Click here to read the affidavit)

That is a statement that Ian Cambridge should not have needed to make. Julia Gillard and/or Slater and Gordon should have told Ian Cambridge how it happened. At the time Ian Cambridge wrote the affidavit the AWU account had been transferred to Maurice and Blackburn lawyers because of the AWU fraud. But this alone should not have stopped Julia Gillard and Slater and Gordon from helping the AWU investigate.

Did she refuse to help because of the police investigations that were afoot at the time? If this is the case it is not a good look to say the least.

At the press conference on Thursday Julia Gillard was asked:

JOURNALIST: *Prime Minister, do you have any information which you are prevented from giving by lawyer-client privilege that could assist the authorities in relation to the funds, you know, that Mr Wilson-*

PM: *No*

Then why did she not give a statement to the police.

The reason there is no lawyer-client privilege stopping her is because of what is called the fraud exception or also known as the crime exception. Lawyer-client privilege means that a lawyer does not have to disclose any communication with the client and they are protected by the law. But if a lawyer helps a client commit a crime, then they can and have to disclose the communication which is covered by the fraud exception

I believe that her admission that there is no "information which you are prevented from giving by lawyer-client privilege" says she knew there was a crime and her communication with Bruce Wilson and Ralph Blewitt was not covered by the lawyer-client privilege. It also asks the question why Julia Gillard did not give any statements to the police or if she did why she has not released them?

At the time of the fraud back in 1995/96 the Western Australia police, Victorian Police and Federal police where all investigating. Bob Kernohan gave a statement to the Federal police in relation to $6,500 he had received from Bruce Wilson which shows up on the Victorian Parliament Hansard website. Kernohan was cleared of any wrongdoing. (Click here to read)

If Bob Kernohan gave a statement, why did Julia Gillard also not give a statement to the police? She now says that she believed the accounts where to be used for a re-election slush fund which turned out to be a lie. So, who lied to her? Was it Bruce Wilson or Ralph Blewitt or both? What did they say exactly? This at the very least would clearly be relevant information that would have helped the police in their investigations and most likely would have helped in a prosecution of Bruce Wilson and/or Ralph Blewitt.

CRIMES ACT 1900 – SECT 316

Concealing serious indictable offence

316 Concealing serious indictable offence

(1) If a person has committed a serious indictable offence and another person who knows or believes that the offence has been committed and that he or she has information which might be of

material assistance in securing the apprehension of the offender or the prosecution or conviction of the offender for it fails without reasonable excuse to bring that information to the attention of a member of the Police Force or other appropriate authority, that other person is liable to imprisonment for 2 years.

(2) A person who solicits, accepts or agrees to accept any benefit for himself or herself or any other person in consideration for doing anything that would be an offence under subsection (1) is liable to imprisonment for 5 years.

(3) It is not an offence against subsection (2) merely to solicit, accept or agree to accept the making good of loss or injury caused by an offence or the making of reasonable compensation for that loss or injury.

(4) A prosecution for an offence against subsection (1) is not to be commenced against a person without the approval of the Attorney General if the knowledge or belief that an offence has been committed was formed or the information referred to in the subsection was obtained by the person in the course of practising or following a profession, calling or vocation prescribed by the regulations for the purposes of this subsection.

(5) The regulations may prescribe a profession, calling or vocation as referred to in subsection (4).

Some of the questions that Julia Gillard has to answer are:

1. Why did you not give a statement / affidavit to the police? If you did why have you not released it as it would clear the air on the whole matter?

2. If you did give a police statement is the story in the statement different to the one the one you have made publicly?

3. Why did you not assist the AWU in their investigations given they were the client?

4. If you did not give a police statement did you refuse on the grounds that you might incriminate yourself?

5. Did you also refuse to help the AWU on the grounds that you might incriminate yourself?

6. Did you claim legal privilege in refusing to help the police? If you did, why did you say on Thursday that legal privilege was not a factor that covered your information in this matter?

7. In 2007 Glenn Milne reported "she has strenuously denied ever knowing what the association's bank accounts were used for." (Click here to read more) But you now say they were meant to be used for a slush fund. Have you told this to the police?

That will do for starters, and I will have follow-up questions once she has answered them.

If you appeal a judgment in court on the grounds of bias by the judge you do not have to show actual bias, you only have to show perceived bias and you will win the appeal. The point is in this matter the media are totally focused on showing Julia Gillard was party to the crime which should be applauded, but they also need to question her role in the concealment of the crime.

Showing Gillard was a party to the crime will be hard to prove unless at least two people spill the beans on Julia Gillard and that is unlikely to happen anytime soon. But what can be proved now is her involvement in the concealment of the crime unless she has some brilliant answers to the issues and questions that I have raised above.

Chapter 13

Julia Gillard and Bruce Wilson AWU fraud investigation gathers pace.

Julia Gillard and Bruce Wilson AWU fraud investigation gathers pace.

BY SHANE DOWLING ON OCTOBER 14, 2012 • (79 COMMENTS)

The Julia Gillard and Bruce Wilson fraud / AWU scandal is gathering pace again. This week Deputy Leader of the Opposition Julie Bishop asked questions of the Prime Minister in Parliament, Fairfax Media have run a number of stories on the matter and Michael Smith and others are still hot on the trail.

There is no stopping it now. Make no mistake about it, the matter will keep on growing until the next election and after.

Below I will put links to a lot of what has been published over the last few days. But that is not the key point I want to make in this post. It is the power of the Internet and the part you play and I will use the Gillard / Wilson / AWU fraud as the example because what is driving this story is you the reader, not only reading the posts but then promoting them online as well.

This is important to understand for the people who feel powerless and think that nothing can be done, not just in this matter but corruption matters overall. You will see it in the comment section from time to time that "there is nothing we can do". Well, that is changing at a rapid pace because of websites like this one and others. If you take out the online websites and community that have been driving the Gillard / Wilson fraud story for over 12 months the story would have died long ago.

There is a very good article on the current state of the media on Crikey titled "Brave News World: media is dead – long live media" Two key parts are where it says:

"The effect of the internet has been as profound as it would have been on any oligopoly suddenly confronted by overpowering quantities of high quality, real-time content priced at zero. It has shivered markets to fragments, atomised and energised audiences, and gnawed business models away at each end, impacting newspapers' abilities both to attract advertising and to charge for news, winnowing television audiences away and eroding the value of free-to-air broadcast spectrum. The proportion of Australians who read a daily newspaper, and who watch an evening news, are roughly half those of 30 years ago."

And: ***THE RACE FOR ONLINE READERS***

Not surprisingly, speed is in fashion. "The way you respond to a story has huge implications," says Hal Crawford, head of news at ninemsn. "If smh.com.au beats us to a breaking news story by two minutes, that can have a huge impact on traffic figures for that month. If you're always slower, the audience will go elsewhere. We don't have a metric yet to measure response times accurately but the difference is palpable. A lot of people hear about stuff first of all from the radio. They then go online to verify the news, which they've only half-heard. So if ABC Radio is running something about a guy who got bitten in half by a shark in Perth, you'd better have it on your site. Doesn't matter how small it is; it has to be there somewhere."

It is quite a long story but a must read for people who use online news sites. (Click here to read the article)

In summary what the above says is that a lot of people are moving to the internet for their news and if the major players like smh.com.au, ninemsn and news do not have the popular content that readers want on their website they lose a lot of traffic. And traffic equals advertising dollars for them.

Fairfax Media

This is probably the main reason that Fairfax Media who own The SMH and The AGE sites have started running with the Gillard / Wilson story this week harder than they had before. They had been losing a lot of traffic to other websites such as the News Ltd sites, mine and Michael Smith's new site who have been running the story. Fairfax's metro papers are dying, and they will soon be online only in the not-too-distant future so they cannot afford to be losing online readership.

Their advertisers know how long people spend on their sites and how long they spend on specific stories. So, if they have garbage stories the readers go elsewhere and Fairfax lose advertising dollars. They can also quickly get a bad reputation which you can see in the comments section of this website and others where Fairfax have been heavily criticised for not properly reporting on the Gillard / Wilson matter. If that is the reason behind Fairfax's decision to start reporting on the matter, then it is because of you the reader.

An example would be this story yesterday on smh.com.au titled "The man who knew too much stirs ghosts of Gillard's past" At the time of writing this it has had 580 Facebook likes and 46 Tweets on Twitter. These numbers are very large even for Fairfax with most of their stories getting nowhere near those numbers. So not only have they received a lot of readers and will show up high on the search engines by having the content, but a lot of their readers have also helped promote the story. By ignoring the story like they have been they have cost themselves money and they must have realised this and changed their mind.

Julie Bishop / Julia Gillard questions

Below is what Julie Bishop asked the Prime Minister in parliament on Thursday about the fraud scandal:

"Did she also inform the appropriate authority of Mr Wilson's misappropriation of union funds?" Ms Bishop wanted to know on Thursday.

Ms Gillard responded by insisting she had exhausted questions about the matter in August.

She also reiterated that police investigations had been conducted in the mid-1990s. No prosecution was ever launched.

Ms Bishop on Thursday subsequently asked why the PM, as a practising lawyer at the time, "didn't inform the appropriate authority of Mr Wilson's fraud when she became aware of it".

The Labor leader fired back: "I remind the deputy leader of the opposition of what I just said. The appropriate authorities were engaged in this matter." (Click here to read more)

I have no doubt Julie Bishop has picked the line of questioning up from a previous post I did on the 26th of August titled "Prima facie case to charge Julia Gillard with concealing a serious indictable offence in the AWU Scandal." (Click here to read) Andrew Bolt did a post a couple of days ago titled "Why did Gillard not go to the police about the AWU scandal?" (Click here to read) Once again if they have picked it up from my post it is because of the readers who promote my posts on Facebook and Twitter etc. I make this point not so I can boast about me and what I have written, but so you can understand the influence that you have.

Julia Bishop asked a broad question of Julia Gillard which allowed her an out to a degree which is fine for a first question. Now Julia Bishop needs to get more specific and ask the questions that I raised such as:

1. Why did you not give a statement / affidavit to the police? If you did why have you not released it as it would clear the air on the whole matter?

2. If you did give a police statement is the story in the statement different to the one the one you have made publicly?

3. Why did you not assist the AWU in their investigations given they were the client?

This gives Julia Gillard less wriggle room to get out of the questions. While other questions are being asked, this is the main line of questioning the opposition and others need to focus on, because why she did not go to the police and give a statement to the police is the hardest thing for Ms Gillard to justify. In fact, it is something she could still do. So maybe she should also be asked if she plans on going to the police with all the new evidence that is coming out.

Remember, you as the online reader have played a major part and to keep on playing your part to drive this issue and other issues. Stop writing in the comment section what a great job I am doing (it is becoming embarrassing and is off topic) and start focusing on the job you are doing. It does not take long to play your part, 5 or 10 minutes a week reading my posts then promoting them on social media which takes 1 or 2 minutes.

I have been sitting on some information and will start writing about it in the next week or two. But here is a question for you. In 1996 Ian Cambridge wrote to the Federal Labor Government asking for a Royal Commission into the Gillard / Wilson / AWU fraud. Not in a million years were they ever going to have a Royal Commission given the Labor Party are an extension of the union movement and Cambridge would have known this. So why did he write to them seeking a Royal Commission? That first came to my attention in 2006 and it hit me straight away what Cambridge was up to.

Some links to reporting the last week:

Michael Smith interview with Ralph Blewitt: Part One (Click here) and Part Two (Click here)

Fairfax Media – Mark Baker – PM vouched for union body caught in corruption scandal (Click here to read) and The man who knew too much stirs ghosts of Gillard's past (Click here to read)

Andrew Bolt Blog – New Document: Gillard Misled on AWU scandal (Click here to read)

The Australian – Hedley Thomas – Tussle over mystery file on AWU slush fund (Click here to read)

Chapter 14

Julia Gillard changes her story again in the AWU fraud scandal at yesterday's press conference

Julia Gillard changes her story again in the AWU fraud scandal at yesterday's press conference

BY SHANE DOWLING ON NOVEMBER 27, 2012 • (55 COMMENTS)

Prime Minister Julia Gillard yesterday called a press conference in relation to the AWU fraud scandal. Ms Gillard claimed she had no evidence of any crimes in 1995/1996 and that is why she did not go to the police or AWU. Well, that is a lie. But even if true she certainly has evidence now and has had so for numerous years, so why does she not go to the Victorian police and make a statement given they are currently investigating the matter.

The evidence Ms Gillard has of a crime by her own admission.

Ms Gillard has said a number of times and in her interview at Slater and Gordon in 1995 that she believed the AWU Workplace Relations Association she helped set up for her then boyfriend Bruce Wilson was a slush fund. As we all know it was an

unauthorised association used to launder fraudulently
gained money through for the benefit of Bruce Wilson and maybe
Ralph Blewitt.

Ms Gillard says she only gave legal advice to Bruce Wilson
and/or Ralph Blewitt in relation to setting up the association. But
for her to believe it was a slush fund either Mr Wilson and/or Mr
Blewitt had to have lied to Julia Gillard. If that is the case that is
evidence that the Victorian and Western Australian police could
use in charging Mr Wilson and/or Mr Blewitt.

This is important evidence because what Mr Wilson and Mr
Blewitt did was fraud and identity theft. Identity theft does not
have to be of a person it can also be of a body corporate such as
illegally using the AWU name.

The laws

I previously did a post where I used a NSW law in relation to
Julia Gillard concealing a serious indictable offence. (Click here
to read the post) Someone pointed out on the comment
section that the offences took place in Victoria and Western
Australia so I found a Victorian law that I believed covered the
crime. But on further reflection I have no doubt that NSW laws
were also breached. The AWU head office is in Sydney NSW
and they are the only ones who have authority to grant the use of
the AWU name. And given the AWU name was used to facilitate
the crime it was a crime against the AWU head office.

Section 10c part 2 of the NSW Crimes Act says: (2) A
geographical nexus exists between the State and an offence if: (b)
the offence is committed wholly outside the State, but the offence
has an effect in the State.

The fraud and theft had a financial impact on the AWU and the
identity theft had an impact on the AWU reputation.

Then we look at NSW laws such as:

Section – 192E Fraud

Section 192J – Dealing with identification information

Section – 192G Intention to defraud by false or misleading statement

Section 193b – Money Laundering

There is no point arguing too much about whether NSW laws were broken as other states have similar laws. But the key point is that the above crimes or similar are what Julia Gillard is currently concealing based on her own evidence that she was lied to by Wilson and Blewitt into believing that the AWU Workplace Relations Association was a slush fund, when in fact it was a breach of the above crimes.

Julia Gillard should go to the police now and make a statement in relation to the lies she was told by Wilson and/or Blewitt when giving advice in setting up the association.

Backing away from the reasons she split up with Bruce Wilson

In yesterday's press conference Julia Gillard said this:

"As for me, obviously at the time these matters came to the attention of the partnership they came to my attention too. I did not have in front of me any evidence of criminality or wrongdoing but there was a lot of rumour about what was happening in the Victorian branch of the AWU at that time."

*"**In those circumstances I came to a personal decision about ending my relationship with Mr Wilson and I did so.** Then of course the Slater & Gordon internal review went through and you see the outcome of that review."*

But in the August press conference she said this:

JOURNALIST: Prime Minister, as I understand it, when these issues were first questioned within the AWU, the matter was looked at, at Slater & Gordon by Bernard Murphy. Now, I

presume he then informed you of these issues. What was your reaction at that time? This is specifically the activities of Mr Blewitt and Mr Wilson?

PM: Well, I'm not in a position, for all the obvious reasons about legal professional privilege, to canvas the contents of files operated by solicitors at Slater & Gordon.

*What I can say to you, Dennis, and what I think your question is trying to drive at is **once I became aware that I had been deceived about a series of matters, I ended my relationship with Mr Wilson**.*

JOURNALIST: Prime Minister, at any point were you aware that this workplace reform association was to receive lumps of money from companies like THEISS and John Holland?

PM: I was not aware of the receipt of these funds. I had no knowledge about the operation of the association. I provided advice, as the association was established, I then knew absolutely nothing about its workings until allegations about its workings became the subject of discussion within the AWU and then more broadly.

And

JOURNALIST: Did you confront Bruce Wilson personally after certain matters were raised with you? What was the atmosphere of that meeting and what are your feelings towards him now?

PM: I ended our relationship and I know that there's some material in today's Australian which would lead people to believe that our national newspapers are for Mills & Boon style recounts of words spoken between people who were formerly in a close relationship. It's not my intention to canvas those matters. And it's not my intention to canvas them because by definition there can be no public interest in them. I ended the relationship. That is the significant fact.

JOURNALIST: Prime Minister, when the scandal erupted and it became known that this money had been stolen by two shysters, who told you? Was it someone at the AWU or was it Bernard Murphy who'd been told by someone else?

PM: Well, I can't go to matters of privilege, but first and foremost, allegations were being raised and dealt with within the AWU. Those allegations came to my attention. I formed a view that I had not been dealt with honestly and based on that view I ended a relationship I had back then, 17 years ago.

So in August they were allegations against Bruce Wilson which one assumes were obviously backed up by evidence as a person does not make serious allegations without evidence, but yesterday Ms Gillard said they were just rumours.

In August Julia Gillard said she was "deceived" by Bruce Wilson and ended the relationship. That clearly says she had hard evidence, not just rumours. But yesterday she says she ended the relationship with Wilson based on the rumours.

Julia Gillard is trying to back away from having knowledge of the crimes in 1995/1996 so she can justify not going to the police or AWU with her knowledge in 1995/96. What is Ms Gillard saying? That in her interview with Slater and Gordon in 1995 over these matters they said to her, "Ms Gillard we have heard rumours about Bruce Wilson, we have no evidence just rumours." From my memory of the transcript Slater and Gordon had documented evidence, such as Slater and Gordon's own files, not just rumours when they interviewed Ms Gillard.

I could write plenty more, but I do not want to lose the focus which is why does Julie Gillard not go to the police now given that the Victorian Police are investigating. Quite simple, Ms Gillard will not go to the police now for the same reason she did not go in 1995, she is lying and if she goes to the police and gives evidence against Bruce Wilson, he might do the same against her.

If they both keep their mouths shut, they will probably get away with the fraud and theft.

Chapter 15

Julia Gillard misleads parliament on who sought the dodgy AWU association

Julia Gillard misleads parliament on who sought the dodgy AWU association

BY <u>SHANE DOWLING</u> ON <u>DECEMBER 2, 2012</u> • (<u>44</u> <u>COMMENTS</u>)

Julia Gillard has misled parliament on who sought the dodgy AWU association, which was used to defraud the AWU, in an attempt to protect her former boyfriend, Bruce Wilson. Gillard and Wilson are playing the blame Ralph Blewitt game to protect themselves.

Bruce Wilson was the brains behind the fraud and setting up the association to facilitate the fraud and Ralph Blewitt was the dummy he had sign the documents to register it which the video shows.

The below video is of the interview that Bruce Wilson did on Tuesday this week for the 7.30 report and of Julia Gillard in parliament on Thursday. They clearly contradict each other.

Julia Gillard and Bruce Wilson AWU frau...

Watch later   Share

Who did you say sought the incorporation?

Watch on ▶ YouTube   ecovered and raring to go for Perth Test   14:39

(The full interview on the 7.30 report with Bruce Wilson goes for 17 minutes. Click here to watch.)

Julia Gillard is limiting what she says about Bruce Wilson as she knows if she says the wrong thing it could be used against him in a court of law and more importantly end her career. In the above video Julia Gillard was fully aware that she was misleading Parliament.

Chapter 16

Justice Rodney Madgwick and the missing court judgement in the Julia Gillard Bruce Wilson AWU fraud scandal

Justice Rodney Madgwick and the missing court judgement in the Julia Gillard Bruce Wilson AWU fraud scandal

BY SHANE DOWLING ON DECEMBER 16, 2012 • (41 COMMENTS)

There is a missing court judgement by Justice Madgwick in the Julia Gillard / Bruce Wilson AWU fraud scandal. The court has advised me that he did not publish a judgement which I find scandalous and not believable, especially when put together with the other documents that have gone missing from other sources in relation to this matter.

There are numerous missing documents in the matter but the missing judgement by Justice Madgwick is probably the most disturbing.

This is the same Rodney Madgwick who has been appointed by the ACTU as Chairman of a panel to make recommendations for improving governance arrangements amid the fallout of the Health Service Union scandal. He obviously has good knowledge of fraud and theft in the unions and how they get away with it given he was the judge in the AWU fraud scandal. The only problem is the court proceedings that came before him achieved nothing. Maybe he has a copy of the missing judgement. (Click here to read more)

Missing documents in the AWU fraud scandal

1. Julia Gillard's old law firm Slater and Gordon say the file they had on the matter has gone missing which would have had documents involving Julia Gillard.

2. The West Australian state archives department has a file that had documents in relation to the dodgy association that Julia Gillard helped her then boyfriend Bruce Wilson set up. They still have the file, but it is now empty.

3. The Federal Court of Australia had 4 files that went missing on the matter. Three have been found (QI 1274 of 1995, QI 1296 of 1995, QI 1297 of 1995) but one is still missing. The missing file, NI 2082/96, is believed to have an original copy of a Slater & Gordon conveyance file for the purchase of the house that was bought with stolen AWU funds. (Click here to read more)

4. The missing Justice Madgwick judgement from 1996 in matter QI 95/1296 for which he issued orders.

The missing judgement would have damaging findings by Justice Madgwick against numerous parties which may include Slater and Gordon. Justice Madgwick seems to have had all 4 matters in his docket and from the files it seems documents filed in one matter were used in all matters which included the Ian Cambridge affidavit. So even though his orders deal specifically with returning redundancy payments that people were not entitled to, it is possible Madgwick made finding on the broader fraud and theft in his judgement which might have included Slater and Gordon.

Justice Madgwick issued court orders against Bruce Wilson, Ralph Blewitt and others in 1996 to recover money, but I am told by the court he did not publish a judgement and there was no judgement in the file. Registrar Segal told me "*it appears from the file no written reasons for judgment were delivered. In other words, there is no "missing" judgment. There was never a written judgment.*" I do not believe this as it would put Justice Madgwick in breach of common law. He has to give written reasons for his judgement as that is what is meant to keep judges accountable and it is required if one of the parties wants to appeal.

Sometimes judgements are not published but that is in minor cases. In this matter a total of $115,000 was ordered to be paid back to the AWU by six different people. Hardly a minor matter. (Click here to read the orders)

I first realised that there was a judgement missing last year when I looked for it on the AustLII website (Australasian Legal Information Institute) which has all legal judgements in the Australia. What I did find was a judgement by Justice Spender who made reference to Justice Madgwick hearing matters in the AWU issue. Spender said "*I want, nonetheless, to make it plain that it is my intention to restore the position as best I can, pending the resolution of the litigation to be heard reasonably shortly by Madgwick J.*"

Inspection of files at the Federal Court of Australia

Thursday last week (6/12/12) I inspected the files at the Federal Court of Australia Sydney registry in the AWU matter. In the days before, when I was organising the inspection, I already knew the judgement was missing and asked for a copy of the transcript. I was told that some of the files have transcript, but I could not inspect them. Registrar Segal said I could buy a copy from the transcript provider. I phoned them and they did not have a copy as they only keep it for a number of years.

The court kept some documents from being inspected, which ones I do not know, and would not allow me to inspect the transcript even though I told them the transcript provider did not have a copy for me to buy.

I thought by the time I went to the registry the file that is still missing might have been found, which it was not and still has not been found.

Michael Francis Moore

During the inspection of the files, I came across a familiar name that has not been mentioned in the scandal as of yet. None other than the former federal court judge Michael Moore. The same man who gets a mention on the front cover of my book, Love Letters from the Bar Table. In correspondence from Robert McClelland to his client Ian Cambridge on the 14th August 1995 he mentions that "*In late February 1995 proceedings were commenced before His Honour Mr Justice Moore in the Industrial Relations Court of Australia alleging certain irregularities in respect of the establishment of the National Construction Branch*" At the time Moore was also a Federal Court judge as he had been appointed as a judge in 1994. I have not been able to find any judgement by Justice Moore in relation to this either. (Click here to read more of his background)

This is the same Michael Moore who resigned in disgrace last year (as he was nothing more than a bad joke in the court) and that was appointed by Bill Shorten firstly to review the Fair Work Act then as administrator of the HSU. It seems Bill Shorten sure likes to look after Mr Moore. (Click here to read posts that I have done on Michael Moore)

This website is not a one trick pony, but I have done numerous posts on the Gillard /Wilson AWU matter of late because it is a case that keeps on giving. The further one looks the more people who become involved and the broader the cover-up and the further into the judiciary it goes. I will keep on the courts case for the missing file.

Chapter 17

Chief Justice Patrick Keane ignores police threat and continues to hide evidence in the Julia Gillard / AWU fraud scandal

Chief Justice Patrick Keane ignores police threat and continues to hide evidence in the Julia Gillard / AWU fraud scandal

BY SHANE DOWLING ON FEBRUARY 24, 2013 • (29 COMMENTS)

The Federal Court of Australia on Chief Justice Patrick Keane's instructions has lied to the Victorian Police and said they cannot find the missing court file relevant to the Julia Gillard /AWU fraud and now the Victorian Police are threatening to obtain a search warrant to find the file NSD2082/96.

It must be remembered that the Victorian Police were given the same type of obstruction by Fair Work Australia in their investigation into Craig Thomson. But more on that in a minute.

How do I know it has happened on Patrick Keane's instructions? Well the file has been missing for six months now and Keane has not rung the police to investigate to protect the courts reputation.

As Chief Justice that is exactly what he should have done. He's the boss as shown in the court structure. (Click here to see the court structure) I also had personal dealings with Keane's predecessor, Chief Justice Black, and I know how he ruled with an iron fist.

It is very obvious the missing file is no accident given that there is also missing documents from a file in a Western Australian government department relevant to the AWU fraud, Slater and Gordon also claim they have lost files and then there is the missing court judgement by Justice Rodney Madgwick which I wrote about previously. (Click here to read the post) Too much to be a coincidence.

On Wednesday 20/2/13 The Australian reported that the court had written to the Victorian Police and told them they could not find the file.

"FEDERAL Court officials have been told by Victorian detectives investigating the AWU "slush fund" scandal that they intend to execute a search warrant at the court's registry to retrieve a legal file concerning Julia Gillard's allegedly corrupt former boyfriend, union official Bruce Wilson." (Click here to read more)

The missing Federal Court file and it's similarity to the FWA/Craig Thomson investigation

Corruption in the Federal Court registry is no different from what the whole country has seen at Fair Work Australia and their deliberate go-slow routine in the Craig Thomson investigation since 2009 and we know the three main players in that. First there was the General Manager of FWA, Tim Lee, who was promoted to the role of Commissioner in September 2011 for his good deeds and then the new General Manager Bernadette O'Neill who did her best to protect Craig Thomson and refused to hand over evidence to the police for a long time.

Victoria Police acting assistant commissioner, crime, Doug Fryer wrote to Ms Bernadette O'Neill when they were investigating Craig Thomson prior to charging him and said to Ms O'Neill in relation to the evidence that FWA had "you have declined to voluntarily provide Victoria Police investigators with access to the information being sought. Your continued refusal . . . unnecessarily hinders our investigation and delays its conclusion." (Click here to read more) Sounds very much like what Chief Justice Patrick Keane and the Federal Court are doing with the missing AWU file.

Also, there was the patsy at FWA, investigator Terry Nassios, who took four years to investigate Craig Thomson. The go slow routine was clearly on the instructions of Lee and O'Neill given they already had a comprehensive report by Slater and Gordon lawyers and accounting firm BDO back in 2009. Mr Nassious resigned as on the 1st February as the shame obviously got to him. He should spill the beans on what really happened at FWA.

Chief Justice Keane's history as a Labor Party boy

Keane is a Labor boy through and through and a friend of Kevin Rudd's. They worked in the Queensland Government together for three years.

Kevin Rudd worked for Wayne Goss when Mr Goss was opposition leader and then when he became premier in 1989 until 1995. From 1989 until 1992 Rudd was Mr Goss's Chief of Staff and then from 1992 until 1995 Mr Rudd was appointed as Director-General of the Office of Cabinet. It has been well written that Rudd was extremely powerful in the Queensland government at the time. (Click here to read more)

Patrick Keane was appointed Solicitor-General for the State of Queensland in 1992 and it is almost guaranteed that Rudd had his fingerprints on Keane's appointment in some manner if not the ultimate decision maker. But putting Keane's appointment aside,

Rudd and Keane would have worked closely for three years and were known to be friends until recent years at least and maybe still are.

In 2005 the Queensland Labor government appointed Patrick Keane as a Judge of the Court of Appeal of the Supreme Court of Queensland. Then in February 2010 while Kevin Rudd was still Prime Minister, Keane was appointed Chief Justice of the Federal Court. I know for a fact that the Prime Minister of day often interferes with judicial appointments and appoint their friends. It has happened before and will happen again. For example, Julia Gillard appointed her former boss at Slater and Gordon, Bernard Murphy, to the position of Federal Court judge in 2011. (Click here to read more)

Keane will start as a High Court Judge in March. I wrote a post last year titled "Gillard appoints Patrick Keane, who has responsibility for the missing files in the AWU scandal, as High Court judge". (Click here to read the post)

The Australian also wrote an article on Keane's High Court appointment and said, *"Justice Keane, a Queenslander who is known to have been close to former prime minister Kevin Rudd, was described yesterday by a Brisbane barrister as "a Labor man." and "He experienced a meteoric rise through the judiciary. In less than three years he moved from the Queensland Court of Appeal to Chief Justice of the Federal Court and now to the High Court."* (Click here to read more)

Keane obviously knows the right people given his quick rise up the judicial ladder and of course one would expect those people want favours back and are getting them based on the above.

The Board of Directors or CEO of any organisation are ultimately responsible for the conduct of their staff and the reputation of that organisation. As Chief Justice, Patrick Keane is equivalent to Executive Chairman, and he has full responsibility for the operation of the Federal Court. His failure to call the police in relation to the missing file is what is really telling. For him to leave it to the Victorian Police to get a search warrant is a disgrace and does untold damage to the court's reputation.

Keane thinks he can slip over to the High Court next month as a Judge and his hands are clean on the missing file matter. That is wrong at least as far as this website is concerned as this site will hold him accountable as he should not have been given his position as Chief Justice in the first place.

Chapter 18

Prime Minister Julia Gillard bribed ACTU Secretary Dave Oliver to keep his support

Prime Minister Julia Gillard bribed ACTU Secretary Dave Oliver to keep his support

BY SHANE DOWLING ON JUNE 23, 2013 • (34 COMMENTS)

Julia Gillard has used a judicial appointment to bribe Australian Council of Trade Unions (ACTU) Secretary Dave Oliver and shore up her internal Labor Party support as Prime Minister. Mr Oliver's wife Suzanne Jones was last month appointed as a judge of the Federal Circuit Court even though she does not have the experience. This happened only 19 months after Mrs Jones was appointed a Commissioner at the Fair Work Commission.

Suzanne Jones appointment would normally be considered a job for "the boys and girls" which all political parties do on a regular basis. The difference here is that there is an immediate and blatant benefit for Julia Gillard which then makes it what it is, a clear bribe by Julia Gillard to Dave Oliver to keep her reign as Prime Minister and beat off any challengers such as Kevin Rudd. This was driven home last week when I read in the SMH *"Gillard's union power base remains her best chance of seeing off another challenge if it comes" "and Dave Oliver of the*

ACTU have showed no signs of withdrawing their support. " ([Click here to read more](#))

Background – The evidence

There is some key supporting evidence that the bribe took place which came out during a Federal Senate Estimates hearing at the end of last month on the 29th and 30th of May which we will get to soon. Firstly though, it is important to understand how the appointment process is meant to work and to know some of the players involved.

The position of Judge for the Federal Circuit Court (formerly the Federal Magistrates Court until April this year) is advertised and applications taken. Then some of the applicants are interviewed. They are interviewed by a panel of three people. In this case Chief Judge John Pascoe, Susan Morgan who is a retired Family Court judge and Ms Louise Glanville, First Assistant Secretary, Attorney-General's Department.

A short list is then sent to the Attorney-General who then takes it to cabinet for a decision and/or approval of who the appointments will be.

Suzanne Jones appointment was reported last month when it was announced by the Attorney-General Mark Dreyfus QC on the 16th of May 2013 and a couple of journalists questioned the appointment for obvious reasons. But it did not go much further than that.

Suzanne Jones appointment as judge of the Federal Circuit Court

Suzanne Jones has no experience in Family Law which will make up 80 to 85% of the cases she is meant to hear and hand down judgements in. There were over 100 applicants, and you would have to assume that some would have had 10, 20 or 30 years Family Law experience but were deemed not good enough, yet Mrs Jones with no Family Law experience was the top choice.

She has had a dream run in judicial appointments. Two in the space of less than 2 years which is unheard of. Her resume briefly:

"From 1977 to 1979, Ms Jones was the associate to Deputy President Isaac of the Australian Conciliation and Arbitration Commission. In 1984, Ms Jones commenced work at the Australian Council of Trade Unions, become a Senior Industrial Officer in 1989 and a National Advocate in 1999."

"In 2001, Ms Jones was admitted to practice in the Supreme Court of Victoria" (Click here to read more)

"Your Honour came to the law a mere 13 years ago following a distinguished career in industrial relations"

"After finishing your law degree in, Your Honour served articles at Maurice Blackburn. Almost immediately after admission, you went to the Bar." (Click here to read more)

Mrs Jones was appointed as a Commissioner of Fair Work Australia in September 2011 and was appointed a Judge of the Federal Circuit Court in May 2013.

Transcript from the Senate Legal and Constitutional Affairs Legislation Committee – Estimates – May 29th and 30th 2013. (Click here for the full transcript for May 29th) and (Click here for the full transcript for May 30th)

May 29th

Senator BRANDIS: We heard from Mr Fredericks that, in relation to the Sydney and Melbourne appointments, there was only ever one short list. In other words, the same names; one finite group of names that did not change. By 'iterations' I mean different versions of a short list with perhaps different names included or omitted.

(Mr Frederick spoke in relation to Federal Court of Australia judicial appointments not the Federal Circuit Court)

Ms Glanville: Because there were four appointments to be made—two to Melbourne, one to Darwin and one to Sydney—there was an initial short list and then, depending on the outcomes of that, there was a subsequent short list.

Senator BRANDIS: So there were two?

Ms Glanville: Yes.

Senator BRANDIS: Was Ms Suzanne Jones on the initial short list?

Ms Glanville: She was on the second short list.

Senator BRANDIS: She was not on the first short list?

Ms Glanville: No.

Senator BRANDIS: How many names were on the first short list?

Ms Glanville: I would have to take that on notice.

Senator BRANDIS: Approximately?

Ms Glanville: I would have to take that on notice.

Senator BRANDIS: How many names were added to the short list when the second short list was prepared?

Ms Glanville: About five, but I would have to check that.

Senator BRANDIS: So Ms Suzanne Jones was one of about five people who did not make the short list but made the second short list?

And

Senator BRANDIS: Can you explain to me, please, why in the case of this particular applicant, who did not make the short list when it was first prepared—Ms Jones; Mr Oliver's wife—she was chosen from the unsuccessful applicants to be on the second short list?

Ms Glanville: It is not that there are unsuccessful applicants; it is that the process—

Senator BRANDIS: There are people who are on the short list and there are people who are not on the short list.

Ms Glanville: There are people who have applied to be federal magistrates, as it was then, and, when there are a significant number of appointments to be made to a number of different jurisdictions, it is a matter of ensuring that there is the right mix of candidates for the needs of the particular jurisdictions.

Senator BRANDIS: That decision can be made at the time the initial short list is prepared. Indeed, you heard Mr Fredericks speaking about the Federal Court, that only one short list had to be prepared. The same principles of selection would presumably apply to another Federal Court, would they not?

Ms Glanville: The reality is that until you commence and conclude the process of what might be your primary candidates of interest you are not sure whether the mix is right and whether the applicants being interviewed have the requisite skills for the positions that are being sought.

Senator BRANDIS: Or connections with the Australian Labor Party?

Senator BRANDIS: Ms Glanville, you have not answered my last question. Why in particular was Ms Suzanne Jones selected from the candidates who were not on the initial short list to be included on the second short list? Why her rather than any of the other candidates who did not appear on the first short list?

Ms Glanville: Because she was part of the group that I referred to that were very close but did not make the first cut. She was discussed as part of that initial process and following the first round of interviews there were then some further candidates interviewed.

Senator BRANDIS: Did people go off the short list as well as go onto the short list between the first short list and the second short list?

Ms Glanville: No.

Senator BRANDIS: So the additional five people who were on the second short list but not the first short list were in supplementation of not in substitution for candidates on the first short list?

NOW WATCH MS GLANVILLE DUCK AND WEAVE:

Senator BRANDIS: When was the first short list sent to the Attorney-General?

Ms Glanville: We do not send the short list to the Attorney-General.

Senator BRANDIS: So you do not follow the practice that Mr Fredericks follows for the Federal Court?

Ms Glanville: There might be the running through of who has applied—

Senator BRANDIS: And who is on the short list?

Ms Glanville: Yes but it is not sent to the Attorney-General as such.

Senator BRANDIS: Is the Attorney-General either directly or through his political staff—

Ms Glanville: It is a similar process to the one that Mr Fredericks described.

Senator BRANDIS: If it is similar to the process that Mr Fredericks described, then the Attorney-General's office would have been made aware of who was on the shortlist. Did that happen?

Ms Glanville: Yes.

Senator BRANDIS: Were they made aware of who was on the first short list?

Ms Glanville: Yes.

Senator BRANDIS: And presumably they were also made aware of who was on the second short list?

Ms Glanville: I will need to check that because in the intervening period there was a change of Attorney-General. To be clear on that I would need to look at what impact that would have had on the process.

It is obvious to me from reading the transcript to this point that the first short list was sent to the Attorney-General Mark Dreyfus QC and he has sent it back saying to add Suzanne Jones. And I have no doubt he has done this on Julia Gillard's instructions given her previous form which I will get to soon.

May 30th

Senator BRANDIS: I was asking when we adjourned last night about the appointment of Ms Suzanne Jones as a judge of the Federal Circuit Court. What was the particular specialisation that Ms Jones, now Judge Jones, brought to the court?

Mr Wilkins: I will refer to Ms Glanville.

Ms Glanville: In appointments to the Federal Circuit Court, the panel looks for generic dispositions—

Senator BRANDIS: What does 'dispositions' mean?

Ms Glanville: Expertise, in other words. Essentially, because the jurisdiction of the Federal Circuit Court is quite broad and perhaps will become broader into the future, the panel looks for a range of areas of expertise. It could be family law, it could be migration law, it could be some taxation law—a variety of those sorts of matters. So, in relation to Ms Jones, that candidate—I do not have her CV with me—comes with a background I think that relates to the general federal law side rather than family law.

Senator BRANDIS: General federal law, really? Does Her Honour have any expertise beyond industrial law?

Ms Glanville: Without having access to her CV and other documentation, I could not comment on that.

Senator BRANDIS: You said that the court deals with a range of matters across the whole of federal law, which of course is true. But it is also true, as we heard from Mr Foster yesterday afternoon, that more than 80 per cent—closer to 85 per cent—of matters are family law matters, and the much smaller proportion of Federal Circuit Court matters are what are called general federal law matters. Does Ms Jones have any expertise in family law?

Ms Glanville: Once again, I would need to look at her CV to give you an answer to that specifically—

Senator BRANDIS: I can tell you, according to the Attorney-General's press release of 16 May, to which he has attached a brief CV of Ms Jones, there is no suggestion that she has any experience in family law matters at all.

Ms Glanville: I accept what you say.

Senator BRANDIS: It is the case, is it not, that, for that particular appointment for that particular position on the court, the court was looking for another specialist family lawyer?

And:

Senator BRANDIS: And what I am putting to you is that, in relation to the particular position on the court that Ms Jones, Judge Jones, was appointed to fill, the court was looking for a family law specialist to replace a family law spot.

Ms Glanville: As I said, in the panel and the convening of the panel, what the panel looks for are applicants who can work across the jurisdictions of the court, and the importance of having the chief judge, John Pascoe, on the panel is to advise on exactly those sorts of issues.

Senator BRANDIS: So is it your evidence to the committee that Chief Judge Pascoe did not acquaint the panel with the fact that the position to which Ms Jones was being appointed was a position in which the court was looking for a family law specialist?

And:

Senator BRANDIS: Does Ms Jones have any family law experience at all?

Ms Glanville: As I said, without looking at her full CV I could not answer that question.

Senator BRANDIS: Well, the answer is 'no'. She was an industrial lawyer and she had been recruited from the Fair Work Commission—

And:

Senator BRANDIS: I can understand, because this is not a perfect science, that it might be able to be explained that a person who, from a very large number of applicants, did not make the shortlist on its first iteration might have ended up getting the job. I can understand, perhaps, how when the court was looking for a specialist family lawyer it ended up with a specialist industrial lawyer with no experience in family law. Each of those circumstances is anomalous but, nevertheless, they might each be able to be explained away. But when both of those sets of circumstances operate in the case of a particular selection—a person is chosen with no expertise or experience in the field where the court is looking to find a replacement, and the person who is chosen is somebody who did not even make the shortlist in its first iteration—and then we learn that the person happens to be married to the president of the ACTU, do not you think, Ms Glanville, that that raises suspicions that perhaps this was not a purely meritocratic process?

It did get a bit heated and the Secretary of the Attorney-General's Department Mr Roger Wilkins AO said this:

Mr Wilkins: I think Ms Glanville has been trying to give her evidence, but if now the suggestion is that there were some corruption involved—

And:

Mr Wilkins: If somebody is suggesting that, particularly if the chief judge was involved—

I am suggesting that Chief Judge John Pascoe is as corrupt as they come as outlined in a previous post titled "The handiwork of Chief Federal Magistrate John Pascoe – witness bribing, price-fixing, succumbing to blackmail to conceal a crime and lying to shareholders etc. Is there anything this man cannot do?" (Click here to read)

Julie Gillard – Bernard Murphy appointment to the Federal Court of Australia

Julia Gillard has strong form on the board of dodgy judicial appointments for her friends. In 2011 Prime Minister Gillard appointed her former boss at Slater and Gordon lawyers, Bernard Murphy, a judge of the Federal Court of Australia.

I wrote a post on it titled "Julia Gillard appoints Bernard Murphy, her partner in crime from Slater and Gordon Lawyers, as a Federal Court of Australia judge."

Some of the highlights from the post in relation to Mr Murphy's appointment which have a similarity to Suzanne Jones appointment:

"This is what it says on the Maurice Blackburn Lawyers website:"

"If you had asked Maurice Blackburn chairman Bernard Murphy this time last year whether he hoped to be a judge, he would have said no. "It hasn't really been on my radar," he admits. "It isn't something that I had thought about until I applied in about October last year." (So what happened between the beginning of 2010 when he had no intention of applying to be a judge and October 2010 when he applied. Well his mate Julia Gillard became Prime Minister).

"A former solicitor is rare enough on the bench; a former plaintiff lawyer is rarer still."

"The man who once recruited Prime Minister Julia Gillard to his previous firm Slater & Gordon has spent 30 years defending the "victim" in court, as he has described clients in the past. More recently, it has been a sophisticated, shareholder victim, in the multimillion- dollar shareholder class actions Murphy has become known for."

Even Chief Judge John Pascoe gets a mention.

"Murphy built Maurice Blackburn's class action practice – the largest in Australia – from a one-man show, winning more than $700 million in damages along the way. And he still holds the record for the largest shareholder class action settlement – $144.5 million in the 2008 Aristocrat case." (This was not only against Aristocrat but also the directors at the time one of which was none other than Chief Federal Magistrate John Pascoe) (Click here to read the full post)

Circumstantial Case

This is what is called a circumstantial case which Justice Gyles set out in Choundary v Capital Airport Group Pty Ltd [2006] FCA 1755 (18 December 2006) at:

3 The appellant was entitled to have that evidence considered at its highest.

and

23 This is a circumstantial case. The Federal Magistrate was required to take into account all inferences most favourable to the appellant, which could reasonably be drawn from the primary facts (see the decision of the Privy Council in *Haw Tua Tau v Public* Prosecutor [1982] AC 136 at 150).

What that basically means if based on the evidence you can reasonably draw those conclusions then the court has to take it as being true unless proven otherwise. People go to jail all the time in circumstantial cases where there is no direct evidence of a crime for every type of crime right up to murder.

As a Commissioner of FWA Suzanne Jones was paid $350,000 and as a Judge of the Federal Circuit Court she is now paid $314,000 which is a decrease. But the court has applied for a pay rise and if approved will take her salary to $360,000 which is an increase. A bribe does not have to be a financial gain. Ms Jones had a choice of staying as a Commissioner of FWA under a Liberal Party government in the near future and going nowhere given her union background or becoming a judge which has a lot more prestige, more diverse work and better opportunities later down the track. So ultimately a lot more money down the track whether or not the expected pay rise as a judge eventuates or not.

One last word from Senator George Brandis: From the transcript:

"What strikes me as surprising about this appointment is that I know from conversations I have had with many senior figures in the court that the court was looking in this particular case for a family law specialist to handle the family law list, which comprises upwards of 80 per cent of its work, and instead, from the large number of applicants for the position it received, it ended up with an industrial law

specialist with no background in family law matters at all. Can you explain how that could have happened, Ms Glanville?"

No, Ms Glanville could not but the title of this post does: Prime Minister Julia Gillard bribed ACTU Secretary Dave Oliver to keep his support.

Chapter 19

Australian social media flexes its muscle and plays a part in taking down former Prime Minister Julia Gillard

Australian social media flexes its muscle and plays a part in taking down former Prime Minister Julia Gillard

BY SHANE DOWLING ON JUNE 30, 2013 • (33 COMMENTS)

Julia Gillard Prime Ministership ended on Wednesday (26/6/13) and it worth looking at the role social media played in her downfall as a lot of people underestimate the power of social media. Looking at all of the evidence there is a strong argument to say that social media played the biggest part in forcing the Labor Party to remove Ms Gillard from office.

If you have heard the quote from Julia Gillard "I was young and naïve" in relation to her involvement in the AWU fraud it is because of social media and if you use social media you would have heard "there will be no carbon tax under the government I lead" to the point of driving you insane. I raise these two examples because one started on this site and they are sound bites that have been used on Twitter, Facebook and the comment sections of Blogs non-stop over the last 2 years.

The mainstream media have found it hard to explain why Julia Gillard's personal unpopularity dragged down the Labor Party vote so much. The answer is social media and its rise and rise in power.

It was not just the mistakes that Julia Gillard made and promises that she back tracked on or lied about. It was the fact that every mistake or lie, real or not, was pounded and pounded on social media 24hours a day, 7 days a week and 52 weeks a year for the entire term of her prime ministership on social media.

What is social media?

Wikipedia describes it as "Social media refers to the means of interactions among people in which they create, share, and exchange information and ideas in virtual communities and networks" and "Social media technologies take on many different forms including magazines, Internet forums, weblogs, social blogs, microblogging, wikis, social networks, podcasts, photographs or pictures, video, rating and social bookmarking" (Click here to read more) It includes everything from Facebook, YouTube, Twitter and Blogs.

Julia Gillard dancing 1998 – Joan Kirner's 60th Birthday –
Picture found on Twitter

Young and Naïve

Two weeks before the 2007 election Julia Gillard did an
interview with News Ltd journalist Glenn Milne in relation to her
involvement with her then in the AWU fraud in the 1990's. One
thing she said was that she was "young and naïve". That is where

it stopped until I published a post on the 7th August 2011 and wrote:

Julia Gillard said: "These matters happened between 12 and 15 years ago," "I was young and naive." Well Julia Gillard was a partner at the law firm Slater and Gordon and in her mid thirties. Slater and Gordon are not in the habit of appointing young and naive people as partners and being in her mid thirties hardly made her young. (Click here to read the post)

From there social media started driving the post and quotes from it until the mainstream media picked up on it. One example is a site called Election Now which did a post on the 26/8/11 *"Julia Gillard 'young and naive' when involved in $1 Million Union fraud case in 2007".* and *"UPDATE: Michael Smith of 2UE and Andrew Bolt appear to run with the kangaroocourtofaustralia."* (Click here to read)

The point is for some 4 years from 2007 to 2011 the mainstream media said nothing. It did not take off until I wrote the post and it was driven by people on social media. Because of social media millions of people now know of her "young and naïve" excuse which was ridiculous as well as the broader AWU scandal. It is sound bites like "young and naïve" that can do the most damage to a reputation and drive an issue. Political Parties use sound bites or slogans all the time for good reason.

The above is just one example of the numerous amounts of information on Julia Gillard's failings that are driven home on social media whether or not the mainstream media do. Only a few years ago there were very few Blogs and no Facebook or Twitter but now they are here they are growing at a rapid pace and their reach and influence is unmatched when enough unite. And unite they did against Julia Gillard.

Websites/Blogs

There are dozens if not hundreds of websites/blogs that specialise in areas such as climate change (Joanne Nova), finance (Barnaby is Right) and this site for example which is judicial corruption. A lot united to some degree in deciding that Julia Gillard and/or the federal Labor Government were a failure. Blogs linked back to each other and picked up on each other's stories even if the mainstream media did not. It was like a loose coalition with the same cause of holding the government and Julia Gillard to account just in different areas of expertise.

Combine the traffic of all the non-mainstream media websites that write about politics, and it would be millions of page views per month and then add Facebook and Twitter etc. and you are looking at 20 to 30 million views a month. It is a powerful force when exposing a corrupt government and Prime Minister.

It does not matter who wins the next election whether that be Kevin Rudd or Tony Abbott. They will be getting the same treatment as Julia Gillard on social media and will become very unpopular very quickly. One lie here and one failure there and the social media will unload unrelentingly. The problem for someone like Tony Abbott if he becomes Prime Minister is that there is so much entrenched corruption when he takes over, he has to deal with it. If Tony Abbott fails to deal with the corruption, then he owns it and will be held accountable accordingly on social media.

Julia Gillard has only been gone a few days and it is almost like she was never there as far as the media is concerned and that is because there are bigger issues confronting this country than Ms Gillard now she has gone. If the political parties do not learn from her downfall and the role social media played in it then they will also suffer. There is a new level of accountability driven by social media which grows by the day and the political parties need to get with the picture. Just sending trolls out to dump their political spin in the comment sections of political websites and blogs will not do.

Individually social media users have no power, but combined they have tremendous power that I believe now outweighs the mainstream media. It is as Paul said in the comment section of a recent post about this site *"This is the real media, right here. Its time everyone accepted this and stopped looking to the dailys, and the TV News to be informed. Make this site known far and wide. That is how new media works."*

A few posts back someone said in the comment section words to the effect "what are we going to do just sit around and whinge on this site and do nothing" which is a fair comment. But this site and its supporters have played a part in holding Julia Gillard and the government to account which collectively with other social media has helped in Julia Gillard's downfall, so we have done more than just whinge.

Chapter 20

Julia Gillard is the 1st PM to face criminal allegations at a Royal Commission. A good day for Australian democracy

Julia Gillard is the 1st PM to face criminal allegations at a Royal Commission. A good day for Australian democracy

BY SHANE DOWLING ON SEPTEMBER 6, 2014 • (24 COMMENTS)

Former Australian Prime Minister Julia Gillard is the fourth Australian PM to give evidence at a Royal Commission but the first PM to face criminal allegations at a Royal Commission. When a leader or former leader of a country is held to account or made to answer allegations of crimes or corruption it is a sign of democracy at work at the highest level. It does not matter whether you like or dislike Julia Gillard you should take notice of her appearance next week as I believe it is a real game changer.

No longer is anyone above the law, at least not as far as the court of public opinion is concerned. Remember it is the online community that drove and kept on driving the AWU fraud and many other crime and corruption issues of recent times.

Julia Gillard's appearance at the Royal Commission is really just the cream on the cake when you look at the fight against corruption in this country. The tide against corruption has been building in Australia for a couple of years now and there is no going back. The list of people who are on the wrong side of that tide has been growing by the day. There are 2 Royal Commissions in progress and one just finished and then there is the ICAC hearings in NSW which has been exposing widespread corruption on both sides of politics. There are also plenty of other issues about to raise their heads and other inquiries not far away, some of which I have written about and some I will write about in the near future.

But let's focus on Julia Gillard and her expected appearance at the Trade Union Royal Commission next week. Julia Gillard is meant to give evidence next Tuesday, Wednesday or Thursday in Melbourne although the Royal Commission has not confirmed the details yet. Although the RC has confirmed that Gillard was advised of a date to give evidence in early September.

Below are two videos of Julia Gillard from 2012 which are worth reviewing before she gives evidence. The first video shows Julia Gillard misleading parliament regarding the AWU fraud and trying to blame Ralph Blewitt. The problem for Ms Gillard is that Bruce Wilson told a different story when he did an interview on the ABC and contradicted what she told parliament. The second shows Ms Gillard avoiding answering a question in relation to when she wrote her acceptance speech when she took over the job of PM from Kevin Rudd. It will be interesting to see if she tries the same technique when she is in the witness stand.

Below is the video showing Julia Gillard misleading parliament and lying about the AWU fraud

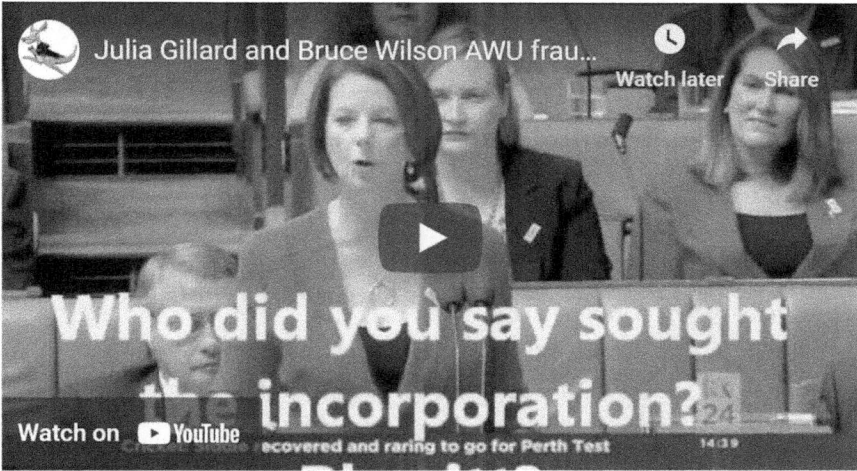

Julia Gillard and Bruce Wilson AWU frau...

Watch later   Share

Who did you say sought incorporation?

Watch on ▶ YouTube

(Click anywhere on the above video to watch)

Below is the video of Julia Gillard refusing to answer a question about preparing her acceptance speech for becoming PM 2 weeks before she stabbed Kevin Rudd in the back. Will she duck and weave and refuse to answer questions at the Royal Commission the same way?

Julia Gillard's Richard Nixon moment

Watch later   Share

Watch on ▶ YouTube

(Click anywhere on the above video to watch)

One of the things that the lawyers for the Royal Commission would have done is to have gone through all the public statements of Gillard and worked out were the lies are. If they have done their job properly then the barrister who will question Ms Gillard, Jeremy Stoljar, should have a career making day. Then again Julia Gillard is very cagey and fast on her feet and more than capable of destroying Stoljar if he is not prepared, as the Canberra press found out a couple of times.

Other witnesses to give evidence next week that I have previously written about include Julia Gillard's old boss and current Federal Court judge Justice Bernard Murphy (Click here to read) and John Cain Jnr (Click here to read). Or for all the KCA posts on the AWU fraud click here.

Corruption is being exposed everyday now and it is the new norm so people should get used to it and feel good about it.

Chapter 21

Julia Gillard should be charged with criminal offences after disgraceful performance at Royal Commission

Julia Gillard should be charged with criminal offences after disgraceful performance at Royal Commission

BY SHANE DOWLING ON SEPTEMBER 11, 2014 • (23 COMMENTS)

Julia Gillard has failed for 18 years to give a legitimate reason why she never made a complaint to the police in relation to the AWU fraud committed by her and her previous boyfriend Bruce Wilson. She failed again at the Royal Commission on Wednesday (10-9-14) and should be charged immediately with concealing a serious indictable offence.

Gillard does not dispute her involvement in the fraud but says she did not do it knowingly and was deceived by Bruce Wilson and when she found out what he was up to she broke off her relationship with him. So why did she not go to the police in 1995 when the fraud and theft were discovered. There is no legal privilege stopping her as she claims she was deceived when she helped Wilson commit crimes. In that situation the crime/fraud exception rule applies which extinguishes legal privilege. Why has she not gone to the police in the last 18 years? Why has she not gone to the Victoria police who are currently investigating the fraud and have been for over 12 months?

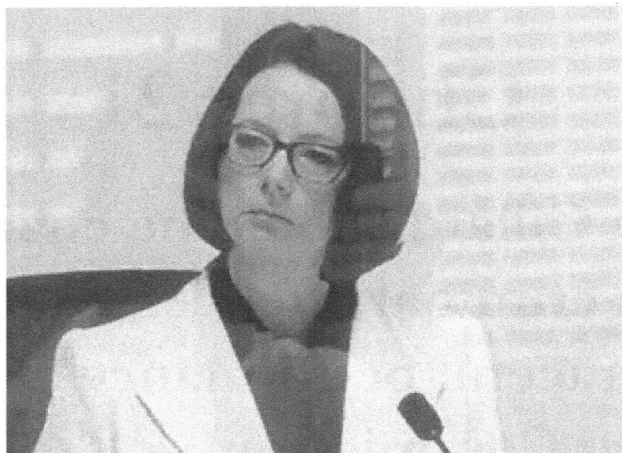

Julia Gillard giving evidence at the
Trade Union Royal Commission in 2014

The only support she is getting seems to be from other fraudsters and thieves in the union/Labor Party movement. No one else wants to go near her. Commissioner Dyson Heydon, who is the one who writes the report, would not have missed a beat, and will do nothing more than embarrass himself if he does not come down hard on Gillard in his report. Every lawyer in the country who has followed the case knows she is at least guilty of the concealment of the fraud.

Watch the news and you will see people being charged with concealing a crime or conspiring to conceal a crime on a regular basis. Gillard should not be given special treatment.

I have raised the fact that Gillard has never gone to the police many times and so have others, so it is not like Julia Gillard has not been put on notice. She has had 18 years and as a lawyer knows the law.

There are a lot of witnesses that contradict Gillard on key evidence and many of them have no reason to give that evidence except that it is the truth. This site has covered the evidence many times (click here to read), but there is no real need. If Julia Gillard really knew she had done nothing illegal, then she would have gone to the police long ago and made a full statement. She could do it today especially given they are currently investigating the fraud. The fact that she has not is a clear admission of guilt.

So, the next time someone wants to argue whether or not Julia Gillard is guilty of any crime, just raise the fact she has not gone to the police and made a complaint and therefore is guilty of the concealment of the fraud at the very least. That also points to her being guilty of other crimes such as the fraud itself. It must be remembered that Julia Gillard and her boss, Bernard Murphy, were sacked over the issue although she claims she resigned which is a lie and Murphy claims he resigned over another issue. They interviewed her and recorded the meeting and had a transcript. This is unheard of and the other lawyers were covering themselves.

Justice Bernard Murphy and Shane Dowling (holding the iPhone) from the website Kangaroo Court of Australia. At the Trade Union Royal Commission – 9-9-14

(The above picture is from an article on the SMH: Click here to see)

Julia Gillard's partner in crime, Bernard Murphy at the Royal Commission on Tuesday 9-9-14

I managed to ask Bernard Murphy a few questions on Tuesday after he gave evidence at the Royal Commission as per the below video.

Background of Murphy becoming a judge:

Julia Gillard became Prime Minister on the 24th of June 2010 after Kevin Rudd lost the support of the Labor Party. On the 21st of August 2010 there was a federal election and several weeks later Julia Gillard formed a minority Government with the support of The Greens and 3 independents.

In October 2010 Julia Gillard's former boss from Slater and Gordon Lawyers applied for the position of a federal court judge. Bernard Murphy was successful and was appointed a judge in April 2011. The whole process was very suspicious and dodgy which I previously wrote in an article in 2011 titled *"Julia Gillard appoints Bernard Murphy, her partner in crime from Slater and Gordon Lawyers, as a Federal Court of Australia judge."* (Click here to read)

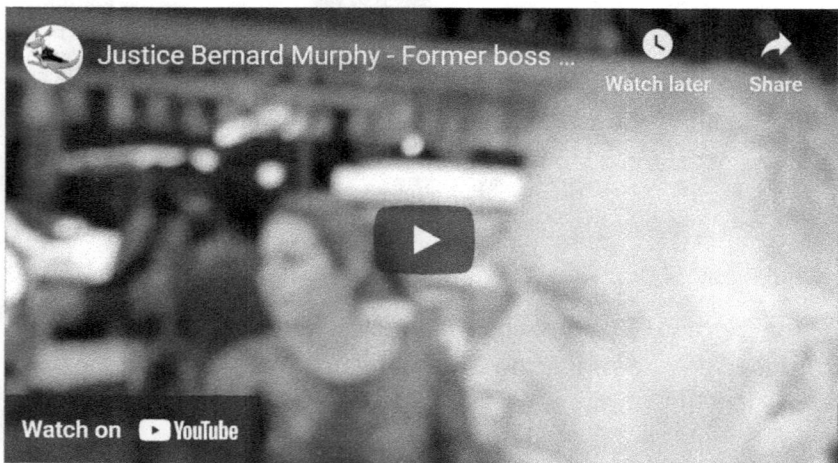

(Click anywhere on the above video to watch) (It is blurred because of walking fast while filming with the iPhone)

There is a lot more evidence to come as the Royal Commission will be hearing from further witnesses in Melbourne next Monday regarding the AWU and then there is the continuing Victoria police investigation into the AWU fraud and the report from the Royal Commission due in December. So, Ms Gillard is not in the clear yet.

Julia Gillard was Prime Minister of Australia and any serious questions of wrongdoing by any Prime Minister could and should be dealt with long before they become PM.

Chapter 22

PM Tony Abbott makes it three Prime Ministers in 3 months and most likely two elections in 12 months

PM Tony Abbott makes it three Prime Ministers in 3 months and most likely two elections in 12 months

BY SHANE DOWLING ON SEPTEMBER 8, 2013 • (46 COMMENTS)

Australia is in for a rough ride politically for the foreseeable future. The make-up of the senate when it is finally decided in the next few days is a major reason which will quite possibly lead to a double dissolution election in the next six months or so. But one thing that needs to be acknowledged is that a challenge to Abbott's leadership by Malcolm Turnbull would already be in the planning.

We have been given the government we had to have given the failings and corruption of the previous government.

Will Abbott make a good Australian Prime Minister? I don't think so. But we should at least give him a honeymoon period to see what he is like as PM. He does have a number of things going for him though. He is following two of the biggest duds the country has ever seen in Kevin Rudd and Julia Gillard so that in itself will make him look good. Secondly the Labor Party will spend quite some time fighting and blaming each other for the election defeat and be in no position to be an alternative government anytime soon.

The Senate issue

The government will not have a majority in the senate and will have a hard time passing many of their promised policies through the senate as the Labor Party and Greens will be in a position to block legislation until June next year. After that the new senators will take office and the exact make-up is unknown at this point, but it will most likely be a situation where a number of independents have the balance in the senate. Whether this will make it easier for the government we will not know until then.

If the government had won control of the senate there would be no talk of a double dissolution election, as all they would do is wait until July next year to pass legislation that was being blocked.

There are many issues that could trigger a double dissolution election. The obvious one being that the government have said they will introduce legislation to abolish the carbon tax in their first week. If Abbott does not hold firm on this, they will lose a lot of support and if they do hold firm it will most likely be blocked by Labor and the Greens and lead to another election early next year.

No Lies Mr Abbott

Tony Abbott needs to have a good look at what happened to Julia Gillard and Kevin Rudd. Social media made sure they were never allowed to forget all their lies and it will do the same for Tony Abbott if and when he starts lying. Based on the history of other PM's it will not take him long. Probably only a few weeks, if that. With social media politics is moving to a new level of accountability and no one is above it.

Malcolm Turnbull challenge

Malcolm has never been one to play second fiddle and he has an ego just as big as Rudd's if not bigger. He is not in politics to be a minister, he is there to be PM. A challenge by Turnbull is a certainty and probably only 18 months away. There will be white anting by Turnbull and his supporters almost immediately. That is how they play the game.

The Labor Party

Kevin Rudd announced his resignation as leader of the Labor Party. The problem Labor has is that they have no one of any real quality to take over. Most of them are crooks or not competent enough. One name that has come up is Bill Shorten who is probably the biggest fraudster left in the Labor Party. If he does become leader he will not go anywhere and be easy fodder for people like me simply because he is that corrupt. I have written numerous posts where he gets mentioned and the most popular is the one titled *"Has Bill Shorten gotten one of his staff members Pregnant? Shorten calls the lawyers."* (Click here to read) The man is a real grub.

Chapter 23

Tony Abbott and his friend Cardinal George Pell. Perceived bias for the Royal Commission into child sex abuse

Tony Abbott and his friend Cardinal George Pell. Perceived bias for the Royal Commission into child sex abuse

BY SHANE DOWLING ON SEPTEMBER 15, 2013 • (76 COMMENTS)

Prime Minister Tony Abbott gave a personal reference in court for the former priest Father John Nester in a child sex abuse case in 1997. Father Nester was later struck off as a clergy by the Vatican. Add this to Tony Abbott's and the Liberal Party's extremely close relationship with Cardinal George Pell who has admitted the church covered up sexual abuse and there is a major problem brewing in relation to the Royal Commission into Institutional Responses to Child Sexual Abuse.

The problem we have is that there is instantly perceived bias by the new federal government regarding the future handling of the Royal Commission and any recommendations the Commission may make affecting the Roman Catholic Church.

Overview

The links between Tony Abbott, the Liberal party and Cardinal Pell has to leave any fair-minded person greatly disturbed and this post will explore that and some other related matters. What becomes obvious is that Tony Abbott and possibly others in the Liberal Party need to make a public statement that they will stand aside from any involvement in the decision-making process of any matter related to the Royal Commission.

Tony Abbott – reference for accused paedophile Priest Father John Nester

Father John Nestor and Tony Abbott both attended the Sydney's St Patrick's Seminary in the 1980s when Mr Abbott was planning on becoming a priest.

Father Nester *"was a priest in the Wollongong diocese in NSW when he was charged with the indecent assault of a 15-year-old altar boy in 1991."*

"Father Nestor was convicted in Wollongong Local Court on February 18, 1997, and sentenced to 16 months in jail, with the magistrate describing the case as a "gross breach of trust"."

"In court, the priest admitted he had – while dressed in boxer shorts and a singlet – slept on mattresses on a floor in the presbytery with the boy and his younger brother sometime between June and September 1991."

On appeal in October 1997 the conviction was overturned. But Father Nester was never allowed to return as a priest.

"The then-Wollongong Bishop, Philip Wilson, now Catholic Archbishop of Adelaide, advised Fr Nestor in writing "significant additional material that I have received ... has been a cause of worry concerning your suitability for a further pastoral appointment in this diocese or any other"."

"Fr Nestor appealed to the Vatican's Congregation for the Clergy, which decreed he be reinstated."

"But in February 2001, the Wollongong diocese appealed and the decree was overturned." (Click here to read more)

During the course of those proceedings Tony Abbott who was then a Federal MP gave a reference in court for Father Nester.

"Tony Abbott insisted on providing a character reference for a Catholic priest later struck off the clergy list by the Vatican following a child abuse case, the former priest says."

"Mr Nestor told AAP at his home in rural NSW that Mr Abbott agreed to provide the character reference in 1997 after being approached by his barrister."

"When the lawyer approached Tony Abbott, he said look, I know you're a parliamentary secretary and you may feel that because of your position you don't want to get involved in this case'."

"Tony said, no, I'm coming down,'. He insisted on coming down and giving the reference, because he's a man of integrity." (Click here to read more)

Tony Abbott told the court Father Nester was a *"An extremely upright and virtuous man. I guess one of things that I liked very much about John when I first him, was his maturity, intellectual, social, emotional he was, to that extent I guess, a beacon of humanity at the Seminary"* (Click here to read the court transcript)

In an interview in March this year the victim questioned why Tony Abbott gave evidence:

"the alleged victim, who asked not to be named, said Mr Abbott should not have provided a character reference for Mr Nestor."

"I was not aware of who Tony Abbott was at the time," he said.

"While I do not necessarily believe that he has done anything wrong, in hindsight it may have been better if he had not involved himself in the matter."

It is understood Mr Abbott communicated with Mr Nestor twice after the court cases, but has had no contact with him for almost 15 years.

"In 1997, Mr Abbott provided a reference for Mr Nestor in an open court. He was subsequently acquitted by a District Court judge," a spokesman for Mr Abbott said.

The alleged victim queried why Mr Abbott hadn't stayed in contact with Mr Nestor.

"If someone was of such good character, why has contact not been kept?" he asked.

He said Mr Abbott's reference may have been a factor in Mr Nestor's successful appeal.

"Certainly a character reference from a member of parliament would hold some sway, no doubt about it," he said.

"It probably did play a big part, but there were other things that played a bigger part. For example, John Nestor never gave evidence at the trial. He was never cross-examined."

He said his case should be examined by the royal commission into child sex abuse. (Click here to read more)

The Nester case and Tony Abbott's involvement at the very least show poor judgement by Tony Abbott given Nester was ultimately struck off as a Priest. More importantly though it raises the possibility that Abbott may be called to give evidence at the Royal Commission if the Commission decides to examine the case. If they do not examine the case then there could be perceived bias by the Commission or a perception of political interference given that Tony Abbott is now the Prime Minister.

The case has all the variables that demand the Royal Commission do review the case. For starters, what was the further evidence that the church obtained that led to Father Nester being struck off as a priest? Was it evidence of criminal conduct that the Church concealed?

Cardinal George Pell

George Pell has a very close relationship with Tony Abbott and the Liberal Party. He has also had allegations made against him that he abused a child which has never been tested in court. Mr Pell has also attended court supporting paedophile priests but has refused when asked by victims to attend court to support them.

Mr Pell and the paedophile allegations

"A decade ago, a Melbourne man claimed he was sexually molested as a 12-year-old at a Catholic youth camp by a student priest he knew as "big George" and later recognised as the Archbishop of Sydney. After a church-appointed inquiry, Pell said he was grateful to God to have been exonerated."

"In fact, retired Victorian Supreme Court judge Alec Southwell had said that both Pell and his accuser gave the impression they were speaking the truth. Taking into account questions about the accuser's credibility (he had a criminal record) and the fact that the alleged incidents occurred so long ago, Southwell found he was "not satisfied that the complaint had been established"."

"Tony Abbott hadn't waited for the judge's decision. *"It should not surprise any Christian that there would be people who want to make unfair, wrong, mischievous, malevolent accusations against the strongest and most public Christian of the time," the politician said when the allegations were first aired. "I'm more than ready to accept Pell's testimony."*

The retired Victorian Supreme Court judge Alec Southwell was on the Church's payroll as it was an internal Church inquiry, so he was hardly impartial. The full report was put on the Churches website in 2002 but has since been taken down. Part of it can be read on the Broken Rites Australia website. (Click here to read)

Pell turns a blind eye to paedophiles and caught lying about it

"As archbishop of Melbourne, he allowed a priest found to have sexually abused a teenager after officiating at his mother's funeral to continue working in another parish. In Sydney, he said in a letter to a man named Anthony Jones that the priest who sexually assaulted him had been the subject of no other complaints, when in fact Pell had written to another of the priest's victims that same day. The letter to Jones was "badly worded and a mistake", he said later." (Click here to read more) It was not a mistake, it was clearly a lie and cover-up and Pell was caught out.

George Pell and the Victorian Parliament inquiry

On the 27th of May 2013 George Pell gave evidence to the Victorian Parliament inquiry into child abuse. Mr Pell has been widely criticised for that evidence. I watched part of it on TV and could not believe how much contempt he seemed to have for the inquiry. Some news reports are below:

CARDINAL George Pell has confessed false documents were created and priests took part in "reprehensible" cover-ups of child sexual abuse.

Cardinal Pell said the fear of scandals drove much of the reaction to rampant abuse in the 1970s and '80s, but that a concern about money was also involved

In a victory for victims, Cardinal Pell said he would ask the Vatican to send all documents it holds on Victorian sex abuse accusations to the inquiry – a promise he had also made to the federal royal commission into abuse. (Click here to read more)

The question I have is what are the documents doing at the Vatican in the first place and why wouldn't there be copies or the originals still in Australia? Sounds like further evidence of the cover-up to me.

"VICTIMS and support groups have called for Cardinal George Pell's resignation following his appearance at yesterday's parliamentary inquiry into child abuse."

"Abuse survivor Stephen Woods, 51, who was sexually assaulted and beaten by three priests when he was a student at St Alipius Christian Brothers Primary School in Ballarat, said that Cardinal Pell should stand down."

"The apology is political. It's still about saving face, it's still about saving the political power of the church, and that's what they are afraid of losing," he said.

"The little care for the victims that he showed, it shows that they still don't get it," he said."

"Mr Woods slammed Cardinal Pell's claims that he had always shown support for victims of child abuse."

"If he had been on the side of victims, how come he admitted that he has never been to court with victims?" he said.

"He's been to court with paedophiles, but he's never been to court with victims.

"He has been asked to go to court with victims, but he has always declined," Mr Woods said. (Click here to read more)

And: "CARDINAL George Pell has conceded it was "a mistake" for him to appear in court during the trial of convicted Victorian paedophile Father Gerard Ridsdale in the 1990s."

"In 1994, Father Ridsdale was jailed after pleading guilty to numerous charges of sexually abusing children in his care in Victoria."

"During the trial Cardinal Pell, Australia's only Archbishop in the Catholic Church, appeared in court supporting Father Ridsdale."

"He said he now understood "how upsetting that may be", saying he did not realise his support for Father Ridsdale would be taken as hostility to the victims." (Click here to read more) So why does he not show up to court to support victims?

And:

He defended his solidarity towards Ridsdale, who he lived with for 12 months and who he accompanied to court when he pleaded guilty to child sex offences.

Cardinal Pell has been questioned extensively on the issue of compensation for victims of Church abuse and over claims he thought it could "bleed the Church dry".

But he says he has only tried to be prudent with the Church's funds.

He was asked how he is able to stay in a $30 million "palace" in Rome, when Australian victims of abuse are limited to just $75,000 in compensation. (Click here to read more)

The $30 million palace was paid for by the Church here in Australia. Money that could have gone to the victims.

George Pell and the Liberal Party connection

On the 31st of May 2013, just days after George Pell gave his testimony and made the admissions that he did at the Victorian Parliament Inquiry into child abuse, Mr Pell was training Federal Liberal Party MP's.

"MAJOR Australian personalities including James Packer, John Howard and Cardinal George Pell – plus a minor British royal – have been giving political pep-talks to Liberal MPs during secret luncheon meetings held across Sydney."

"The exclusive gatherings, known as the "Chartwell Society", have seen a cross-factional band of ambitious MPs taking tips from major figures on the world stage during regular, invite-only gatherings.)

"The most recent function was held on Friday at the Australian Hotels Association plush Macquarie St boardroom with Cardinal George Pell attending as the guest of honour at a gathering of 11 Coalition MPs."

"Separate gatherings have been held at universities, churches and corporate boardrooms." (Click here to read more)

The Friday above would have been the 31st of May 2013, just days after Pell gave evidence to the Victorian Parliament. What was the Liberal Party thinking? They should have stayed right away from him until the Royal Commission has handed down its recommendations.

The politicians who met Pell are the same people who are going to have input into the government's response to the recommendations that the Royal Commission makes on the abuse of children. The Catholic Church will have adverse findings against them as everyone knows they were involved in a massive cover-up in Australia and globally for many years. How can any fair-minded person see these politicians as being impartial now? And what did Pell teach them?

George Pell is a very sick and perverted person of no moral fibre whatsoever given the above. The child abuse allegations against him need to be reviewed by the Royal Commission and if they fail to do so one has to wonder why. Will they put it in the too hard basket given Pell's position in the church and his political connections? Probably.

The Royal Commission into Institutional Responses to Child Sexual Abuse

The Royal Commission can be affected by government decisions in many ways. The government could close it early or the Royal Commission could ask the government for further funding and if the government refuses, then there would be a perceived bias by many given the relationship between Tony Abbott, the Liberal's and George Pell.

Tony Abbott and George Pell have a history of working together in politics. Before the 2004 election Tony Abbott gave an infamous interview on the ABC's Lateline where he was caught lying and deceiving in relation to a meeting with George Pell. A couple of days after the meeting George Pell was a signatory to a letter criticising the Labor Party. (Click here to read the transcript) or (Click here to watch on YouTube)

Conclusion

There are hundreds if not thousands of victims who have been waiting for justice for a long time and we know the precedent *"Not only must Justice be done; it must **also be seen to be done**." R v Sussex Justices, Ex parte McCarthy* ([1924]) Judges have to stand down from hearing a matter if there is only perceived bias, not actual bias. And so should Tony Abbott stand aside and have nothing to do with the Royal Commission decision making.

The terms of reference for the Royal Commission are fairly narrow given the subject matter and there will no doubt be many who are not satisfied with the outcome and will blame the government for any short comings of the Royal Commission. That is another reason why it is important that Tony Abbott and others who have a close relationship with Cardinal Pell abstain for any decision-making in relation to the Royal Commission.

This website will drive this issue for at least another post or until we get a result. I will send correspondence to the Royal Commission and Tony Abbott and see what we get back.

Chapter 24

Tony Abbott versus the world. The leadership battle heats up

Tony Abbott versus the world. The leadership battle heats up

BY SHANE DOWLING ON FEBRUARY 4, 2015 • (44 COMMENTS)

For how much longer Tony Abbott will continue as Prime Minister no one knows but it could be over soon with a ballot highly likely next week as late on Tuesday night (3/2/15) members of his own party called for him to resign.

People are blaming the many mistakes Abbott has made but there are 2 mistakes that have not received a great deal of focus from the media that are worth looking at because both were and still are very damaging.

One was the Knighthood of Angus Houston who is the former leader of the Australian Defence Force and someone I have written about a couple of times. The second was Tony Abbott's attack on social media users in an attempt to downplay criticism of the Knighthood of Prince Philip.

Angus Houston

When Angus Houston was the Chief of the Defence Force (2005-2011) he was up to his neck in denying justice and compensation to women who were sexually abused and other abuse victims were also denied justice.

I wrote an article in April 2011 titled *"How the Defence Minister Stephen Smith and others cover up the sexual abuse of women"* (Click here to read the article) and followed it up in July 2011 with another article on the matter titled *"Going Jack – Air Chief Marshal Angus Houston"* (Click here to read the article)

Abuse victims who had their complaints stonewalled and swept under the carpet for years by Angus Houston would have been horrified when Tony Abbott read out Houston's name for the Knighthood. This would have lost Mr Abbott and the Liberal Party plenty of support. While the Knighthood of Prince Philip was embarrassing nationally so was the Angus Houston appointment to a lot of people who know his many failings.

In April 2011 the government set up the Defence Abuse Response Taskforce because the problem had become so bad. (Click here to read more) Angus Houston resigned in July 2011 as a disgrace and should never have received any award let alone a Knighthood.

Live Canberra

Australia Day
Abbott: I think Angus Houston and Prince Philip are suitable recipients of these knighthoods

(Click anywhere on the above video to watch)

Attacking social media is fatal for politicians because they are then taking on the world

For any politician to attack or insult social media users is political suicide. On Australia Day Tony Abbott attacked all social media users who did not agree with the Knighthood of Prince Philip and what made it even worse is that many of them are Liberal voters. Abbott said *"Social media is kind of like electronic graffiti and I think that in the media, you make a big mistake to pay too much attention to social media"* (Click here to read more)

Abbott attacked social media even further in the above video and said that social media *"has as much credibility as graffiti"*. He was in effect attacking everyone who uses social media. What makes the comment strange is that the government spends millions to monitor social media and Abbott would have to be aware of it as it is run by the Department of Prime Minister and Cabinet. The SMH reported:

"The Abbott government has created a hub of 37 communication and social media specialists to monitor social media and offer strategic communications advice costing taxpayers almost $4.3 million a year." (Click here to read more)

The phones of the federal Liberal MPs would have been ringing continuously from their own supporters complaining about Prime Minister Abbott. You can attack the opposition all day every day but once you start attacking your own supporters you are stuffed. And that is why Tony Abbott is in so much trouble. It is pretty much all his own doing.

If Tony Abbott loses the expected ballot next week whoever ends up leader will probably not be much better than Abbott. Sometimes you have to hit rock bottom before things get better. I thought we had bottomed out with Gillard and Rudd, but it looks like we have further to go and it could last a few years.

Chapter 25

Tony Abbott's Liberal Party take bribes for favours once too often. Time for a Royal Commission!

Tony Abbott's Liberal Party take bribes for favours once too often. Time for a Royal Commission!

BY <u>SHANE DOWLING</u> ON <u>JULY 2, 2015</u> • (<u>32</u> <u>COMMENTS</u>)

Everywhere you look lately there is evidence of the Liberal Party taking bribes for access to their politicians. The most recent allegation by the ABC and Fairfax Media is that the Liberal Party have been taking bribes off the Mafia. Add that to the recent NSW ICAC Liberal Party bribery scandal and the *"Treasure for Sale"* defamation case *"partial win"* and things aren't looking good for the Liberals.

There is a massive storm heading the way of Tony Abbott and the Liberal Party and it is worth having a look at one of the key reasons why which is how the Liberals fund the party and the favours they do in return. You only have to put a few of the headlines together from the media over the last 12 months to realise there is deep-seated corruption in the way the Liberal Party is funded.

Four Corners / Fairfax Media investigation

The ABC's Four Corners program televised an episode on Monday (29/6/15) titled *"The Mafia in Australia: Drugs, Murder and Politics"*. *(Click here to watch)* It is part-one of a two-part series that reveals how the mafia is linked to the Liberal Party. At the same time Fairfax Media ran a story titled *"Key Liberal fundraising body took Mafia money for access"* which start off:

"Mafia figures donated tens of thousands of dollars to the discredited NSW Liberal Party fundraising vehicle, the Millennium Forum, as part of an ultimately successful campaign to allow a known criminal to stay in Australia." (Click here to read more)

A key part to the story is that the mafia paid the Liberal Party $1,000's for the then Immigration Minister Amanda Vanstone to allow mafia member and convicted criminal Frank Madafferi to stay in Australia.

The story is an old story as any internet search will tell you and one that also includes Labor Party politicians. But it is fair and reasonable for the ABC and Fairfax to focus on the Liberal Party and this time they have dug deeper than before.

In 2009 it was reported

"According to an investigation by The Age, in late 2003 three Sydney Italian businessman – Pat Sergi, Tony Labbozzetta and Nick Scali – saw the NSW Liberal senator Marise Payne about assisting the Melbourne-based Madafferi to obtain a visa. Payne contacted the office of the then immigration minister Amanda Vanstone twice to discuss Madafferi's visa case. In 2005 Vanstone allowed Madafferi to stay on humanitarian grounds. Last August Madafferi was arrested over his alleged involvement in the world's largest ecstasy bust but is yet to face trial." (Click here to read more)

The original investigation and article in 2009 was written by The Age which said:

"Exactly how much money was given to the Liberal Party and for what purpose remains unclear. At the very least, the donations have created a perception that help was bought by, in at least some cases, some very questionable figures." (Click here to read more)

There will be ongoing bad publicity from this as part two of the Four Corners program is next Monday. It might be a lot worse than the first one for the Liberal Party.

Kerry Stokes

A couple of weeks ago (18/6/15) The Australian Financial Review ran a story about Kerry Stokes and the influence he has with the government.

It starts off:

*"A series of angry phone calls from Seven proprietor **Kerry Stokes** to **Tony Abbott** and **Julie Bishop** early on Wednesday morning resulted in a push for media industry reform being permanently shelved."* (Click here to read more)

It must be true because regular readers know what Kerry Stokes is like with suing.

It raises many questions that Prime Minster Tony Abbott needs to answer.

1. Why does he take direct calls from Kerry Stokes? Is it because Stokes donates to the Liberal Party? Is it because Stokes owns Channel 7 and other media?

2. Why did the PM shelve media industry reform after the phone call with Kerry Stokes? What did Kerry Stokes say to the PM to make him shelve reform in the media industry?

Kerry Stokes - walkies...

(Picture from The Australian Financial Review article titled *"Kerry Stokes' fury over media reform felt in* Canberra") (Click here to read)

ICAC

In the last year or so at least 12 members of the Liberal Party have been either sacked or resigned from the party because of revelations of corruption at the NSW Independent Commission Against Corruption (ICAC). Most of it related to money the politicians were corruptly receiving from people who obviously wanted favours. This included the resignation of the then NSW Premier Barry O'Farrell last year. (Click here to read more)

The fall out and damage from the ICAC investigations and ongoing court cases will do damage to the Liberal Party for years to come.

Joe Hockey v Fairfax Media – Hockey v Fairfax Media Publications Pty Limited [2015] FCA 652 (Click here to read the judgment)

While Joe Hockey might have won the defamation case and been awarded $200,000 (Click here to read) he has done millions of dollars damage to the credibility of the Liberal Party. The case was always about Joe and his ego and he didn't care what damage he did to the Liberal Party.

He was awarded a *"partial win"* as many commentators are saying. The article he complained about which is titled "Treasurer for sale" (Click here to read) is still on the internet and always will be I suspect.

What Hockey's court case did was highlight the fact that if you want access to politicians like Joe you need to pay big dollars.

I wrote in May last year:

"Didn't the Liberals learn anything from the Craig Thomson defamation proceedings. If Fairfax Media do not settle and I suspect they will not, then a lot of media attention is going to be

on Hockey and his financial dealings for a long time and most likely right up to the next election. A lot of people see the dealings as being dodgy even if they are not illegal. I can't and most people cannot afford a lazy $22,000 to get a meeting with Hockey". (Click her to read more)

There is a lot of money flowing into the Liberal Party and everyone who donates seems to want something in return. Worse still, is the fact that the Liberal Party politicians seem happy to do favours for the cash. Even for members of the mafia.

The call for a Royal Commission into the Liberal Party and its fund-raising is going to get louder and louder. The Liberal Party have spent taxpayer's money investigating the Unions/Labor Party and that is fine. But now there needs to be a Royal Commission into the Liberal Party and their grubby backroom financial deals. While a Royal Commission will obviously be a few years away and will never happen while the Liberals are in power there is nothing that I can see that would stop the Australian Senate setting up an inquiry straight away.

The battle to force the Liberal Party to clean up corruption within their own party has well and truly begun and it will not stop until it is won. It seems very few people within the Liberal Party realise it yet.

Chapter 26

Tony Abbott and Brandis both secretly met with paedophile protector George Pell. Why?

Tony Abbott and Brandis both secretly met with paedophile protector George Pell. Why?

BY SHANE DOWLING ON JULY 26, 2015 • (38 COMMENTS)

Federal Attorney-General Senator George Brandis QC secretly met with known paedophile protector and alleged paedophile Cardinal George Pell in May this year. It was only reported on Monday (20/7/15) because Brandis has spent the last 3 months trying to conceal it.

It is almost identical to Tony Abbott lying in an interview in 2004 on the ABC's 7.30 Report about a secret meeting he had with George Pell before the 2004 Federal Election.

George Brandis should have never been anywhere near George Pell for many reasons. Not the least of which is that Pell is a sick and perverted person and a key witness at the $500 million Royal Commission into Institutional Responses to Child Sexual Abuse.

It causes major headaches for a lot of people including Prime Minister Tony Abbott who is also a long-time friend of Cardinal Pell. I find it impossible to believe that George Brandis would have met with Cardinal Pell without Tony Abbott's knowledge and approval. Be that as it may, Prime Minister Abbott certainly knows about the meeting now and has said nothing which also suggests he has known for a long time.

The problem will not be going away as many sexual abuse victims are very upset about it and George Pell is due to give evidence at the Royal Commission again sometime before Christmas. It is guaranteed that Pell will be asked about the May meeting with Brandis when he is next at the Royal Commission and that will raise further questions for Brandis and Tony Abbott.

Channel Ten Report on Monday 20/7/15

(Click anywhere on the above video to watch)

Channel 10 have a slightly longer report on their website where at the beginning they talk about Pell being accused of protecting paedophiles and at the end about **Brandis' office** *"only disclosing the lunch after persistent enquiries from Channel 10"*. (Click here to watch)

George Brandis knew he should not be meeting with George Pell

It is not like George Brandis did not know Pell was a witness at the Royal Commission. Pell already gave evidence in March and August last year and was put on notice in May this year that he would be required for further evidence later this year.

Also, when the Royal Commission makes recommendations to the government Brandis will be having a substantial say in what recommendations they will implement. As a QC Brandis is fully aware that he should never have met with George Pell for legal reasons such as perceived bias.

Tony Abbott's friendship with George Pell and the Liberal Party connection

In September 2013 I wrote the below in an article:

"Tony Abbott and George Pell have a history of working together in politics. Before the 2004 election Tony Abbott gave an infamous interview on the ABC's Lateline where he was caught lying and deceiving in relation to a meeting with George Pell. A couple of days after the meeting George Pell was a signatory to a letter criticising the Labor Party." (Click here to read more)
Below is the video showing Tony Abbott lying.

Tony Abbott lies about meeting George ...

Watch later   Share

Watch on ▶ YouTube

(Click anywhere on the above video to watch) (For the longer transcript version click here)

Given Tony Abbott has previous history of telling a lie trying to conceal a meeting with George Pell did he tell George Brandis to try and conceal his meeting with Pell?

Questions that need to be answered regarding the George Brandis / Cardinal George Pell meeting

What does Abbott know about the meeting? What did Brandis say to Pell at the meeting? Did Brandis say to Pell that there is no need for Pell to worry as any negative recommendations by the Royal Commission against Pell and the Church will be swept under the carpet? Did Brandis pass on any messages to Pell from Tony Abbott at the lunch or pass on any message to Tony Abbott from Pell after the lunch?

Give credit where it is due

It must be noted that in September 2014 at the request of the Royal Commission the Federal Government led by Prime Minister Tony Abbott extended the Royal Commission for 2 years until 2017. (Click here to read more)

Alleged paedophile George Pell and his support for paedophile priests

(Above picture: Confessed paedophile Gerard Ridsdale and his supporter George Pell go to court)

This article is not about George Pell and his recent actions are well-known so I won't go too in-depth but his background is highly relevant to the article so I will cover a few parts. George Pell supported serial paedophile Gerard Ridsdale even when he was facing criminal charges as the above photo shows.

I wrote an article in March last year regarding Pell's evidence at the Royal Commission which starts off:

"Cardinal George Pell, who was investigated in 2002 for sexually assaulting a 12-year-old-boy in 1961, gave evidence yesterday (24/3/14) at the Royal Commission into Institutional Responses to Child Sexual Abuse. It is a bit rich to call what came out of George's mouth "evidence" given almost every second word would have to classified as perjury." (Click her to read more)

(Click anywhere on the above video to watch)

Another article I wrote in September 2013 which has a lot of background information is titled *"Tony Abbott and his friend Cardinal George Pell. Perceived bias for the Royal Commission into child sex abuse"* (Click here to read)

Is George Brandis a paedophile?

As we now know paedophilia goes to the highest levels of government in England so when members of parliament act as strange and in the circumstances that Brandis has, I think it fair to ask the question about them.

One thing that is certain is that Brandis having lunch with Cardinal George Pell has given some credibility to a person who will go down in history as one of the biggest paedophile protectors the world has ever seen. And why Brandis has done that is something he needs to explain to the public.

Brandis is divorced with 2 children and his own sexuality is the subject of rumour or at least that is what the Sydney Morning Herald said in an article in 2013.

"Those who know him well insist occasional gossip about Brandis's sexuality is baseless." And *"Don Markwell says he*

and Brandis have discussed sex only once in more than 40 years of friendship." (<u>Click here to read more</u>)

I would like to know what those rumours are and whether or not a dodgy meeting with Pell is relevant.

The only rumour that I know of is that George Brandis is gay and was caught in bed with another man at university. If that is true who cares and he wouldn't be the first gay person to get married and have children. But maybe the other rumours are a lot more than that.

Why George Brandis met with Cardinal Pell and why he tried to cover it up is unknown so all we can do is speculate to try to get to the truth and so we should as it is disgusting and needs to be exposed.

There will be suspicion about anyone who meets with George Pell. Even worse if they are the Federal Attorney-General

Everyone knows that the Catholic Church are protecting paedophiles on a huge scale. Now and in the past. I wouldn't go anywhere near George Pell in a million years unless it was to try to expose his criminal conduct further.

George Brandis as put the credibility of the $500 million taxpayer funded Royal Commission in jeopardy.

Time for action

Tony Abbott and Brandis need to come clean now. The longer they wait the worse it will become. The above story is dynamite waiting to go off and it will sometime in the not-too-distant future I expect.

If this was a court case afoot the first question people would ask is: Has George Brandis and/or Tony Abbott interfered in the administration of justice. The Royal Commission isn't a court case, but it is the next best thing and people will be wondering for a long time if Brandis and/or Abbott have interfered with it. At least until they say what happened at the meeting with Brandis and Pell.

Chapter 27

Canning by-election. Will it decide the fate of Tony Abbott and Bill Shorten?

Canning by-election. Will it decide the fate of Tony Abbott and Bill Shorten?

BY SHANE DOWLING ON SEPTEMBER 5, 2015 • (18 COMMENTS)

In a couple of weeks there will be a by-election in Western Australia which, if the Liberals lose, could see a new Prime Minister and a new leader of the Labor Party not long after. Continued internal rumblings in the Liberal Party suggest Prime Minister Tony Abbott is just hanging on to the job and many predict he will be gone if the safe Liberal seat of Canning is lost.

What most people are not talking about is that Labor Leader Bill Shorten would almost certainly lose his position as well as he is not popular with the voters. The only thing that keeps Shorten in the job is that the voters like Tony Abbott even less and the polls have been saying this for a long time. (Click here to read more)

Background – The by-election

There is a by-election in the federal seat of Canning in Western Australia on the 17th of September 2015 because of the death Liberal MP Don Randall. There are 12 candidates and there needs to be a 11.8% swing against the Liberals for them to lose. Most polls are currently saying the swing is about 10% which makes it very close. (Click here to read more)

Tony Abbott

Below is a fair summary of Abbott's position:

"Depending on the result, the Canning by-election might signal the beginning of a comeback for Abbott and his Government – just as Aston did for John Howard. It might mean the end of his leadership. Or it might mean nothing at all. The figures on the night will determine that. And this time if a leader falls it won't be in the dead of night leaving an electorate stunned. It will have a basis in fact, the result of a real poll." (Click here to read more)

Tony Abbott's poor position has mostly been his own doing although some ministers have badly let him down. He has not been a good Prime Minister and if Labor had someone besides Bill Shorten as their leader who was half decent Abbott probably would have been replaced by now.

The Conversation website says:

"Fight is what Abbott does best – but this penchant for pugilism is his great weakness as well as a strength."

"The prime minister, who won power two years ago on Monday, is most at home in combat, whether on the domestic campaign trail or escalating Australia's commitment to a battle abroad."

"A Liberal parliamentarian, highly critical of Abbott, describes his current approach to government as "doing what comes naturally – he's trying to be a warrior. He's relying on a small circle of advice; he's going back to areas he's comfortable with."

"In February a deeply disillusioned Liberal backbench, angry at the command-and-control style of the Prime Minister's Office (PMO) and especially chief-of-staff Peta Credlin, fearful about

the bad polls, appalled at the Prince Philip knighthood
"captain's pick" and shocked at Campbell Newman's
Queensland defeat, gave Abbott a huge scare with a spill motion
that mustered a substantial 39 votes, to the 61 against." (Click
here to read more)

This instability in Australian politics obviously has short-term problems but in the longer term should be good for the country as it is sending a message to all politicians that poor performance won't be tolerated. It is being driven to a large extent by a less tolerant and better educated public who demand more from their politicians.

How long Tony Abbott survives is unknown, but the Canning by-election could have a huge bearing on it.

Bill Shorten

If Abbott is replaced by Malcolm Turnbull, then the polls would probably do a huge reversal in the short-term at least and make it almost impossible for Labor's Bill Shorten to survive. Then again maybe no one in Labor would want the leadership 12 months out from a federal election if they thought Labor were certain to lose it.

Bill Shorten's performance as leader will also be gauged to some degree depending on how well Labor does or doesn't do in the Canning by-election. Although Shorten has a lot of problems coming his way such as a second appearance at the Trade Union Royal Commission which might decide his future irrespective of the Canning by-election. The Canning election will be Shorten's first real test with voters as Labor leader, but it is hard to gauge whether or not he will have any influence at all.

A change of leaders for both parties might be good for the country as federal politics to a large degree has seemed to stall making positive changes over the last few years. Some issues seem to have been around forever and never get solved.

In a normal situation almost no one would care about the Canning by-election but it could be a real game changer depending on how the votes go and could decide the fate of a number of politicians. If Abbott goes so would quite few Ministers as well and if Shorten goes so will a number of Shadow Ministers.

Chapter 28

Malcolm Turnbull the rain man who speaks with forked tongue.

Malcolm Turnbull the rain man who speaks with forked tongue.

BY SHANE DOWLING ON SEPTEMBER 9, 2012 • (93 COMMENTS)

Malcolm Turnbull has called for more truth in parliament. I agree, so in this post we have a look at what a dirty rotten lying scoundrel Malcolm Turnbull is.

In a speech that Mr Turnbull gave in Perth last Wednesday it was reported *"Malcolm Turnbull has decried the state of political discourse in Australia, saying it had deteriorated to such an extent that the nation suffered "a deficit of trust" and there was an urgent need for honesty in politics."* (Click here to read more)

Before Malcolm starts preaching, he needs to have a good look at himself. His own party dumped him as leader in 2009 and from all reports trust and honesty were an issue. Mr Turnbull has also refused to answer a number of questions in relation to a grant he gave when he was Environment Minister in the Howard government to his friend Matt Handbury.

Mr Turnbull's electorate fund-raising is done though an organisation he set up in 2007 called the Wentworth Forum. The

SMH reported *"Regarded as the country's most sophisticated political fund-raising machine, the forum offers membership packages that give the most generous supporters more opportunities to gain access to Mr Turnbull."*

"It costs $5500 to be a "member", $11,000 to be a "sponsor", $16,500 to be a "patron", $25,500 to be a "benefactor" and $55,000 to be a "governor"."

"A governor can host boardroom events, and gets two tables at big functions featuring Mr Turnbull, and attendance at an exclusive dinner for supporters."

"An analysis of forum donations, fund-raising events and memberships between 2007 and last December shows Mr Turnbull received more than $1.4 million. He personally contributed about $10,000 in catering for forum events. Most of the money was raised before the 2007 federal election." (Click here to read more)

Matt Handbury was one of the donors to Mr Turnbull's Wentworth Forum.

Before the 2007 election and two weeks after the election was called Malcolm Turnbull announced that the government would spend $11 million funding a trial of rainfall technology. The company in question was Australian Rain Corporation which was then part-owned by Matt Handbury.

It says on Mr Turnbull's Wikipedia profile *"During the 2007 election campaign, Turnbull announced that the then Government would contribute $10 million to the investigation of an untried Russian technology that aims to trigger rainfall from the atmosphere, even when there are no clouds. Literature suggests that the technology is based on bogus science. The Australian Rain Corporation presented research documents written in Russian, explained by a Russian researcher who spoke to local experts in Russian."*

"Although Turnbull claimed that Australian Rain Corporation is Australian-based, investigations have shown that it is in fact 75 per cent Swiss-owned. It was also revealed that a prominent stakeholder in the Australian Rain Corporation, Matt Handbury, is a nephew of Rupert Murdoch. Turnbull has refused to answer questions regarding Matt Handbury's contribution to the Wentworth Forum, the main fundraising organisation for Turnbull's 2007 election campaign." (Click here to read more)

It was even raised in parliament in 2009 during the infamous Godwin Grech / Utegate scandal. On the 22nd of June 2009 the following statement by Tony Burke Minister for Sustainability, Environment, Water, Population shows up on Hansard:

"There is an interesting organisation involved in what is described as 'rainfall enhancement technology'—a company named the Australian Rain Corporation. Apparently they have decided to corporatise rain! The Australian Rain Corporation sought money and the National Water Commission commissioned an independent review of the technology that they were putting forward by a former senior CSIRO officer and professor of physical sciences and engineering from the ANU. The National Water Commission insisted that the Australian Rain Corporation give a presentation of this technology to a panel of physicists. They then provided it with the research papers and made the presentation in Russian. The independent review concluded: 'There is no convincing evidence that the Atlant technology operates as believed by its proponents.' But in the end the department recommended that the member for Wentworth provide them with $2 million for a trial, which was arguably a generous offering, given what had been said about the technology. What did the Leader of the Opposition, as a minister, do with a recommendation to give them $2 million? He wrote to the Prime Minister seeking a lazy $10 million for the Australian Rain Corporation. You have to ask: What would be the circumstances of taking a departmental recommendation for $2

million and turning it into $10 million? Why would the Leader of the Opposition have done that as a minister?"

"This is where we discover that an executive of the Australian Rain Corporation happened to be a next-door neighbour of the Leader of the Opposition. The same person, the same neighbour, was a member of his electorate fundraising committee, the Wentworth Forum, with membership costing a cool $5,000 to get yourself into the room. If you want to find deals for mates, there are stories of deals for mates and there are stories that rest very squarely with the Leader of the Opposition. This is the same person who was able to run around saying, 'Well, we've got this email. You'd better publish it,' and who went to members of staff, intimidated them and said that he had documentary evidence. All we ask of the Leader of the Opposition is: prove that you have been telling the truth. We know what will happen. We know we will be greeted with the same deathly silence that we get now. We know that he is pretending to write and focus on something else, but we know full well that the Leader of the Opposition has been caught out and caught out badly." (Click here to read more) And on the 23rd June 2009 it was raised again in parliament by Tony Burke. (Click here to read)

Another article says: *"Rainmaker Ian Searle, the father of cloud seeding in Australia for the Tasmanian Hydro scheme, has also expressed doubts, as has Israel's internationally respected cloud physicist Professor Daniel Rosenfeld."*

"There is no single scientific paper, only the patent, and one can patent anything claiming it's to do anything that he likes, as long as no one else has made the same claims before," Professor Rosenfeld said.

"Mr Searle says all the literature he has seen on the technology shows it to be a bogus science." (Click here to read more)

At one point the government were talking about having an inquiry into the grant to Australian Rain Corporation but it never eventuated. As it turned out when the Rudd government came to power in November 2007 the new Environment Minister Penny Wong cancelled the grant but $2.97 million had already been paid and there were likely other costs in terminating the funding agreement. (Click here to read more)

There are a lot of unanswered questions that Malcolm Turnbull needs to answer about the Australian Rain Corporation grant. So far he refuses.

Other issues about his honesty have also been raised such as: *"Mr Turnbull's connection to the logging industry in Solomon Islands began in 1991 and 1992, when he owned shares and also chairman of the then Hong Kong listed Axiom Forest Resources that own logging operations and forest concessions in the country."*

He rejected accusations that he had once played a huge role in bad logging practices in Solomon Islands, claiming "he was trying to encourage local landowners to change logging practices and ways".

Mr Turnbull then further claimed ".... the company (Silvania) brought in some of the best foresters in the world. There was a lot of work done on reforestation, on plantations".

A report by the Australian International Development Aid Bureau – now Ausaid – in 1994 described the logging practices of Axiom subsidiary Silvania Forest Products as:..."more like a clear-felling operation and bearing little relation to an attempt at even retaining a token sample of future commercial crop on the site."

A separate report also described Silvania's forest practices as "amongst the worst in the world." (Click here to read more)

If Malcolm Turnbull wants more honesty in government, he needs to start with himself. At the next election if the polls are true and the Liberals/Nationals win power one of the first things that they need to do is get rid of Turnbull. He is a major liability, not an asset. Judgement day is coming for all corrupt politicians no matter what side of politics they are on.

Chapter 29

Malcolm Turnbull's rap sheet. $10 million fraud & theft, branch stacking & his slush fund

(This article does cover some of the previous article)

Malcolm Turnbull's rap sheet. $10 million fraud & theft, branch stacking & his slush fund

BY SHANE DOWLING ON SEPTEMBER 20, 2015 • (41 COMMENTS)

Prime Minister Malcolm Turnbull is now in power, so it is worth looking at some of dodgy and corrupt conduct in his background. He has a history of fraud and theft of $11 million when he was Environment Minister in 2007, running a slush fund and branch stacking to get elected to federal parliament in 2004.

Add that to some other "handiwork" when he was in private business and it is not exactly the squeaky clean image that Australia deserves as its Prime Minister.

The Slush fund

I wrote an article in 2012 which is still relevant titled *"Malcolm Turnbull the rain man who speaks with forked tongue"* which details the fraud and theft when Turnbull gave a $11 million grant to his friend Matt Handbury. Mr Handbury, who is a nephew of Rupert Murdoch, was also involved in helping Turnbull run his election slush fund.

The 2012 article said in part:

Mr Turnbull's electorate fund-raising is done though an organisation he set up in 2007 called the Wentworth Forum. The SMH reported *"Regarded as the country's most sophisticated political fund-raising machine, the forum offers membership packages that give the most generous supporters more opportunities to gain access to Mr Turnbull."*

"It costs $5500 to be a "member", $11,000 to be a "sponsor", $16,500 to be a "patron", $25,500 to be a "benefactor" and $55,000 to be a "governor"."

"A governor can host boardroom events, and gets two tables at big functions featuring Mr Turnbull, and attendance at an exclusive dinner for supporters."

"An analysis of forum donations, fund-raising events and memberships between 2007 and last December shows Mr Turnbull received more than $1.4 million. He personally contributed about $10,000 in catering for forum events. Most of

the money was raised before the 2007 federal election." (Click here to read more)

The fraud and theft

Matt Handbury was one of the donors to Mr Turnbull's Wentworth Forum.

Before the 2007 election and two weeks after the election was called Malcolm Turnbull announced that the government would spend $11 million funding a trial of rainfall technology. The company in question was Australian Rain Corporation which was then part owned by Matt Handbury.

It says on Mr Turnbull's Wikipedia profile *"During the 2007 election campaign, Turnbull announced that the then Government would contribute $10 million to the investigation of an untried Russian technology that aims to trigger rainfall from the atmosphere, even when there are no clouds. Literature suggests that the technology is based on bogus science. The Australian Rain Corporation presented research documents written in Russian, explained by a Russian researcher who spoke to local experts in Russian."* (Click here to read the full article)

The branch stacking in 2003 to get Turnbull elected to Parliament in 2004

Malcolm Turnbull was elected to federal parliament in 2004 in the Sydney seat of Wentworth. Firstly though Turnbull had to win Liberal Party preselection by beating the then Liberal Party federal MP Peter King. So Turnbull did what any proud crook would do. He started branch stacking and even enlisted James Packer for help. The Age reported in October 2003:

"A federal Liberal MP yesterday accused the party's federal treasurer, Malcolm Turnbull, of a "millionaires' plot" to unseat him, as sources confirmed that media magnate James Packer has been recruited to join a branch being stacked with Turnbull supporters."

"Peter King, who holds the blue ribbon Sydney seat of Wentworth, is under siege from Mr Turnbull, who has more than 700 new members signed up or about to be signed up for the Point Piper branch."

"In an extraordinary race for numbers before the cut-off date for branch members to be eligible to vote in the preselection, Mr King's camp has sent out a letter appealing for people to join the party."

"Mr King said this appeared to be "the largest branch stack in Liberal history". and that it was "disgraceful" that a federal office bearer appeared to be personally perpetrating it." (Click here to read more)

And who says money doesn't talk?

Stabbing Prime Minister Tony Abbott in the back.

Some people say that Abbott was stabbed in the back but that is a bit rich given the whole country knew when the leadership vote in February happened this year that Abbott had been put on notice by his own party.

If Turnbull had not replaced Tony Abbott as Prime Minister there is a good chance that Labor's Bill Shorten would have become Prime Minister which Turnbull points out in the below video.

Turnbull announces his challenge and the reasons he said justified it

(Click anywhere on the above video to watch)

Malcolm Turnbull says in the above video one of the reasons that he challenged Abbott for the leadership is because Abbott lost 30 polls in a row which he says pointed to the fact that they would lose the next election. While it is not comparing apples with apples it is worth noting that Turnbull also lost 30 polls in a row when he was opposition leader in 2008 to 2009 and was then replaced by Abbott.

21st September, 2008 – Turnbull loses his first Newspoll. It would be the first of 30 straight Newspoll losses.

29th November, 2009 – Turnbull loses his 30th Newspoll out of 30.

1st December, 2009 – Turnbull loses leadership to Tony Abbott.

It's a big effort to lose 30 polls in a row and both Tony Abbott and Malcolm Turnbull have done that. The difference is that Tony Abbott was Prime Minister when he did it and was up against a very unpopular Labor leader in Bill Shorten. While Turnbull was opposition leader and up against Prime Minister Kevin Rudd who was a very popular leader in 2008 and 2009.

All the old dirt like the Godwin Grech / Utegate affair will rise again

Malcolm Turnbull has his critics of which I am one and there is even a new website called "Stop Turnbull". Everything in Turnbull's past will be raised again on social media and Turnbull's relationship with the media proprietors won't do him much good just as Abbott's relationship with Rupert Murdoch couldn't save him. Turnbull needs to meet his critics on social media head on and address the issues raised.

New cabinet

I'm no fan of Malcolm Turnbull but he is going to have to stuff-up extremely badly to get beaten by Bill Shorten at the next election and the Labor Party know it and will likely get rid of Shorten as soon as they can. But if Turnbull acts in the same incompetent and negligent way he did last time he was leader of the Liberal Party then things could change fast.

The first major mistake that Malcolm Turnbull looks like making is appointing Arthur Sinodinos to the ministry as a reward for helping him become Prime Minister. Mr Sinodinos lost all his credibility when he gave evidence at the NSW Independent Commission Against Corruption regarding his involvement in government corruption.

It is only a couple of weeks ago that Sinodinos had a legal case dropped against him. The SMH reported

"Liberal senator Arthur Sinodinos is free of a major legal headache after shareholders in a company embroiled in a corruption inquiry dropped a costly case against him."

"Senator Sinodinos, a former chairman of infrastructure company Australian Water Holdings, was one of several former directors being pursued by the disgruntled shareholders to recover their investment."

"The company and former chief executive Nick Di Girolamo, a prominent Liberal Party fundraiser, were the subject of a high-profile Independent Commission Against Corruption inquiry last

year into allegations the company improperly billed the state-owned Sydney Water for lavish expenses including limousines and airfares. " (Click here to read more)

It would be a massive mistake to appoint Sinodinos as a minister and set Turnbull's new government up for immediate criticism. Especially on social media where many, including this website, have zero tolerance for corruption.

Chapter 30

Malcolm Turnbull sued Fairfax for accusing him of killing his ex-girlfriend's cat #KittyGate

Malcolm Turnbull sued Fairfax for accusing him of killing his ex-girlfriend's cat #KittyGate

BY SHANE DOWLING ON OCTOBER 11, 2015 • (8 COMMENTS)

In 1981 Malcolm Turnbull was accused by Fairfax Media of killing the cat of his ex-girlfriend Fiona Watson. Turnbull sued and won but as our new Prime Minister it is interesting to consider why he even bothered to sue in the first place, and more importantly will he continue to threaten journalists with legal proceedings?

Of further interest is the fact that Turnbull wrote a letter to the cat as you can see below which was either a novel way of trying to win his girlfriend back or a sign of a nutter.

Background to #KittyGate

The cat story was written by Richard Ackland in 1981 and at the time Turnbull was attempting to be preselected for the federal seat of Wentworth. Four years earlier Turnbull's girlfriend Fiona

Watson had dumped him and Turnbull wrote letters to her cat in what seems to be an attempt to win her back. It was rumoured that Malcolm Turnbull had killed the cat in 1978.

In the 1981 article Richard Ackland said: *"if Turnbull is preselected he could face some hostile questions from the Animal Protection League."*

Turnbull sued and was successful. One of the letters is below.

"For those having trouble with the hieroglyphics here it is:"

Dear Nessie,

Tell you [sic] miss that I love her very much, tell her that when I came to see her on Sunday and she wasn't there I cuddled you up and it broke my heart that it wasn't her.

Tell her I know a lot about her current boyfriends will tell her not to see me, they will stroke her back and tell her to forget me.

But, Nessie, we know she never will and you tell her, my little cat, how much we were in love.

all my love

Malcolm

The article also says:

"Turnbull routinely dropped the "defamation" word. Journalists who interviewed him for profiles invariably were threatened that he'd sue their pants off if he didn't like what was published."

"He waged a torrid war of libel threats against the former editor of The Economist, which had published something innocuous about the murky matter of FAI and HIH." (Click here to read more)

The fact that he sued and won a defamation proceeding regarding the cat is maybe why the media do not write about it much.

Will Malcolm Turnbull continue to threaten journalists now he is Prime Minister?

Numerous former Prime Ministers have threatened or tried to intimidate the Australian media not to publish stories they didn't want the public to know about. The most recent example is Julia Gillard who threatened News Ltd and Fairfax Media executives in 2012 regarding her involvement in the AWU / Bruce Wilson fraud and theft. (Click here to read more)

Given Malcolm Turnbull has some form in threatening the media one has to wonder if he will do it again as Australian Prime Minister if it suits his purpose. Turnbull was the Communications Minister prior to becoming the Prime Minister and had promised to change media ownership laws which was quickly shot down by former PM Tony Abbott on the instructions of Channel 7's owner Kerry Stokes. (Click here to read more)

So how will the media game play out now Turnbull is the Prime Minister? Will Turnbull tell Stokes and Murdoch that they better play ball, or he will change the media ownership laws that will cost them money?

It is interesting to note that Turnbull's good mate is Bruce McWilliam who is an executive at Seven West Media and a non-executive director of its major shareholder Seven Group Holdings.

The AFR had this to say about McWilliam in 2014:

"There's nothing uninteresting about McWilliam's history as a legal adviser to Australia's media barons. By and large, McWilliam spent the 1980s working for Kerry Packer, the 1990s working for Rupert Murdoch and the noughties (up to now) working for Kerry Stokes."

*"Then there's his 40-year association with federal Communications Minister Malcolm Turnbull, and his extensive property interests; last year, McWilliam sold the iconic Bang & Olufsen House on Sydney Harbour for $33.5 million. He met his wife Nicky – herself an accomplished lawyer – at **Rodney Adler's wedding** in 1987; they now have three children."*

and: *"McWilliam, the son of a Wollongong dentist, met Turnbull in 1974 on his first day at Sydney University. After working at CPH together, they founded their **law firm Turnbull McWilliam** in 1985 (which continued to advise Packer's media interests)."* (Click here to read more)

And it was Bruce McWilliam who said good things about Malcolm Turnbull on a recent episode on Malcolm Turnbull titled *"The making of Malcolm"*. (Click here to read more)

As a side note I have been told that it is Bruce McWilliam who has responsibility for Kerry Stokes' defamation proceedings against me. (Click here to read more) Which means Prime Minister Malcolm Turnbull's good mate Bruce McWilliam is up to his neck in bribing NSW Supreme Court Judges. I'll write more on that issue another time.

It should also be noted that Malcolm Turnbull has never threatened to sue me for the article I wrote in 2012 about his thieving ways when he was a Minister in the Howard government in 2007. (Click here to read the article)

Will Kitty Gate be raised in Parliament again?

The evidence supporting the claim that Malcolm Turnbull killed the cat is extremely weak at best but that won't stop people raising it and it has previously been mentioned in the federal parliament.

In June 2009 federal Labor MP Tony Burke raised the cat story in parliament when Turnbull was opposition leader. News.com.au reported at the time:

"Turnbull, who has sued a few times on this (leading to a sign over the subbing desks in the Fairfax offices in Sydney insisting the "cat should never be mentioned"), insists the pussy was run over and laughs off the cat story."

"But in the hothouse climate of Parliament this week, the cat was back."

"Agriculture Minister Tony Burke, who's becoming more famous for dirt-throwing than dirt tilling, was asked an innocent question on animal protection." (Click here to read more)

The chances of Kitty Gate being raised again in parliament would have to be low as Bill Shorten wouldn't want a dirt fight given his own dirty laundry and skeletons in the closet. Then again, maybe Shorten will think he has nothing to lose.

Chapter 31

Malcolm Turnbull's own $11 million donation/bribery scam comes back to haunt him

Malcolm Turnbull's own $11 million donation/bribery scam comes back to haunt him

BY SHANE DOWLING ON MARCH 26, 2016 • (24 COMMENTS)

Malcolm Turnbull's own $11 million donation scam during the 2007 election is set to become a political issue again given the Arthur Sinodinos donation scandal that broke in the media on Wednesday. Add that to the Mafia/Liberal Party bribery scandal that was reported last year it is highly likely that Malcolm Turnbull is facing the political crisis of his career.

All the pieces to the donation/bribery puzzle are starting to come together which is bad news for the Liberal Party and the timing could not be worse as it is just a few months before the federal election.

Current donation scandal

The NSW Liberal Party had been using an ACT based slush fund called the Free Enterprise Foundation to bypass NSW laws banning property developers from donating to political parties. The NSW Liberals told the property developers to donate to the Free Enterprise Foundation and then the Free Enterprise Foundation would donate to the NSW Liberal Party. This scam was used extensively to help the Liberals fund the 2011 state election campaign.

The NSW Election Commission enforces the political donation laws and audits the financial records of the donations. The political parties have to name who has donated to them for donations greater than $1,000. So, all the NSW Liberals were doing was putting down the name Free Enterprise Foundation which hid the real companies donating.

The NSW Independent Commission Against Corruption (ICAC) investigated the Liberal Party and its 2011 election funding relationship with the Free Enterprise Foundation in 2014. The investigation was part of Operation Spicer which had public hearings and the NSW Election Commission followed the hearings closely and started their own investigation as they believed election laws had been broken in 2011.

On Wednesday (23-3-16) the NSW Electoral Commission published its report and in effect made a finding of corrupt conduct against various Liberal Party officials and Senator Arthur Sinodinos who was the NSW Treasurer at the time. (Click here to read the Summary of Facts report or click here to read the full report)

At any time the Liberal Party could have easily stopped the NSW Electoral Commission investigation by simply handing over a list of the donors. For whatever reason the Liberal Party have chosen not to do this and have fought extremely hard not to hand over the names of the donors. The fight can be seen in the letters between the NSW Electoral Commission and the Liberal Party's lawyers at the end of the full report. (Click here to read the full report)

The media storm hit Wednesday with the Labor Party calling for Arthur Sinodinos to be sacked or stood down. (Click here to read more) Arthur Sinodinos threatened legal action against the NSW Electoral Commission.

"Sinodinos said the commission's report had led to media reports labelling him corrupt and is demanding it retract all references to him in the publication."

"In light of these matters, my lawyers on my behalf have invited the commission to immediately retract all references to me in the publication. The commission has been invited to publish a correction to that effect on its website." (Click here to read more)

At this point the NSW Electoral Commission hasn't succumbed to Arthur Sinodinos' legal threats and I doubt very much they will. It must be remembered that Sinodinos hopped in the witness stand in 2014 at ICAC and could barely remember anything regarding his $200,000 job as Chairman of Australian Water Holdings (AWH) when he was in cahoots with Eddie Obeid and his family ripping off the taxpayers millions of dollars.

"The allegations of questionable donations to the party have dogged Sinodinos ever since his string of "don't recalls" and "don't recollects" reverberated through the hearing room during ICAC's Operation Spicer inquiry."

"Paul Nicolaou, the party's former chief fund-raiser, told the inquiry that Sinodinos was chairing a finance committee meeting in 2010 when the idea of washing illicit donations through the FEF was first raised."

"Sinodinos said that if he had been present when this was floated "it went over my head"." (Click here to read more)

Malcolm Turnbull in full flight on the ABC defending Arthur Sinodinos

Arthur Sinodinos tries a swifty

At 10pm on Easter Friday Arthur Sinodinos' lawyers (Arnold Bloch Leibler) released the threatening letter sent on Thursday (24-3-16) to the NSW Electoral Commission. Releasing the letter at that time is an old political trick and was clearly designed to have it receive as little media attention as possible which shows the lack of confidence that Sinodinos and his lawyers have in what they said in the letter. (Click here to read the letter)

I haven't read the whole letter but why bother. If Sinodinos and his lawyers don't have any confidence in the letter, why should I.

The bottom line is:

"The NSW Liberals refusal to formally disclose the names of the donors led the commission to withhold $4.4 million in campaign and administrative funding claimed by the NSW Liberals from the 2015 state election. It has also frozen future public funding to the division until it complies." (Click here to read more)

So why would the Liberal Party not hand over the names when millions of dollars are riding on it? One answer might be that it names the Mafia as reported last year.

Key Liberal fundraising body took Mafia money for access

"Mafia figures donated tens of thousands of dollars to the discredited NSW Liberal Party fundraising vehicle, the Millennium Forum, as part of an ultimately successful campaign to allow a known criminal to stay in Australia."

"A senior Millennium Forum figure, who is already under investigation by ICAC for allegedly funnelling illegal developer donations to the NSW Liberal Party, also helped criminal Frank Madafferi's lawyer meet then immigration minister Philip Ruddock on the visa issue." (Click here to read more)

The Mafia being on the list is one of the few reasons I could think of as to why the Liberal Party won't release the names. Whoever it is on the list they are sure worried about being named and the Liberal Party are worried about naming them.

Rain man Malcolm Turnbull should have seen the storm clouds coming

I wrote about Malcolm Turnbull's own dodgy election funding in an article in 2012 titled *"Malcolm Turnbull the rain man who speaks with forked tongue"*. The article focused on how Turnbull, when he was Environment Minister in the John Howard government, awarded an $11 million grant to a dodgy company run by Matt Hanbury who was one of his key fundraisers. It said in part:

Mr Turnbull's electorate fund-raising is done through an organisation he set up in 2007 called the Wentworth Forum. The SMH reported *"Regarded as the country's most sophisticated political fund-raising machine, the forum offers membership packages that give the most generous supporters more opportunities to gain access to Mr Turnbull."*

"It costs $5500 to be a "member", $11,000 to be a "sponsor", $16,500 to be a "patron", $25,500 to be a "benefactor" and $55,000 to be a "governor"."

"A governor can host boardroom events, and gets two tables at big functions featuring Mr Turnbull, and attendance at an exclusive dinner for supporters."

"An analysis of forum donations, fund-raising events and memberships between 2007 and last December shows Mr Turnbull received more than $1.4 million. He personally contributed about $10,000 in catering for forum events. Most of the money was raised before the 2007 federal election." (Click here to read more)

Matt Handbury was one of the donors to Mr Turnbull's Wentworth Forum.

Before the 2007 election and two weeks after the election was called Malcolm Turnbull announced that the government would spend $11 million funding a trail of rainfall technology. The company in question was Australian Rain Corporation which was then part owned by Matt Handbury.

It says on Mr Turnbull's Wikipedia profile *"During the 2007 election campaign, Turnbull announced that the then Government would contribute $10 million to the investigation of an untried Russian technology that aims to trigger rainfall from the atmosphere, even when there are no clouds. Literature suggests that the technology is based on bogus science. The Australian Rain Corporation presented research documents written in Russian, explained by a Russian researcher who spoke to local experts in Russian."*

"Although Turnbull claimed that Australian Rain Corporation is Australian-based, investigations have shown that it is in fact 75 per cent Swiss-owned. It was also revealed that a prominent stakeholder in the Australian Rain Corporation, Matt Handbury, is a nephew of Rupert Murdoch. Turnbull has refused to answer questions regarding Matt Handbury's contribution to the Wentworth Forum, the main fundraising organisation for Turnbull's 2007 election campaign." (Click here to read more)

If we are going to have a close look at what Sinodinos did or didn't do then we should also have a good look at other corrupt donation/fraud schemes such as the one above run by Malcolm Turnbull.

Looks like good-bye to the Double Dissolution election

This story is just starting to blow and in a couple of months it will be powering along. Corruption will be one of the biggest issues if not the biggest issue at the next federal election. It will be driven by social media if not the mainstream media and the Liberals are in a lot of trouble of their own making. There is no doubt that Senator Arthur Sinodinos has to go, it is just a matter of when and how much damage he does to the government before he does.

Chapter 32

Malcolm Turnbull: The frivolous litigant who "poisoned the fountain of justice" said Justice Hunt

Malcolm Turnbull: The frivolous litigant who "poisoned the fountain of justice" said Justice Hunt

BY SHANE DOWLING ON JUNE 4, 2016 • (12 COMMENTS)

In 1984 Justice Hunt in the NSW Supreme Court said Malcolm Turnbull had *"managed effectively to poison the fountain of justice"* in relation to defamatory statements Mr Turnbull had made in the media while representing Kerry Packer during the Costigan Royal Commission. Some say it probably also helped end Turnbull's career in law.

Malcolm Turnbull likes to portray that he was a young super barrister who won a huge case (Spycatcher) and then moved on to business with his career but the reality seems to be different and it is worth reviewing his short legal career.

Background

The real story is that in 1984 Malcolm Turnbull and his corrupt mate Bruce McWilliam instituted frivolous and vexatious defamation proceedings on behalf of Kerry Packer against Douglas Meagher who was counsel assisting the Royal Commission. They used the media and lied, deceived, ducked and weaved and trashed the reputation of Mr Meagher to help legendary tax cheat Packer dodge prosecution during the Costigan Royal Commission.

The proceedings were so frivolous and vexatious they only lasted a couple of days and it backfired badly as the Judge hearing the case unloaded with both barrels mostly directed at Malcolm Turnbull.

It's worth noting that Malcolm Turnbull has a glass jaw when it comes to criticism of himself. He is well known to threaten journalists with defamation proceedings, and he sued Fairfax Media in 1981 which I wrote about in an article last year. Turnbull's partner in crime Bruce McWilliam also gets a fair mention in the article. (Click here to read the article)

The Costigan Royal Commission

The Costigan Commission (officially titled the Royal Commission on the Activities of the Federated Ship Painters and Dockers Union) was an Australian royal commission held in the 1980s.

Headed by Frank Costigan QC, the Commission was established by the Australian government in 1980 to investigate criminal activities, including violence, associated with the Painters and Dockers Union. The Commission was seen by many as politically motivated in keeping with a long running anti-union agenda by the governing party of the day.

However, its enquiries led away from union activities towards investigation of so-called "bottom of the harbour" tax evasion schemes. This involved the asset-stripping of companies to avoid tax liabilities and was facilitated by criminals among the Painters and Dockers but benefited wealthy individuals. (Click here to read more)

Malcolm Turnbull and Bruce McWilliam

Turnbull worked for Packer at Australian Consolidated Press Holdings Group from 1983 to 1985. McWilliam also worked with Turnbull when they defended Packer during the Royal Commission.

Not long after in 1986 they set up their own law firm Turnbull McWilliam which Turnbull left in 1987 and established an investment banking firm, Whitlam Turnbull & Co Ltd. (Click here to read more)

Kerry Packer and Malcolm Turnbull. Photo was probably taken in the early 1980's.

Kerry Packer and the Royal Commission

Packer was investigated by the Royal Commission, but they hid his identity and gave him the name *"The Squirrel"*. It was leaked to the media, and they changed the name to The Goanna.

In September 1984, the now defunct National Times reported an amazing story sourced from a Royal Commission set up to investigate possible corruption in the Federated Ship Painters and Dockers Union. There's no doubt the union had some questions to answer, since some of its members had ended up being shot dead at close range or otherwise disposed of, but the investigation had not gone according to plan. Kerry Packer was the publisher of the Bulletin magazine, which had first raised the corruption issue. But when the investigation expanded to follow up the union's links to drug trafficking, money laundering, tax evasion, murder and pornography, Packer's name bobbed up; it appeared he had been mixing in bad company. The Bulletin story had boomeranged on its own proprietor.

Aware of the extreme sensitivity of the information it was gathering, the Royal Commission – headed by QC Frank Costigan, noted for his fairness and fearlessness – disguised Packer's identity, calling him "The Squirrel" instead. The National Times replaced this with the reptilian name "The Goanna", but otherwise published the Royal Commission documents in full.

The Frivolous and Vexatious defamation proceedings on behalf of Kerry Packer

Several days after the National Times story appeared, anyone driving into the city from what was then the increasingly gentrified suburb of Balmain in Sydney's inner west could see a big painted sign. "The Goanna = Kerry Packer", it said in metre-high white lettering. It wasn't long before Packer's lawyer, the brilliant and often unpredictable Malcolm Turnbull, was threatening legal action – not against the obvious target, the National Times and its publisher Fairfax, but against Douglas Meagher, counsel assisting the Royal Commission. Turnbull claimed defamation on the grounds that Meagher and Costigan have conducted themselves most reprehensively in failing to stop an unauthorised and illegal leak of information which was inevitably going to do immense or irreparable damage to the reputation of Kerry Packer.

It was a novel approach, but Justice Hunt in the NSW Supreme Court wasn't impressed. His court wasn't going to be party to an attempt to bully a Royal Commission, and Justice Hunt was scathing about Turnbull's conduct. (Click here to read more)

In one of the most aggressive performances seen in Australia, Turnbull taunted Costigan to sue him – according to Justice

David Hunt in the NSW Supreme Court, Turnbull accused Douglas Meagher QC and Costigan of being unjust, capricious, dishonest and malicious.

Turnbull's scorched-earth use of the media made him unpopular with elements in the NSW Bar and was a factor in his leaving. He later moved full-time into merchant banking. (Click here to read more)

Below is the front page of The Sydney Morning Herald on Tuesday the 18th December 1984 which gives Malcolm Turnbull a hiding for the defamation case (Click here to see the full paper)

Judge dismisses defamation action as an abuse

Packer's 'ulterior motive'

By TRUDY STOREY

Mr Kerry Packer's suit for defamation against Mr Douglas Meagher, QC, counsel assisting the Costigan Royal Commission, has been struck out by the Supreme Court as an abuse of the legal process.

Giving his reasons yesterday, Justice Hunt said the circumstances in which the action had been launched strongly suggested that Mr Packer may have wanted to punish Mr Meagher for his part in compiling the Costigan report.

"There may have been a vindictive desire on the part of the plaintiff [Mr Packer] to make the defendant [Mr Meagher] as uncomfortable as possible for as long as possible . . . in order to punish him," Justice Hunt said.

Whether or not such a desire existed, he was satisfied the ulterior motive in bringing the action was to investigate the conduct of the Costigan commission and not to vindicate Mr Packer's reputation.

Mr Packer has alleged that Mr Meagher was responsible for leaking to *The National Times* confidential case summaries prepared by the royal commission.

The defamation action was filed eight days ago. On Friday morning, Mr Packer sought to discontinue it but in the afternoon he

applied to withdraw the notice of discontinuance.

Yesterday, Justice Hunt refused the application for discontinuance and struck it out as an abuse of the legal process.

He also struck out the entire defamation suit as an abuse of process, and ordered Mr Packer to pay Mr Meagher's costs.

The judge said this was an exceptional case and one which he hoped would never be repeated.

An act of grave impropriety had been alleged against Mr Meagher and the legal process of the court had been abused in the proceedings.

Justice Hunt said he was satisfied that the filing of the notice of discontinuance had been filed to deny Mr Meagher his chances of obtaining public vindication.

"The defendant should have that public vindication. He has successfully and publicly called the plaintiff's bluff".

Justice Hunt said that Mr Malcolm Turnbull, who had described himself as the general counsel for Consolidated Press Holdings Pty Ltd, of which Mr Packer is chairman, alleged to the media on December 8 that he had every reason to believe Mr Meagher was responsible for the leaking of the Costigan summaries.

"Having managed effectively to poison the fountain of justice immediately before the commencement of the present proceedings", Mr Turnbull had added that he did not believe the leak came from the National Crime Authority, but from the Costigan commission, the judge said.

Justice Hunt said he did not propose to comment on the "propriety or other otherwise" of Mr Turnbull's statement.

On December 10 Mr Turnbull had said on the ABC radio program *AM* that he had evidence to support his claim, but declined to disclose it.

Two days later Mr Packer's lawyers had been served with an affidavit by Mr Meagher denying the allegations and had been asked to supply particulars of publication of the matter Mr Packer complained of.

Mr Packer's counsel had failed to give particulars of the allegation.

"The plaintiff's failure to give those particulars has never been explained, nor have the particulars ever been supplied, not withstanding several requests during the hearing that they be identified, at least generally."

Continued Page 2

Packer's 'ulterior motive' in action

From Page 1

The allegation that Mr Meagher had published the material in *The National Times* could not have been expressed in more general terms by the plaintiff, he said.

Mr Meagher had had no idea from Mr Packer's statement of claim about the nature of the proposed case against him on the issue of publication.

Last Thursday Mr Turnbull had announced in a press statement that the action was being discontinued because different litigation in another jurisdiction was being considered.

Justice Hunt said it had been submitted by Mr Meagher's counsel on Friday that the filing of the discontinuance notice had been deliberately timed just before the court vacation to ensure Mr Meagher would have to wait until February, when the court resumes, to clear his reputation.

Counsel for Mr Packer had said Mr Packer was immensely damaged by the allegations in the Costigan report. He was entitled to vindicate his reputation and repair the damage.

But Justice Hunt said several matters led him to believe Mr Packer never had a case against Mr Meagher on the publishing allegation.

The matters included:

● Mr Packer's discontinuance of the proceedings as soon as Mr Meagher had pressed for particulars of the allegations.

● The failure of, Mr Packer's counsel to identify the particulars they relied on.

● The failure of Mr Packer to give evidence about the issues raised.

A solicitor for Consolidated Press Holdings, Mr Bruce McWilliam, said last night the company would appeal against Justice Hunt's judgment.

(Click on the above news articles to make them larger)

Malcolm Turnbull lied, deceived and defamed others to defend a guilty man

Much of the Goanna material was, as Packer described it in an 8000-word statement crafted by Turnbull and issued in 1984, "grotesque, ludicrous and malicious". But the tax findings were not lightly based, nor easily dismissed. Even though the then attorney-general Lionel Bowen declared that Packer had been cleared of all allegations against him, Meagher later revealed that briefs for prosecution were prepared against Packer in relation to tax evasion after the commission was wound up. Costigan had told him three "very senior counsel" based in Sydney "each looked at them independently and recommended prosecution", but it didn't occur.

"Packer was a man of great influence," Meagher said. "He wasn't cleared. Not at all." (Click here to read more)

While Kerry Packer might have got away with tax fraud his son James isn't so lucky. The Australian Tax Office has recently taken James to court for $362 million in taxes he has tried to avoid paying into the public purse. (Click here to read more)

Summary

Malcolm Turnbull was never scrutinised before he became Prime Minister, so it is time to have a good look at his past and who he is now. Turnbull has represented tax cheats and in doing so he defamed people, lied, deceived and trashed the rule of law. Knowing some of his history it is no surprise he hasn't achieved much as PM and many Liberal supporters don't like him. Is that the sort of person Australia needs or wants as Prime Minister?

Declaration: Bruce McWilliam who is mentioned above is running frivolous and vexatious defamation proceedings against me on behalf of Kerry and Ryan Stokes and their lawyer Justine Munsie which is being funded by Channel 7. That has had no influence on what I have written above.

Chapter 33

Has PM Malcolm Turnbull's wife Lucy been outed as Australia's best known lobbyist?

Has PM Malcolm Turnbull's wife Lucy been outed as Australia's best known lobbyist?

BY SHANE DOWLING ON AUGUST 13, 2016 • (15 COMMENTS)

Last week Malcolm Turnbull announced new measures which would force bank CEO's to front a parliamentary committee supposedly to keep the banks honest. At the same time Malcolm Turnbull was making this announcement his wife Lucy was having coffee with the Chairman of the ANZ bank David Gonski which is highly suspicious to say the least.

On Monday this week Tony Abbott was on the ABC's Four Corners program calling for reform in the Liberal Party *"alleging the NSW branch is controlled by factional warlords who are also lobbyists for commercial interests"*. Add Lucy Turnbull's secret meeting with the ANZ Bank Chairman to Abbott's comments then there is clearly serious questions for the Turnbull's to answer. (Click here to read more or watch the Four Corners episode)

"*In NSW the Liberal Party is corrupt*" – former Howard government minister Jackie Kelly

Before we have a closer look at Malcolm and Lucy Turnbull's suspect behaviour it is worth noting that the internal focus on corruption in the Liberal Party seems to have started with former federal MP Jackie Kelly. In June this year Ms Kelly said on national TV that "*In NSW the Liberal Party is corrupt*" and "*The Liberal Party is full of lobbyists*". The below video is Jackie Kelly on The ABC's The Drum Friday June 3, 2016 which is what seems to have started the internal debate in the Liberal Party which Tony Abbott and others raised in the Four Corners show on Monday.

Malcolm Turnbull and Scott Morrison announce a crackdown on Banks

Last Thursday it was reported: "*Prime Minister Malcolm Turnbull and Treasurer Scott Morrison have announced the nation's major banks will have to face the House of Representatives Economics Committee at least once a year to explain their treatment of customers.*"

"*It follows this week's decision by the Reserve Bank to cut official interest rates to a record low 1.5 per cent — a cut that has not been passed on in full by the major banks."* (Click here to read more)

Lucy Turnbull's secret meeting with ANZ Chairman

The Australian reported the same day: *"Guess who first lady **Lucy Turnbull** was having coffee with at exactly the same time her husband, Prime Minister **Malcolm Turnbull**, joined his Treasurer **Scott Morrison** to announce a tough new "accountability" measure for the big four banks?*

*Step forward **David Gonski**, the chairman of ANZ — one of the big four banks with which the PM was apparently getting tough.*

So where would Lucy and Gonski elect to meet?

Where else but the coffee shop at 1 Bligh Street, home of the commonwealth government's offices in Sydney — the very spot that the PM and his Treasurer held their press conference to make their supposedly tough-on-banks announcement.

No wonder the Labor Party is having such fun using bank bashing as a proxy for going after Turnbull, once the head of investment bank Goldman Sachs down under.

*And no wonder ANZ's boss **Shayne Elliott** (who Gonski - appointed last year) was so quick to endorse the PM's "necessary initiative".* (Click here to read more)

Questions for Malcolm Turnbull

Lucy Turnbull is not an elected official so the public cannot demand that she answers questions. But Malcolm Turnbull is the Australian Prime Minister and the public have a right to know in regards to why his wife was meeting with the Chairman of the ANZ bank at the same time he was announcing a crackdown on the banks.

Some questions for Malcolm are:

1. When having coffee with the ANZ Chairman David Gonski was your wife Lucy telling him not to worry as the crackdown on the banks was just for show to fool the public into believing the government was actually doing something about banking corruption?

2. Given that in 2015 your "*estimated net worth was in excess of A$200 million*" did Lucy use the meeting to get better rates from ANZ for your business dealings and/or personal dealings with the bank?

3. Given that Lucy now runs your business interests estimated to be worth over $200 million do you think it is appropriate for you and Lucy to coordinate your political meetings with her business dealings?

4. Does Lucy Turnbull get some sort of benefit from the ANZ for pushing the ANZ's agenda with Malcolm Turnbull? Is Lucy Turnbull a lobbyist for the ANZ?

Those are the sorts of questions all the journalists from the major media companies in the Canberra Press Gallery should be asking Malcolm Turnbull.

Four Corners – former Australian Prime Minister and current MP Tony Abbott

Tony Abbott didn't miss on Monday night in regards to corruption and perceived corruption in his own party. He said:

TONY ABBOTT, FORMER PRIME MINISTER: "Wouldn't it be nice to see a bit of democracy inside our party? If Mike Baird wants it, if Malcolm Turnbull wants it, if John Howard wants it, if Barry O'Farrell wants it, if Tony Abbott wants it, it surely is good enough for the factional warlords to have it!"

MARIAN WILKINSON: The Liberals dismal loss of seats in NSW gave Abbott the opening and he seized it.

MARIAN WILKINSON: Can you just take us to that night and why you thought it was important to use that venue to make your call?

TONY ABBOTT: As a re-elected Member of Parliament, you've got the opportunity to say something, not just to your electorate, but to the nation, and in particular to the wider Liberal Party. Ah and this is a very important message.

MARIAN WILKINSON: Now relegated to the backbench, Abbott is declaring war on party powerbrokers who oppose his right-wing faction. His targets are a small group of well-connected lobbyists who he says can wield influence over choosing MPs and Senators for both the federal and state parliaments.

TONY ABBOTT: I want to empower the membership and make every member count. And the best way for that to happen is to say you count when it comes to choosing the Liberal Party's representatives in the parliament. Now, the difficulty at the moment ah is that because there's a smaller, ah less representative party, ah it's easily controlled ah by factional warlords. Some of these factional warlords have a commercial interest ah in dealing with politicians, whose pre-selections they can influence. Now, this is a potentially corrupt position, ah and the best way to see off the factionalists ah is to open up the party. The more members we've got the harder it will be for the factional warlords to control.

MARIAN WILKINSON: In an interview with Four Corners, Abbott threw down a challenge to the Liberal Party.

TONY ABBOTT: The point, Marian, that I made as soon as I became Prime Minister was that you could be a lobbyist or you could be a powerbroker, but you couldn't be both. Now, a lobbyist is someone who makes money out of getting people in front of politicians. A powerbroker is someone who controls or influences the pre-selections of those politicians. Now, ah if you are making money out of the people whose pre-selections you control or influence, there is obviously a potential for corruption. And that's the last thing that we should have inside the Liberal Party. (Click here to read more or watch the show)

Tony Abbott did not expressly mention Malcolm Turnbull and Lucy Turnbull using Malcolm's position as Prime Minister to further their financial interests but by Tony Abbott raising the issues he has then it was always going shine the light to some degree on the Turnbulls which I am sure Abbott would have known. This is nothing new as former Prime Minister Kevin Rudd and his wife Therese Rein sold their Australian assets when he was elected PM so there would be no allegations of corruption which I investigated extensively in 2013. (Click here to read more)

Former federal Liberal MP Sophie Mirabella rises again

Right on cue, it was announced on Friday (12/8/16) that Gina Rinehart, Australia's second richest person, has hired former Liberal Party politician and failed candidate from the latest federal election, Sophie Mirabella, as a *"lobbyist and spin doctor in Canberra"*.

"The dumped Indi MP was named on Friday as the first general manager of government and media relations for Ms Rinehart's company Hancock Prospecting." (Click here to read more) While Sophie Mirabella's appointment to her new job is not exactly corrupt it is not far off it and most voters would find it quite disgusting. From previous numbers I have seen I suspect Mirabella would be getting paid somewhere between $500,000 and $1 million by Rinehart to make sure the federal government does what Rinehart wants.

Cleaning up corruption within the Liberal Party will be an ongoing battle and very important for Australia's democracy given they are one of the major parties so I will keep a close eye on it and it's good to see people within the Liberal Party driving the issue.

Chapter 34

Prime Minister Malcolm Turnbull refuses to deny sexual affair with staff member

Prime Minister Malcolm Turnbull refuses to deny sexual affair with staff member

BY SHANE DOWLING ON MARCH 10, 2018 • (12 COMMENTS)

Malcolm Turnbull is refusing to deny allegations he had an affair with Debbie Huber when she was an employee of his in the 1980's. Ms Huber's family are currently involved in an ongoing tax-fraud battle worth over $100 million with the Australian Taxation Office and Debbie Huber seems to have been given favourable treatment so one wonders if the Prime Minister intervened on her behalf?

The third element to this article is that Debbie Huber worked for the Federal Director of Public prosecutions in the 1980's at a time when authorities were investigating Kerry Packer who Malcolm Turnbull worked for and who was later a client of Turnbull's law firm he set up with fellow Packer employee and lawyer Bruce McWilliam. Debbie Huber went on to work for Turnbull when he set up the law firm.

On Friday 9/3/18 I emailed questions to the Prime Minister, Bruce McWilliam, Nicky McWilliam and sent questions on Facebook to Debbie Huber and no one has responded which is standard if people have something to hide. Both Bruce and Nicky read the emails as they sent read receipts, but the Prime Minister's office refused to confirm when I phoned them asking if they intended to respond.

Malcolm Turnbull has a long history of what I will politely call questionable conduct. In 2015 I published an article titled "*Malcolm Turnbull's rap sheet. $10 million fraud & theft, branch stacking & his slush fund*" which outlines some of Malcolm's handiwork.

Debbie Huber on the right with her sister

Malcolm Turnbull's days as a lawyer, setting up law firm Turnbull McWilliam and investment bank Whitlam Turnbull & Co Ltd.

It says this on Wikipedia regarding Malcolm Turnbull and the period of his alleged affair with Debbie Huber:

After graduating from Oxford, Turnbull returned to Australia and began working as a barrister. He left the bar in 1983. Firstly he attempted preselection in the safe Liberal seat of Mosman. However, he lost to Phillip Smiles. Then he chose to become general counsel and secretary for Australian Consolidated Press Holdings Group, from 1983 to 1985.

(Australian Consolidated Press Holdings Group was owned by Kerry Packer)

During this time he defended Kerry Packer against the "Goanna" allegations made by *the Costigan Commission. Turnbull attempted to use the press to goad the counsel assisting the commission, Douglas Meagher QC, into suing him and Packer for the withering public attack both undertook to sully Meagher's and Costigan's names. Turnbull accused Meagher and Costigan of being "unjust, capricious, dishonest and malicious". Turnbull led Packer to sue Meagher for defamation, an action that was struck down by Justice David Hunt as being an abuse of process, and that Turnbull had managed "to poison the fountain of justice". The "Scorched Earth" tactic made Turnbull enemies in the NSW Bar Association, something that led to Turnbull leaving the Bar Association.*

In partnership with Bruce McWilliam, he established his own law firm, Turnbull McWilliam. During 1986, Turnbull defended Peter Wright, a former MI5 official who wrote the book Spycatcher, and successfully stopped the British government's attempts to suppress the book's publication in Australia. Turnbull later wrote a book on the trial.

"The fact of the matter is that nothing is achieved in this world, particularly politically, other than with persistence, and persistence involves repetition and it involves argument and re-argument... The public interest in free speech is not just in truthful speech, in correct speech, in fair speech... The interest is in the debate. You see, every person who has ultimately changed

the course of history has started off being unpopular." Turnbull's closing submissions, 18 December 1986

In 1987, Turnbull established an investment banking firm, Whitlam Turnbull & Co Ltd, in partnership with Neville Wran (a former Labor Premier of New South Wales) and the former State Bank of New South Wales chief executive, Nicholas Whitlam (son of Gough Whitlam, a former Labor prime minister). Whitlam parted company with the others in 1990 and the firm operated as Turnbull & Partners Ltd from then until 1997, when Turnbull moved to become a managing director and later a partner of Goldman Sachs. (Click here to read more)

Bruce McWilliam and allegations he destroyed evidence for Kerry Packer and called in favours from Malcolm Turnbull for Channel 7

Most people would not know who Bruce McWilliam is but his past becomes relevant in relation to Malcolm Turnbull and Debbie Huber. So, we'll have a look at some key parts of Bruce's dodgy past.

1980 – 1983: Bruce worked at Allen Allen and Hemsley as a solicitor and then left to join Consolidated Press Holdings (CPH) the Packer company with his friend Malcolm Turnbull (who is now the Prime Minister).

1983 – 1985: During this period, Bruce McWilliam & Malcolm Turnbull undertook many transactions for CPH as lawyers and advisers.

1985 – 1987: In 1985 Bruce McWilliam and Malcolm Turnbull set up their own law firm 'Turnbull McWilliam'.

1987: Bruce left to return to Allen Allen and Hemsley as a partner while Malcolm Turnbull formed his investment bank. (Click here to read more)

It says in a SMH July 2017 profile article by journalist Tim Elliott on Bruce McWilliam:

McWilliam's best friend, Prime Minister Malcolm Turnbull, lives a couple of doors down the road; the two go kayaking together in front of their houses. For McWilliam, who grew up in working-class Dapto near Wollongong, Point Piper is "the greatest suburb on Earth".

Though few members of the general public would have heard of him, McWilliam has for almost 40 years worked at the centre of Australia's cutthroat media industry, having served as a close adviser and confidant to a succession of Australia's most powerful men, including Kerry Packer in the 1980s, Rupert Murdoch in the 1990s and Kerry Stokes in the 2000s. Former Nine Network boss Sam Chisholm describes him as a "consigliere", a catch-all term which nonetheless fails to convey the full scope of McWilliam's remit.

Over the years, he has done everything for his bosses save bear their children: he has cut their deals and run their errands; he has policed their interests and defended their reputations; he has, in a very real sense, helped them make their billions. On occasion, he has even organised their social calendar. (When Rupert Murdoch married Wendi Deng in 1999, McWilliam found them a villa in Tuscany for the honeymoon. Murdoch then invited him to visit.) Peerlessly well connected and unwaveringly discreet, McWilliam is a consummate keeper of secrets whose arsenal includes irresistible charm, legal thuggery and much in between.

"Bruce is probably the most aggressive corporate lawyer we have ever seen," says James Warburton, who worked with McWilliam as Seven's sales boss in the late 2000s and is now CEO of Supercars. "Bruce is paid to make problems go away," another former Seven executive says. "He's like Mr Wolfe in Pulp Fiction, that calm, dapper guy who gets rid of the dead body from the back of the car and hoses it out."

McWilliam's friendship with the prime minister has indeed on occasion proved problematic. In 2014, officers from the

Australian Federal Police raided Seven's offices searching for evidence of a suspected seven-figure deal with convicted drug smuggler Schapelle Corby. It emerged that McWilliam had rung then Communications Minister Malcolm Turnbull, who had in turn phoned Attorney-General George Brandis and Justice Minister Michael Keenan, leading to suggestions that Turnbull had interfered in an AFP investigation on behalf of his friend. Turnbull denied this. When News Corp journalist Jennifer Sexton rang to discuss the matter with McWilliam, he hung up on her. (Click here to read more)

Debbie Huber – Federal Director of Public Prosecutions – Working for Malcolm Turnbull and Bruce McWilliam

Debbie Huber is so far refusing to answer questions. But I'm told by my sources that Debbie Huber worked for Federal Director of Public Prosecutions in the 1980's. This is supported by an article in The Sydney Morning Herald on 20th May 1986 which says:

"Miss Debbie Huber, prosecuting on behalf of the Director of Public Prosecutions, told the court there was some degree of indecision as to whether the case against Levinge would proceed under a State prosecutor or the Director of Public Prosecutions." (Click here to read more)

In the July 2017 SMH article on Bruce McWilliam above it quotes Debbie Huber in relation to the law firm Turnbull McWilliam:

"Deborah Huber worked at the firm as a litigator. "We all had a sense that Malcolm was going to be important, and Bruce was always supportive of him," she says. " (Click here to read more)

Then there is also her Facebook page post from the 17th June 2016 where she says *"as most of you know, I worked with Malcolm for many years (as a lawyer not a politician)"*

as most of you know, I worked with Malcolm for many years (as a lawyer not a politician) so this isnt mean spirited. he is a good man and a semitophile. But once you enter politics you are fair game!

Turnbull spends night stranded in Kirribilli: 'I now understand middle Australia'

Prime Minister Malcolm Turnbull says he now understands the "horrors of middle class living", after he found himself stranded at his modest Kirribilli

CHASER.COM.AU

So, let's put the timeline together. Malcolm Turnbull's law firm only lasted 18 months from 1985 to 1987. We know Debbie Huber worked at the law firm because she is quoted in the SMH article as having "worked at the firm as a litigator." which makes sense as she was a litigator at the Federal Director of Public Prosecutions. So that means she must have joined Malcolm's law firm just before is closed.

But we also know from the Facebook post that Debbie Huber worked for Malcolm for "*many years*" which means she went on to work for Malcolm at his investment bank Whitlam Turnbull & Co Ltd which he set up after closing the law firm. This is also supported by the below photo that Debbie Huber post on her Facebook page of her and Lucy Turnbull on the 9th of September 2016 which I am told was taken in the board room of Whitlam

Turnbull & Co Ltd. From the comments I believe the photo was taken in the 1980's.

Debbie Huber and Lucy Turnbull in the 1980's

Some of the details raised by my sources:

In the mid to late 1980's Ms Debbie Huber worked for the Federal Director of Public Prosecutions (NSW branch). She worked on a number of high-profile prosecution matters including the DPP file on the so-called Goanna files which related to allegations of drug importation and the late Kerry Packer. Those files were inherited from the Royal Commission.

Huber's boyfriends around the time included Rodney Adler and a number of other well-known businessmen.

Ms Huber was introduced by a senior AFP officer to Malcolm Turnbull who was retained by Kerry Packer and was a principal briefly in his own law firm with Bruce McWilliam and then in the firm of Whitlam Turnbull.

Ms Huber formed a close personal relationship with Malcolm Turnbull and went to work with Malcolm, first at Malcolm's law firm and then in the firm of Whitlam Turnbull. This caused some concern in DPP circles given her association with the sensitive Goanna and Tax prosecution files.

Ms Huber was quite upfront about her personal relationship with Mr Turnbull and spoke to many legal and DPP acquaintances about it. A number of interesting anecdotes survive including Malcolm taking Debbie to purchase a birthday present for Lucy.

Ms Huber recently (during the Nudie tax case) posted on her Facebook page photos and comments confirming she worked for Malcolm for years and a photo of herself and Lucy from the period in the Whitlam Turnbull boardroom. It is not clear whether govt departments were intimidated by her public display of her prior association with Turnbull.

Many employees at Whitlam Turnbull including a Mr xxxx xxxx had concerns about the relationship. Malcolm and Debbie were apparently caught in the act with Malcolm wearing only red socks.

Eventually Malcolm Turnbull and Debbie Huber came to a parting of the ways after discussions about Ms Huber's personal trading.

Ms Huber recently attracted media attention arising out of her court appearances in an ATO criminal case involving her in laws and the Nudie juice entities. Ms Huber admitted certain transactions however it appears from media reports that the Federal Government has provided her with a form of indemnity against prosecution. However it is proceeding against other family members.

It is extremely unusual for a form of indemnity against prosecution to be granted to a key participant in an alleged tax evasion. The value of the Nudie Group was estimated to be $300 million and evaded tax was estimated at $100 million.

Irrespective of the alleged affair the Prime Minister has very serious questions to answer.

Nudie Juice tax fraud and destruction of evidence

The Nudie tax fraud involves Debbie Huber's family avoiding tax of over $100 million, using fraudulent overseas loans to avoid the tax and destroying evidence. Basically it is identical to what Kerry Packer was accused of during the Costigan Royal Commission and it was Malcolm Turnbull who Justice Hunt said "poisoned the fountain of justice" in trying to help Packer. And it was Bruce McWilliam who Costigan accused of destroying evidence on behalf of Packer. Since that time Bruce McWilliam has had a long history of attempting to destroy evidence for court cases or potential court cases which I can personally attest.

Has Prime Minister Malcolm Turnbull intervened for Debbie Huber with the ATO like the PM did for Bruce McWilliam and Channel 7?

Debbie Huber is still good friends with Bruce McWilliam and his wife Nicky as she is friends with them on Facebook and Bruce would have given journalist Tim Elliott Debbie Huber's contact details for his article on Bruce. I regard this as very important evidence as Bruce has called in favours from Malcolm before with Channel 7 at least and maybe even the recent reduction in TV license fees.

So, has Debbie Huber used Bruce Williams play book and received preferential treatment from the ATO? When Debbie Huber posted the above article on Facebook about Malcolm Turnbull in June 2016 and the picture of herself with Lucy Turnbull in September 2016 was she trying to send a message to the ATO that she knows people in high places and they should not mess with her? Did she contact Malcolm / Lucy Turnbull or Bruce / Nicky McWilliam and discuss the Nudie Juice matter?

These are legitimate questions that all those named are refusing to answer.

Huge conflict of interest working for Malcolm Turnbull and Kerry Packer

Did Malcolm Turnbull employ and have a sexual relationship with Debbie Huber to get information from her for his client Kerry Packer?

In a 2016 article I published titled *"Malcolm Turnbull: The frivolous litigant who "poisoned the fountain of justice" said Justice Hunt"* I quoted the following passage:

"Much of the Goanna material was, as Packer described it in an 8000-word statement crafted by Turnbull and issued in 1984, "grotesque, ludicrous and malicious". But the tax findings were not lightly based, nor easily dismissed. Even though the then attorney-general Lionel Bowen declared that Packer had been cleared of all allegations against him, Meagher later revealed that briefs for prosecution were prepared against Packer in relation to tax evasion after the commission was wound up. Costigan had told him three "very senior counsel" based in Sydney "each looked at them independently and recommended prosecution", but it didn't occur."

"Packer was a man of great influence," Meagher said. "He wasn't cleared. Not at all." (Click here to read the full article)

That raises the question of whether Debbie Huber had any knowledge of the three "very senior counsel" who "recommended prosecution" of Packer when she worked for the Director of Public Prosecutions and did she disclose it to Packer, Turnbull or McWilliam.

Also, did Debbie Huber use her knowledge of tax evasion and fraudulent overseas loans to assist her family members to avoid tax in the Nudie Juice matter?

Alleged affair between Malcolm Turnbull and Debbie Huber

No one is denying the affair. So, the question many will be asking is Malcolm Turnbull a hypocrite given he had sex with a staff member, but he has recently banned sex between ministers and their staff after the Barnaby Joyce scandal broke. Malcolm Turnbull spoke of the need to have a higher standard in parliament. If that's true he needs to address the issues I have raised.

I'll leave it there for now and will do a follow-up article soon. You won't read the above article elsewhere so please read below and support independent journalism.

Chapter 35

Further pieces of the puzzle that Malcolm Turnbull abused the law in covering-up crimes by Kerry Packer

Further pieces of the puzzle that Malcolm Turnbull abused the law in covering-up crimes by Kerry Packer

BY SHANE DOWLING ON MARCH 17, 2018 • (5 COMMENTS)

Further pieces of the puzzle have been revealed of Prime Minister Malcolm Turnbull's corrupt conduct in the 1980's trying to conceal the crimes of Kerry Packer from the Costigan Royal Commission and later from the CDPP. Putting the pieces together it now seems certain that the former and first Commonwealth Director of Public Prosecutions (1984-1989) Ian Temby QC is the one who ultimately covered up Kerry Packer's crimes.

And other key details previously reported last week have been confirmed by the below newspaper article published in 1989 in The Sydney Morning Herald. This is on top of corruption allegations that I published last week that were made against Malcolm Turnbull and his partner Bruce McWilliam in the 1980's in their attempts to cover-up the criminal conduct of Kerry Packer. (Click here to read more)

The below newspaper article confirms that Malcolm Turnbull's alleged former mistress Debbie Huber worked for the Commonwealth Director of Public Prosecutions Ian Temby at the time he would have been considering criminal charges against Kerry Packer.

The article below says in relation to Debbie Huber after her time at University:

"She then joined the Sydney law firm Stephen Jacques and Stephen, as it was then called. Later she became a prosecutor for the Commonwealth Director of Public Prosecutions, Mr Ian Temby QC, handling such cases as the Tina Wong prosecution and a number of narcotics trials."

"I loved prosecuting" she said. "It was fun work but there comes a time in every litigation solicitor's life when they get sick of telling barristers of what to say and then having to listen to them say it."

Ms Huber thought about going to the bar, but instead joined Malcolm Turnbull's legal firm, handling such clients as Mr Geoffrey Edelsten, Mr Alexander Barton and Mr Kerry Packer.

Ms Huber stayed with Mr Turnbull for a while after he formed the Whitlam-Turnbull investment bank, but not seeing her future in that field, left to join Russell Reynolds. (Russel Reynolds was a recruitment firm for law firms.)

As I said in the last post the reason my sources told me she left Malcolm Turnbull's investment bank was when there were questions asked about her "personal trades".

Still achieving ... Ms Deborah Huber, now a personnel consultant, and Dr Mark de Souza.

(Click here to see the full page)

It was huge conflict of interest for Debbie Huber to work for Malcolm Turnbull's law firm Turnbull McWilliam and their client Kerry Packer given Ms Huber had just recently left the CDPP who at the time were considering criminal charges against Kerry Packer resulting from evidence uncovered during the Costigan Royal Commission.

The Costigan Royal Commission which ran from 1980 to 1984 *"was established by the Australian government in 1980 to investigate criminal activities, including violence, associated with the Painters and Dockers Union"*

During the Costigan Royal Commission Fairfax Media published a news story on Kerry Packer: "In 1984 Fairfax newspaper The National Times published leaked extracts of the Commission's draft report which implicated a prominent Australian businessman codenamed the "Goanna" in tax evasion and organised crime, including drug trafficking, pornography, and murder. Australia's richest man, media magnate Kerry Packer revealed himself to be the subject of these allegations which he strenuously denied." (Click here to read more)

When the Royal Commission ended, the evidence was sent to the Commonwealth Director of Public Prosecutions who did nothing with it. As I wrote last week:

"Much of the Goanna material was, as Packer described it in an 8000-word statement crafted by Turnbull and issued in 1984, "grotesque, ludicrous and malicious". But the tax findings were not lightly based, nor easily dismissed. Even though the then attorney-general Lionel Bowen declared that Packer had been cleared of all allegations against him, Meagher later revealed that briefs for prosecution were prepared against Packer in relation to tax evasion after the commission was wound up. Costigan had told him three "very senior counsel" based in Sydney "each looked at them independently and recommended prosecution", but it didn't occur."

"Packer was a man of great influence," Meagher said. "He wasn't cleared. Not at all." (Click here to read the full article)

So with the new details about Ian Temby QC being the Commonwealth Director of Public Prosecutions from 1984 to 1989 we know he is the one who had the final say on whether or not to prosecute Kerry Packer. So why didn't he prosecute Packer given: *three "very senior counsel" based in Sydney "each looked at them independently and recommended prosecution", but it didn't occur*? Was a favour called in or did money change hands?

Did Malcolm Turnbull communicate directly with Ian Temby regarding Kerry Packer after the Royal Commission finished in 1984 or did Debbie Huber do that on behalf of Kerry Packer?

A lot of questions still need to be answered but the above article was a good find from a KCA supporter as it confirms many details and sheds new light on other areas. I'll keep investigating. And just for the record I haven't received any answers to the questions or allegations that I emailed last week to Prime Minister Malcolm Turnbull, Bruce McWilliam, Nicky McWilliam or the questions I sent to Debbie Huber on Facebook.

As a side issue I ran into the Commonwealth Director of Public Prosecutions Sarah McNaughton SC in the lift as I was going to serve court paperwork on Friday (16/3/18).

I said: Hi Sarah.

Sarah McNaughton replied: Do I know you?

I said: Yes I'm Shane Dowling & I sent you an email & you didn't respond. I'm going to your office to serve court documents.

Sarah McNaughton got off at Level 1 instead of her office on Level 10. I had a look out the door of the lift on Level 1 and saw it was a Telstra office. So, unless Sarah McNaughton was upgrading her mobile phone, she did a runner. She was probably worried I would video her, ask questions and upload it to the internet which I have done to lawyers in the past. McNaughton is currently involved in trying to stitch me up with criminal charges for an email I sent in September 2016 to judges of the NSW Supreme Court asking questions for an article I was about to publish. The frivolous and vexatious criminal charges for the email, for what amounted to the crime of journalism, were dropped a few days later on the 28th of March 2018)

Chapter 36

Prime Minister Malcolm Turnbull personally linked to a second multi-million-dollar fraud of taxpayer's money

Prime Minister Malcolm Turnbull personally linked to a second multi-million-dollar fraud of taxpayer's money

BY SHANE DOWLING ON JULY 28, 2018 • (20 COMMENTS)

Malcolm Turnbull has been caught sticking his hand in the government till for $12 million dollars for some dodgy outfit called the United States Studies Centre which directly benefits his wife, his son-in-law James Brown and the Murdoch Family. This is not the first time that Malcolm Turnbull and the Murdoch Family have personally conspired to fraudulently rip-off taxpayers for millions of dollars for their own benefit.

In 2007 Malcolm Turnbull and Matt Handbury, who is Rupert Murdoch's nephew, were involved in an $11 million rainwater scam but more on that in a minute. And of course, there is the $30 million that Turnbull's government gave Rupert Murdoch's Foxtel to further broadcast "women's and niche sports". The problem is that nobody knows exactly what the money will specifically be spent on.

The SMH reported in February 2018 *"News Corp is refusing to explain exactly how it will spend taxpayers' money more than six months after the Turnbull government granted Foxtel $30 million."* (Click here to read more) And nothing seems to have changed. But back to the latest scam.

Malcolm Turnbull's new scam

The financial review reported on Monday (23-7-18) that:

The United States Studies Centre, a foreign policy think tank with close links to the Turnbull and Murdoch families, has been given $12 million by the federal government.

The think tank, based at Sydney University, was established by the American Australian Association to promote the US alliance, train students, develop policy and provide an intellectual counterweight to American critics in Australian universities.

The grant, which was announced on Sunday, will be provided through the AAA, which was co-founded by Rupert Murdoch's father, Sir Keith Murdoch. Part of the money will go to USAsia Centre, which is the US Study Centre's sister organisation located at the University of Western Australia.

The grant is an example of how politically connected organisations are often effective at lobbying governments for funding.

Prime Minister Malcolm Turnbull's wife, Lucy Turnbull, is the United States Studies Centre's "patron".

Their son-in-law, James Brown, was the think tank's research director from 2015 until a few months ago, when he resigned to devote time to the unpaid role as president of the NSW division of the Returned and Services League of Australia, which is going through a financial scandal.

Mr Brown, a former army captain, remains a non-resident fellow of the think tank.

"I suspect what has happened here is they were meant to get this money in the budget last year but because of the controversy surrounding James Brown and the treatment of Tom Switzer it was too hot to give them the money," a former associate of the US Studies Centre said.

Government spokespeople declined to discuss, on the record, the close ties between the think tank and the Turnbull family.

Negotiations for the four years of funding were handled by the American Australian Association, and Ms Turnbull and Mr Brown weren't involved, US Studies Centre CEO Simon Jackman said.

The structure of the US Studies Centre was decided in the dining room on the third floor of the headquarters of News Corp in New York City in 2006. Prime minister John Howard promised $25 million start-up capital. (Click here to read more)

If the $12 million grant was approved last year that means Malcolm Turnbull's son-in-law was the "think tank's research director" at the time the government approved the grant and Malcolm's wife was "patron". It is such a blatant conflict of interest and something that Malcolm Turnbull and the government should have declared publicly before the $12 million grant was approved.

Rupert Murdoch, his wife Jerry Hall and eldest son Lachlan Murdoch leave Kirribilli House after Saturday's summer drinks with Prime Minister Malcolm Turnbull. January 2017

Once a thief, always a thief and nothing will change Malcolm Turnbull. If you look at one issue by itself, it is bad but once you start collating all the corruption Turnbull is involved in it starts to tell the full story. It's another one of the hundreds of reasons why we need a federal corruption body like ICAC to investigate corruption like this. Until then the best thing voters can do is helping publicise the corruption on social media.

Chapter 37

Prime Minister Scott Morrison appoints Australia's most ethically bankrupt lawyer to advise on Federal ICAC

One of the most important strategies for corrupt politicians, so they are never held to account, is to try and make sure they control the government bodies that are meant to hold them to account. And Scott Morrison does this well which this article covers regarding a proposed federal Independent Commission Against Corruption (ICAC).

Prime Minister Scott Morrison appoints Australia's most ethically bankrupt lawyer to advise on Federal ICAC

BY SHANE DOWLING ON JANUARY 24, 2019 • (16 COMMENTS)

In December 2018 Prime Minister Scott Morrison appointed Australia's most ethically bankrupt lawyer the recently retired NSW Deputy Senior Crown Prosecutor Margaret Cunneen to advise on a Federal ICAC.

Margaret Cunneen's appointment doesn't get any grubbier as she has a long history of lying and deceiving in public office, associating with criminals such as murderer Roger Rogerson and even perjuring herself at the Child Sex Abuse Royal Commission to try to conceal her involvement it getting alleged paedophile Scott Volkers off charges.

Add that NSW ICAC's own investigation into unsettled corruption allegations against Cunneen and she is the last person in Australia who the government should have advising on how to set up a Federal ICAC. So why has she been appointed? Firstly, the Liberal Party in NSW have had to sack numerous MP's, and others resigned, in recent years because of NSW ICAC investigations and Scott Morrison and the Liberals don't want a repeat of that at the federal level so they want a toothless tiger for a Federal ICAC. And secondly, as payback to help Cunneen, to try to restore her destroyed reputation, for her dirty work over the years in helping her corrupt Liberal Party connected mates such as Alan Jones, News Corp journalists and others.

Cunneen has a long history of corruption and most of the below I wrote in 2015 (Click here to read the article) but it is worth repeating with some updates given her Federal ICAC appointment.

Interviews with Fairfax Media and The Australian and the big contradictions in answers

In 2011 Margaret Cunneen gave an interview with journalist Kate McClymont at the Sydney Morning Herald (SMH) and gave certain answers in relation to her personal association with major criminal Roger Rogerson. In February 2015 Cunneen gave an interview with 2 journalists from The Australian and gave a different answer. (Click here to read)

This was not a one-off lie. Cunneen has also been caught lying about her relationship with Stephen Fletcher who is facing criminal charges for allegedly paying off over 10 NSW police officers to use their betting accounts. (Click here to read the Police Integrity Commission report – Operation Montecristo) One has to wonder, given Fletcher was allegedly paying the police officers to use their betting accounts, was he also paying them for anything else more sinister?

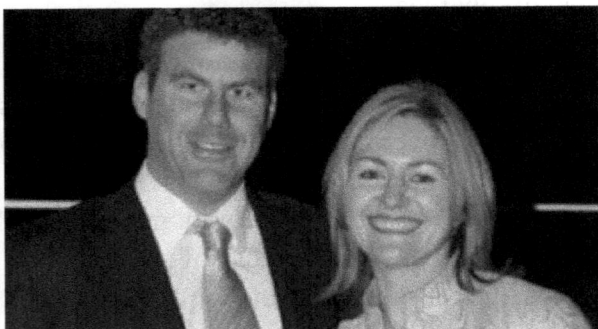

Stephen Fletcher and Margaret Cunneen

Margaret Cunneen lied about her relationship with Fletcher in 2011 and implied she would have nothing to do with him again. But last year Fletcher went on holidays with Cunneen's son Stephen Wyllie and his girlfriend Sophia Tilly after the infamous car crash. So why was Cunneen lying? The ABC last year reported Stephen Fletcher was Margaret Cunneen's long-term boyfriend.

Convicted criminal Roger Rogerson and Margaret Cunneen

Margaret Cunneen helping convicted criminal and former corrupt police officer Roger Rogerson profit from his crimes at a book signing. Mr Rogerson is currently in jail awaiting trial for murder. Margaret Cunneen should be investigated as to why she is associating with criminals and helping a criminal profit from his crimes. Margaret Cunneen is a Deputy Senior Crown Prosecutor in NSW. For further information see: Kangaroo Court of Australia at: http://kangaroocourtofaustralia.com

Roger Rogerson is a former corrupt police officer sentenced in 2016 to life in jail for murder. He is a major league crook and always has been. When he was a police officer he took bribes to protect every type of criminal from murderers to drug dealers. He was kicked out of the police force in 1986. Rogerson was charged in the late 1980's for drug dealing and attempted murder amongst other crimes and he has killed at least two people and probably more. (Click her to read more)

So the question is: Why was Margaret Cunneen at Roger Rogerson's book signing helping him profit from his crimes in 2009?

When asked about it in 2011 Cunneen said: *"But I know Roger independently. I've known him since he was a detective ... He was never convicted of anything while he was a police officer."* (Click here to read more)

Is Cunneen for real? Roger Rogerson is and was a major criminal and she should have never been anywhere near him, and she knows it. In February 2015 Cunneen had changed her story to that she decided not to:

"continue to snub people who have gone to prison and paid their debt to society. I, and other prosecutors who attended, thought it important that prosecutors don't subscribe to lifelong punishment." (Click here to read more)

What dribble! She is trying to hide her scandalous friendship with Rogerson. But her answer raises some very serious questions such as: Who were the other prosecutors who attended the book signing? And: Is the prosecutor who convicted Roger Rogerson of his murder charge one of prosecutors who attended his book signing as a fan? Has Cunneen ever used her position to leak information to Rogerson or helped him in any way?

Based on what Margaret Cunneen told the journalists about the other prosecutors being at the book signing then all the staff at the Office of the Director of Public Prosecutions need investigating by ICAC just to be safe.

Scott Volkers

In 2004 Margaret Cunneen gave extremely dodgy legal advice that helped the Queensland Director of Public Prosecutions justify not re-charging swimming coach Scott Volkers on paedophile charges. The Queensland DPP could not justify why the charges were dropped against Scott Volkers in the first place and needed dodgy legal advice to make sure he was not re-charged otherwise the Queensland DPP would be looking very stupid if not corrupt.

Scott Volkers was accused of abusing 3 girls between the ages of 12 and 14 but charges were dropped in 2002. He was re-investigated by police, but the QLD DPP decided not to charge him again.

Margaret Cunneen gave some scandalous advice to the QLD DPP that attacked the evidence of the girls and said *"a conviction would be difficult to achieve because the girls were unlikely to have had developed breasts and thus the groping allegations would be difficult to substantiate."* (Click here to read more)

and: *"She also questioned whether a female abuse victim could have experienced an orgasm while being abused."*

"It is difficult to accept that Gilbert could have been sufficiently relaxed for orgasm to occur," Ms Cunneen wrote in legal advice to the Queensland DPP." (Click here to read more or watch the 7.30 Report interview)

Margaret Cunneen's advice was disgraceful and there was obviously no legal or medical evidence to support it. It was a clear and pathetic attack by Margaret Cunneen to discredit witnesses and justify not re-charging Scott Volkers.

I think the Volkers matter is important because it really pulls back the curtain and we can see what Cunneen is like behind closed doors. She clearly does favours for friends and gives them the dodgy advice they want to justify their decisions if need be.

The Cunneen / Volkers scandal was uncovered at the Royal Commission into Child Sexual Abuse last year and Cunneen should have been sacked then. Cunneen tries to make out she is some sought of hero for victims of sexual abuse. What a lie that is, which the Volkers matter shows. How many other criminals has Cunneen helped walk free?

Scott Volkers charged 9/11/18

On the 9th of November 2018 Australian swimming coach Scott Volkers was committed to stand trial on five counts of indecent treatment of a child. (Click here to read more)

Margaret Cunneen and her mate Eddie Obeid

Margaret Cunneen not only had a secret meeting with jailed former NSW Labor MP Eddie Obeid behind the court while his trial was afoot but has also used the media to defend a corrupt coal deal he was involved in. (Click here to read more) For Cunneen to have made public statements defending Eddie Obeid it clearly raises the suspicion she was on his payroll. Then to have a secret meeting with him at the courthouse when his trial was in progress is a scandal. Did she pass on a message to her fellow prosecutor on behalf of Eddie Obeid to go easy on him?

Crown prosecutor Margaret Cunneen shaking hands with corrupt former MP Eddie Obeid outside the NSW Supreme Court in Darlinghurst in February 2016 while Mr Obeid was on trial for corruption.

News Corp, 2GB's Alan Jones and other media support Margaret Cunneen

You won't hear to many Australian media outlets criticise Margaret Cunneen's Federal ICAC appointment. In December 2015 I wrote an article titled *"Rupert Murdoch's News Corp caught bribing Australian Crown Prosecutor for news stories"* which started off:

Rupert Murdoch and News Corporation are heading for another major scandal regarding bribing government officials and this time it is in Australia and involves NSW Crown Prosecutor Margaret Cunneen.

Murdoch's News Corp has a long history of bribing government employees for stories. This was exposed by the UK phone-hacking scandal which also revealed the bribing of UK police and other officials. (Click here to read more)

In the same article I wrote about Alan Jones involvement in supporting Margaret Cunneen and said:

Alan Jones and Chris Merritt on 2GB Monday April 20, 2015 (Click on the audio below to listen)

Audio Player

Use Up/Down Arrow keys to increase or decrease volume.

Alan Jones interviewed The Australian newspaper's Legal Affairs editor Chris Merritt a couple of days after the High Court handed down it's judgment in the Margaret Cunneen / ICAC matter.

They went hard attacking ICAC and defending Margaret Cunneen. In the tape you will hear Alan Jones refer to journalist Janet Fife-Yeomans as a source who we now know is one of the beneficiaries from Margaret Cunneen's leaks.

Channel 7 and Ray Hadley on 2GB are also Cunneen supporters

Interviews with Ray Hadley on 2GB and Channel 7

In April 2015 Cunneen did soft interviews with Ray "Jelly Back" Hadley and Channel 7 News. She did not get asked any tough questions nor did "Jelly Back" raise Stephen Fletcher, Roger Rogerson or her disgraceful conduct in the Scott Volkers matter.

Margaret Cunneen complained that *"murderers and terrorists"* would not be treated the way she was. Well she should know, look at the above photo of her and Roger Rogerson and how well she treated him. She looks like a love-struck groupie with her big smile not a Senior Crown Prosecutor who should have nothing to do with criminals.

If you want the truth about Margaret Cunneen and how scandalous her appointment to advise on a Federal ICAC is you have to go to online websites or social media because half the old media are in bed with her.

When you hear Prime Minister Scott Morrison talk about the Federal ICAC just think of Margaret Cunneen because it shows what a fraud the whole Federal ICAC plan is?

Chapter 38

Prime Minister Scott Morrison, his best mate David Gazard and the $50 billion submarine scam

Prime Minister Scott Morrison, his best mate David Gazard and the $50 billion submarine scam

BY SHANE DOWLING ON FEBRUARY 16, 2019 • (21 COMMENTS)

Prime Minister Scott Morrison's best mate and closest political advisor, David Gazard, is profiting $millions from the $50 billion submarine contract Australia finalised this week with the French state-owned shipbuilder Naval Group. Naval Group is still under investigation for bribing Malaysia's former leader Najib Razak US$128 million.

What is becoming clear is that the $50 billion submarine contact is a money grab for numerous Liberal Party cronies which is disturbing given Naval Group was previously investigated by the Australian Senate in 2016 for bribery in Australia via one of their subsidiaries.

Firstly, we'll look at the bribery allegations against Naval group and Naval Group's former Australian operations CEO Sean

Costello who was a former Liberal Party staffer and then David Gazard's relationship with Prime Minster Scott Morrison and Naval Group.

Bribery Allegations against Naval Group – Formally known as DCNS and one of their subsidiaries is Thales. So, they are all the same company.

The bribery allegations against Naval Group have never been publicly addressed by the Government and they should have. Naval Group have history of employing consultants to pay bribes which makes the Liberal Party connections to the $50 billion submarine contract even more worrying.

On the 1st of May 2016 I published an article titled "Bribery allegations against Australia's $50 billion submarine contract winner" and wrote:

Australia has just awarded a $50 billion defence project to build Submarines and even before the ink is dry on the contract hundreds of thousands of dollars if not millions of dollars have landed in the pockets of Liberal Party crony and former staffer Sean Costello. To make matters worse the French company DCNS which has won the $50 billion contract is currently under investigation by a French court for bribing Malaysian officials to win their submarine contract in 2002.

DCNS is alleged to have bribed officials linked to Malaysian Prime Minister Najib Razak and the corruption also involves allegations of murder. This is on top of other previous allegations of bribery against DCNS.

Another suspicious element of the Australian tender is that DCNS employed former Liberal staffer Sean Costello as its CEO for the bid. Mr Costello was chief-of-staff for former Defence Minister David Johnston who was sacked from his position in 2014.

The below video is Sean Costello on the Lateline show 26/4/16. Costello resigned as CEO of DCNS Australia in March 2017 less than a year after they won the contract. DCNS won the contract in 2016 but the final detailed contract was only signed this week.

Australia's dodgy $50 billion Submarine c...

The video above is Sean Costello on the Lateline show 26/4/16 and raises many questions. (Click here to watch the full story)

DCNS, Malaysia bribes, murder and the French court case

It has been reported in the media since January 2016 that the French are investigating DCNS for bribing Malaysian officials including the Prime Minister Najib Razak. The SMH reported:

A case involving allegations of high-level bribery, blackmail, betrayal and the murder of a glamorous Mongolian socialite in Malaysia has resurfaced in France, only days after Malaysia's prime minister Najib Razak was cleared of corruption charges at home.

French prosecutors have charged a French businessman involved in Malaysia's $US2 billion ($2.8 billion) purchase of two French-Spanish built submarines with paying illegal kickbacks to a Malaysian official linked to Mr Najib, according to the French newsagency AFP. (Click here to read more)

In March 2016 the ABC's Four Corners screened an episode on Malaysian Prime Minister Najib Razak called "State of Fear" which covered the many corruption scandals surrounding the Prime Minister. It also covered the Submarine bribery scandal and said this:

LINTON BESSER: Accusations against prime minister Najib date back almost a decade.

The first scandal was in 2002, when Najib Razak was defence minister overseeing a $1 billion submarine deal between Malaysia and France. It embroiled some of Najib's closest confidants in allegations of kickbacks, cover-ups and another murder.

French authorities have indicted the former head of French arms firm Thales. They acted after an investigation by Malaysian anti-corruption campaigner Cynthia Gabriel into a US$108 million commission paid to a Malaysian company.

CYNTHIA GABRIEL, ANTI-CORRUPTION CAMPAIGNER: It wasn't just this payment that was of question: ah, it was a couple of other payments as well that were made that seemed murky and seemed very shady; that did not have very clear, um, ah, reasons for why, ah, the payments were made.

LINTON BESSER: The middleman in the submarines deal was a senior adviser and friend to the prime minister. His name is Razak Baginda.

CYNTHIA GABRIEL: We don't know who he is, apart from him being a close associate and friend of, ah, Najib.

Ah, so I think today we are not certain if he was actually on a formal contract with the Defence Ministry, or whether he was just negotiating a very large multi-million dollar contract, only because he was the friend of Najib Razak.

TERENCE GOMEZ: The allegation is that kickbacks were given to the middle-men who negotiated the deal in France. That is the allegation. That allegation now has to be investigated properly.

LINTON BESSER: What thrust the corruption scandal into the global spotlight was another murder. This time, the victim was a 28-year-old model from Mongolia named Altantuya Shaariibuu. She worked as a translator.

It's also been alleged she was having an affair with Najib, something he's always denied.

But his adviser, Razak Baginda, was sleeping with her.

CYNTHIA GABRIEL: He did admit that they were having a romantic relationship for a while. And then the events that led to her death suggested that he was trying to get rid of her.

LINTON BESSER: The model, Altantuya, wanted a cut of the money from the submarine deal. (Click here to read more or watch the show)

The French arms firm, Thales, mentioned above owns 35% of DCNS and was allegedly involved in the bribery.

DCNS's involvement in bribery and scandals has long been known as their Wikipedia profile shows:

The DCN / DCNS plays a major role in "one of France's biggest political and financial scandals of the last generation [that left] a trail of eight unexplained deaths, nearly half a billion dollars in missing cash and troubling allegations of government complicity" connected to a sale of warships to Taiwan in the 1990s.

Apart from the issues surrounding the sale of ships to Taiwan mentioned above, French prosecutors started investigating a wide range of corruption charges in 2010 involving different submarine sales, with possible bribery and kickbacks to top officials in France. In particular interest by the prosecutors are sales of Scorpène submarines to countries like India and Malaysia.

The investigation in Malaysia has been prompted by human rights group Suaram as it involved current Prime Minister Najib Tun Razak when he was defence minister and his friend Abdul Razak Baginda whose company Primekar was alleged to be paid a huge commission during the purchase of two Scorpène submarines. French investigators are interested in the fact that Perimekar was formed only a few months before the contract was signed with the Malaysian government and DCNS and that Primekar had no track record in servicing submarines and did not have the financial capability to support the contract.

Investigations have also revealed that a Hong Kong-based company called Terasasi Ltd in which the directors are Razak Baginda and his father, sold classified Malaysian navy defence documents to DCNS. (Click here to read more) (Click here to read the full article)

The US$128 million bribery of Najib Razak is still being investigated and this week (12/2/19) it was reported a French lawyer went to Malaysia for meetings with officials still investigating the corruption. (Click here to read more)

The Australian Senate Inquiry

On the 5th May 2016 I published an article titled "Australian Senate corruption inquiry investigating $50 Billion Submarine contract winner" and said:

The Australian Senate are already investigating corrupt conduct by French arms firm Thales who are the parent company of DCNS which won the $50 billion Submarine contract. They are in effect one company and why the government didn't address this issue when they announced DCNS as the winner of the Submarine contract is scandalous.

The corrupt conduct by Thales under investigation by the Senate is the rorting and rigging of a $1.5 billion contract with Airservices Australia who are a government body responsible for airspace management in Australia which includes the management of airport control towers etc.

The Australian Senate inquiry

The Australian Senate have been investigating financial fraud and corruption at Airservices Australia since 2014 which also involves Thales and its Australian CEO Chris Jenkins. The inquiry has heard evidence of widespread fraud, nepotism and blatant corruption.

The Senate inquiry was still in progress in 2016 and in 2015 they referred the matter of dodgy consultancy contracts to the Australian National Audit Office who investigate financial corruption on behalf of the government. It says on their website:

"Our purpose is to provide the Parliament with an independent assessment of selected areas of public administration, and assurance about public sector financial reporting, administration, and accountability. We do this primarily by conducting performance audits, financial statement audits, and assurance reviews." (Click here to read more)

The National Audit Office were due to report in May 2016 and did publish recommendations that achieved very little. (Click here to read the recommendations)

The Airservices Australia multi-million-dollar consultancy sting

The big sting was a dodgy multi-million-dollar consultancy contract that was overseen by Airservices chairman Sir Angus Houston who is a former Chief of the Air Force and Chief of the Defence Force.

How the sting worked

Airservices Australia hired a consulting organisation called International Centre for Complex Project Management (ICCPM) to negotiate a $1.5 billion contract with Thales to upgrade Australia's air traffic control program. The problem is that ICCPM is very dodgy to say the least. The former chairman, and still a director of ICCPM, is Thales CEO Chris Jenkins.

It should be no surprise that Thales was awarded the contract in February 2015 which is called the Onesky project. (Click here to read more)

It doesn't get any more corrupt than this

So the net effect is that you have an organisation overseen by Chris Jenkins in his role as chairman/director (ICCPM) negotiating with Chris Jenkins in his role as CEO (Thales) to get the best deal for Airservices Australia.

Airservices Australia should have had nothing to do with ICCPM as they are in effect a division of Thales. Airservices should have had the expertise to negotiate themselves and if they didn't they should have employed people directly with the experience. (Click here to read more)

I don't have a copy of the Senate findings but from memory they did bugger all. Another reason why we need a Federal ICAC.

Scott Morrison and the David Gazard connection

Scott Morrison and David Gazard

David Gazard is the man who Scott Morrison went to for advice during the leadership showdown between Tony Abbott and Malcolm Turnbull in September 2015. The SMH reported in 2016 in an article titled *"Scott Morrison's relentless rise to power"*:

"On the evening of September 14, 2015, Tony Abbott's prime ministership was hanging by a thread. Abbott had made Morrison a last-minute offer to join him on a leadership ticket and to take over Joe Hockey's job as Treasurer. Hunkered down in his Parliament House office over a home-made curry, Morrison gamed his next move with his close friend David Gazard, a former Howard and Costello staffer, while Costello offered advice over the phone." (Click here to read more)

That shows that David Gazard is one of Scott Morrison's closest advisors and friends if not his closest.

Update: A few minutes after publishing this article it was brought to my attention that another company called ECG Financial has the same 2 directors, David Gazard and Jonathan Epstein, as ECG Advisory Solutions. Also, ECG Financial has a Chairman who is none other than former federal treasurer Peter Costello who is also mentioned above as the other person that Scott Morrison sought advice from in September 2015 during the leadership challenge. (Click here to see their website)

The ABC reported (11/2/19):

A long-awaited contract for the $50 billion Future Submarine program will be signed in Canberra today by France and Australia, following months of tough negotiations and the recruitment of a high-powered lobbyist.

The ABC can reveal one of Prime Minister Scott Morrison's key political confidants was recently hired by the French state-owned shipbuilder Naval Group to help improve a rocky relationship with the Defence department, and to secure a crucial Strategic Partnering Agreement (SPA).

"ECG Advisory Solutions", a lobbying firm founded by former Liberal party candidate David Gazard, has been advising Naval Group since last year on how to handle the difficult SPA negotiations with Australia.

Mr Gazard, who was chief of staff to former New South Wales Liberal leader John Brogden, began his friendship with Mr Morrison when he was the Liberal Party's State Director for the 2003 election.

In a statement, Naval Group confirmed the arrangement but did not disclose how much Mr Gazard's company was being paid for its lobbying services.

Mr Morrison discussed progress on the SPA with French President Emmanuel Macron at the G20 summit in late November, and told reporters they had agreed to elevate it "back up to leader-level to ensure it's finalised in the near term". (Click here to read more)

In December 2018 the Financial Review reported:

The other significant "mate of Morrison" who straddles the business and political worlds is David Gazard, a former staffer to Howard and Peter Costello turned lobbyist.

One Liberal source says Gazard is "number one" in terms of who Morrison talks to first but Gazard, who calls the PM one of his best friends, maintains he is way down the pecking order. (Click here to read more)

The $50 billion contract, and the direct involvement of Prime Minister Scott Morrison and his mate David Gazard has got the smell of the Malaysian bribery scandal all over it. Naval Group were having trouble finalising the details of the $50 billion deal with Australia so they hire Prime Minister Scott Morrison's best mate as a "consultant" and pay him $millions to get the deal finalised.

How do I know David Gazard is getting paid $millions? I don't. But former federal MP and trade minister Andrew Robb is being paid $880,000 a year, even if he does nothing, for a consulting deal with a company closely linked to the Chinese government. (Click here to read more) So it would be a fair guess that David Gazard is being paid $million if not more for "consulting" on the $50 billion submarine deal. The exact deal and how much David Gazard is being paid is something that Prime Minister Scott Morrison has an obligation make public. For Scott Morrison to say it has nothing to do with him is not believable. The French didn't employ Morrison's mate for nothing.

Naval Group has a long history of employing dodgy consultants to bribe government officials. And in November 2018 Prime Minister Scott Morrison decided the $50 billion deal would be finalised *"back up to leader-level to ensure it's finalised in the near term"*. That is about the same time that David Gazard was hired by Navel Group. It raises many questions.

Did Scott Morison suggest to French President Emmanuel Macron that the French government-owned Naval Group should employ David Gazard and pay him $millions to finalise the $50 billion submarine contract? Should Australia trust any of them with our $50 billion? I don't think so.

The scandal involving Morrison, his mate David Gazard and the $50 billion submarine contract should be front page news and the end of Morrison's career as there are too many unanswered questions but once again the old media have failed to hold the government to account as you won't read the above anywhere else.

Chapter 39

Prime Minister Scott Morrison and his puppet master Peter Costello

Prime Minister Scott Morrison and his puppet master Peter Costello

BY SHANE DOWLING ON FEBRUARY 24, 2019 • (11 COMMENTS)

Former Federal Treasurer Peter Costello has his fingerprints all over Prime Minister Scott Morrison as his puppet master, the $50 billion submarine contract scam and the federal government via his chairmanships of ECG Financial Pty Ltd, Nine and the $150 billion Future Fund. There is also documented evidence that Peter Costello has been deliberately hiding his lobbying activity from state and federal governments.

My investigation and ASIC company searches show that Peter Costello is a current financial owner of ECG Financial Pty Ltd and was previously a financial owner of the sister company ECG Advisory Solutions which I reported last week has made $millions from a dodgy deal to give advice in the $50 Billion submarine contract. There's also a prima facie case that Prime Minister Scott Morrison helped orchestrate the deal for ECG and his mates Costello and David Gazard who is a director and 50% shareholder of ECG Advisory via his company GPJT Pty Ltd.

There is clearly musical chairs being played by Peter Costello and others to hide the truth and the fraud and thefts. Specifically, what is being hidden is that Peter Costello makes a lot of money lobbying the government for large companies.

How it works:

There are 2 companies and one of them, ECG Advisory Solutions, is also a registered lobbying company and that seems to have become a problem as it was being widely published on the lobbyist registers that Peter Costello's private company was a shareholder in the company but he was not listed as one of the lobbyists. Yet he is the Chairman of the sister company ECG Financial.

Where this obviously became a problem for Costello is for example the $50 billion submarine deal where it was reported that Prime Minister Scott Morrison's mate David Gazard was appointed as an adviser. (Click here to read more) That is extremely concerning and needs investigating but it would have been a million times worse if the media had of also reported that Peter Costello and/or his company had been appointed as an advisor. They must have realised a few years ago that having the Peter Costello link was a possible problem so he sold his shares is ECG Advisory but kept his shares in the sister company ECG Financial.

The companies and their shareholders as per ASIC searches today (23/2/19).

ECG Advisory Solutions – Registered 3/8/2011

Shareholders:

Peter Costello and his wife own shares via their company Phomadse Pty Ltd which was registered 2/6/2010

David Gazard owns shares via his company GPJT Pty Ltd which was registered 1/8/2011

Jonathan Epstein owns shares via his company Jonnik Pty Ltd which was registered 30/6/2011

Merle Want – Her shares were held in her personal name.

Peter Costello and Merle Want are no longer shareholders in ECG Advisory Solutions and seem to have sold in 2014. David Gazard and Jonathan Epstein now own 50% of the company each.

ECG Financial Pty Ltd – Registered 20/12/12

Peter Costello and his wife own 50 % of the shares via their company Phomadse Pty Ltd which was registered 2/6/2010

Jonathan Epstein owns 50% of the shares via his company Jonnik Pty Ltd which was registered 30/6/2011

Lobbying state and federal governments

Peter Costello had a shareholding in ECG Advisory Solutions which is listed with state and federal governments as a lobbyist company. The 2 lobbyists listed for the company are David Gazard and Jonathan Epstein who are both former employees of Peter Costello when he was Federal Treasurer.

The problem stands out per below in the 2013 Victoria Lobbyist register. You can see David Gazard and Jonathan Epstein as the lobbyists but at the bottom you can also see Peter Costello's company Phomadse Pty Ltd as a shareholder.

View Lobbyist Profile

Company Details

Name: ECG Advisory Solutions
A.B.N: 93354249142

Lobbyist Details

Name: Jonathan Epstein
Position: Director
Name: David Gazard
Position: Director

Client Details

Name: Folkestone Funds Management Limited
Transurban Group
Mantle Mining Corporation Ltd
Westpac Banking Corporation
Primary HealthCare Ltd
ASG Group
Exergen Pty Ltd
Coles
Orica
SP Ausnet
Peet Ltd
DP World Australia Ltd
JDRF
Cambridge ESOL
Wesfarmers
National Retail Association

Owner Details

Name: GPJT PTY LTD
JONNIK PTY LTD
PHOMADSE PTY LTD

Details Last Updated: 01/02/2013

In 2014 Peter Costello's private company Phomadse Pty Ltd was also named in a report for regulating lobbying in NSW which might have been a reason he sold his shares in ECG Advisory Solutions at about the same time. (Click here to read more)

Would anyone really believe that Peter Costello is a shareholder in a lobbying company but he doesn't lobby himself? He is always meeting with government MP's. For example he met with Finance Minister Mathias Corman this week, had coffee with Josh Frydenberg when he became Treasurer to give him some advice and Costello is well-known for being a mentor to Prime Minister Scott Morrison. These same people wouldn't spare 5 minutes for the average person and Costello isn't spending time with them for nothing.

Treasurer Josh Frydenberg has met with former treasurer Peter Costello to get advice on his new job. 2018

And what about the conflict of interest given Peter Costello's position as Chairman of the $150 billion Future Fund.

In relation to Nine and the Future Fund this was said to the Senate this week: *"Former treasurer Peter Costello will manage any potential conflicts of interest as chair of the Future Fund and chair of the newly-merged Nine and Fairfax, a Senate committee has heard."*

But Costello made no statement regarding his conflict with his lobbying company and the Future Fund. Why? Because he has tried to hide it.

The Future Fund says on their website:

The Future Fund is Australia's sovereign wealth fund. We invest for the benefit of future generations of Australians.

We were established in 2006 to strengthen the Australian Government's long-term financial position. Every dollar that we make is a dollar that adds to Australia's wealth and contributes to its future. (Click here to read more)

Does the future fund invest in any of the companies that Peter Costello or his company lobby for and does Costello declare it to the Future Fund board?

Peter Costello was recently re-appointed as Chairman of the Future Fund and it would be almost certain his mate Prime Minister Scott Morrison had a hand it given they also stacked the Administrative Appeals Tribunal with Liberal mates this week.

It's worth having a quick look at last weeks post as this article ties in strongly with it. I started off last weeks article titled "Prime Minister Scott Morrison, his best mate David Gazard and the $50 billion submarine scam" with:

Prime Minister Scott Morrison's best mate and closest political advisor, David Gazard, is profiting $millions from the $50 billion submarine contract Australia finalised this week with the French state-owned shipbuilder Naval Group. Naval Group is still under investigation for bribing Malaysia's former leader Najib Razak US$128 million.

What is becoming clear is that the $50 billion submarine contact is a money grab for numerous Liberal Party cronies which is disturbing given Naval Group was previously investigated by the Australian Senate in 2016 for bribery in Australia via one of their subsidiaries.

Firstly, we'll look at the bribery allegations against Naval group and Naval Group's former Australian operations CEO Sean Costello who was a former Liberal Party staffer and then David Gazard's relationship with Prime Minster Scott Morrison and Naval Group.

And I also said:

"ECG Advisory Solutions", a lobbying firm founded by former Liberal party candidate David Gazard, has been advising Naval

Group since last year on how to handle the difficult SPA negotiations with Australia.

Mr Morrison discussed progress on the SPA with French President Emmanuel Macron at the G20 summit in late November, and told reporters they had agreed to elevate it "back up to leader-level to ensure it's finalised in the near term". (Click here to read the article)

The $50 billion submarine scam uses the same routine of mates looking after mates as exposed this week with the Helloworld travel agency $billion tender scam involving the former Federal Treasurer Joe Hockey and the Finance Minister Mathius Corman.

Peter Costello is Chairman of ECG Financial Pty Ltd and he and his wife own 50% of the company via their private company Phomadse Pty Ltd. Both ECG Financial and ECG Advisory have the same Melbourne address and phone numbers on their websites which is no great surprise but worth noting as it's another piece of evidence that confirms that they are really the same company.

On the Nine Entertainment Co website it says this:

Peter Costello

Independent Non-Executive Chairman

Peter Costello was appointed to the Board in February 2013 as an independent, Non-Executive Director and in March 2016 became Chairman of the Board. He is also a member of the Audit & Risk Management Committee.

Mr Costello is currently Chairman of the Board of Guardians of Australia's Future Fund and serves on a number of domestic and international advisory boards. **His business ECG Financial Pty Ltd** is a boutique advisor on mergers and acquisitions, foreign investment, competition and regulatory issues which affect business in Australia. Mr Costello served as a member of the House of Representatives from 1990 to 2009 and was Treasurer of the Commonwealth of Australia from March 1996 to December 2007.

Prior to entering Parliament Mr Costello was a barrister. He has a Bachelor of Arts and a Bachelor of Laws LLB (Hons) and a Doctorate of Laws (Honoris Causa) from Monash University. In 2011, Mr Costello was appointed a Companion of the Order of Australia. (Click here to see on their website)

On the Federal Government's website you can see the companies that ECG Advisory Solutions currently lobby for. It has been recently updated to add Navel Group.

1	Wesfarmers
2	Coles Supermarkets
3	Transurban Group
4	Youth Care WA
5	Peet Limited
6	Australia Pacific Airports Corporation Ltd
7	National Automotive Leasing and Salary Packaging Association
8	BP Australia Pty Ltd
9	TPG Capital
10	Oaktree Capital
11	Challenger Limited

12	Auctioneers and Valuers Association of Australia (Incorporated)
13	Australian Finance Group
14	Workpac Group
15	Brewers Association of Australia
16	Afterpay Touch Group Ltd
17	Naval Group

(Click here to see the lobbyist list)

ECG Advisory Solutions use a different business name for the federal register called The Trustee for ECG Advisory Trust. How that works I'm not sure but maybe there's an accountant reading this who can suggest in the comment section below why they would do that. Tax dodging maybe?

Peter Costello has to resign as Future Fund chairman and the other issues raised need answers from the government. The former politicians who keep hanging around government and won't go away are there for their financial greed, not the good of the country.

Chapter 40

Prime Minister Scott Morrison and his dirty deal with the Labor Party and Sam Dastyari

Prime Minister Scott Morrison and his dirty deal with the Labor Party and Sam Dastyari

BY SHANE DOWLING ON APRIL 5, 2019 • (14 COMMENTS)

Prime Minister Scott Morrison worked in marketing for many years before he entered parliament in 2007 so it's no surprise he comes across as a used car salesman when he announces new government spending, programs, and initiatives. But he has a history of stabbing Liberal Party competitors in the back on a regular basis with the most extreme being the leaking of lies to win the Liberal Party pre-selection for the seat of Cook in 2007 with the assistance of the Labor Party.

There is a radio interview below with disgraced former senator Sam Dastyari who spills the beans on Scott Morrison colluding with the Labor Party in 2007 and what Sam Dastyari says is hard to ignore given most of it, if not all of it, is backed up by other media reports.

Scott Morrison's political background

Scott Morrison was a power broker and former state director (2000 to 2004) of the NSW Liberal Party and was elected to Parliament in 2007.

In September 2008, Morrison was appointed to Malcolm Turnbull's coalition front bench as shadow minister for housing and local government.

In December 2009, after Tony Abbott outed Malcolm Turnbull as Opposition Leader, Morrison became shadow minister for immigration and citizenship coming into the shadow cabinet for the first time. The promotion suggests that Scott Morrison helped Tony Abbott roll Malcolm Turnbull.

In September 2015 Malcolm Turnbull challenged and defeated Tony Abbott for the Prime Ministership. Scott Morrison was promoted to Treasurer which points to Scott Morrison stabbing Tony Abbott in the back in a deal with Turnbull.

In August 2018, after a long and sustained effort to destabilize his government by members of his own party, Malcolm Turnbull lost the Prime Ministership. In a subsequent ballot process Scott Morrison was elected Prime Minister. All the evidence suggests that Morrison again had a hand in the outing of Malcolm Turnbull which if it is the case shows Morrison as being a regular turncoat.

Morrison's dirty deal to get rid of competitor Michael Towke

Scott Morrison has a history of being involved in dirty election campaigns and his bid to be preselected by the Liberal Party for the 2007 election is regarded as one of the dirtiest in-house Liberal Party brawls. It was reported in 2018:

Mr Morrison won the seat of Cook in 2007, after the retirement of Mr Baird, amid the most bitter political factional war ever seen in the shire.

The Liberal Party preselection for the safe seat attracted a big field of candidates, but was won easily by Michael Towke, a young Lebanese Catholic, who had been working quietly for months building up numbers in the branches.

Mr Morrison was eliminated in the first ballot, gaining only eight votes, and Mr Towke went on to win with 82 votes.

However, the state executive of the party refused to endorse Mr Towke's preselection after a media campaign suggesting Mr Towke had fudged his CV and rumours spread about his family and early ALP involvement.

News Limited later paid Mr Towke $50,000, plus costs, and removed offending articles from the internet after he sued for defamation.

Mr Towke claimed party officials did not want him as a candidate after the 2005 Cronulla riots because of his Lebanese background.

A second preselection resulted in Mr Morrison being endorsed.

Mr Morrison has previously rejected any knowledge of muckraking or playing the race card. (Click here to read more)

Former federal Senator Sam Dastyari also tells the story on radio about Morrison and Towke and normally I wouldn't put much faith in what Sam Dastyari says but it is consistent with what Michael Towke has said and what numerous journalists have reported. Dastyari says:

Ever wondered how Scott Morrison first got into politics? Well, it involves the dumping of Michael Towke and the southern Sydney seat of Cook in what Sam Dastyari describes as the "biggest dirt campaign".

"I've seen a lot of dirty things in politics, but I've never had the Liberal party come to us [Labor] and ask for dirt to fight one of their own internal opponents," he said.

"I would never underestimate Scott Morrison... because I would never underestimate a guy who would turn to one of his political opponents to take out one of his own... a guy who will do that will do anything. (Click here to listen to the full interview)

(Click anywhere on the below video to watch an edited version of the interview)

The SMH reported in 2016:

Morrison is never adrift for long. In 2007, he set his sights on a rich Liberal prize: the federal parliamentary seat of Cook, centred on Sutherland Shire, scene of the Cronulla race riots two years before. (The seat was being vacated by his old patron, Bruce Baird, who had moved into federal politics.)

Baird's retirement triggered an almighty battle between the Right and Left factions of the NSW Liberal Party, both seeking to install their choice of successor. The initial winner of the preselection contest was a young Lebanese Catholic, Michael Towke, who had been quietly stacking branches for the Right faction for months while posing as a footsoldier for the Left.

By the time Morrison showed up, Towke was already in possession of a sizeable bloc of branch votes and the Left was running several stellar candidates of its own.

Morrison, who had either misread the numbers or taken very bad advice, fell between the two factions. He found himself eliminated in the first round, garnering only eight votes. Towke emerged the victor with more than 80 votes. This was a potentially fatal blow to Morrison's political ambitions, but the minute the result became known, party heavyweights in Canberra were on the phone demanding it be sorted out. How could a virtual unknown have defeated a former party state director?

Towke soon found himself the target of a media campaign suggesting he had inflated his CV. Rumours were peddled that his family had unsavoury associations and that he had fudged an early history with the ALP. Liberal head office bombarded him with lengthy interrogations about his credentials, while Towke hired lawyers to fend off a raft of allegations. On August 3, 2007, the party's NSW executive refused to endorse his preselection. At the same time, Towke says, he was gagged by the party, leaving him unable to defend himself.

Several days later, he was summoned to a secret backroom meeting at NSW party headquarters. Memories differ sharply about who was in attendance and what was said. But *Good Weekend* can reveal the existence of a secret deed drawn up by the party on August 15, in which Towke agreed to withdraw from the preselection in return for the party publicly acknowledging him to be a "fit and proper person".

Towke alleges the pressure from the party hierarchy to sign the document was relentless. He says he was instructed to support Morrison's candidacy, while being bound to keep the deed confidential. Even now, few who were senior in the party at the time admit knowing of its existence. Those contacted by *Good Weekend* declined to go on the record, though one insisted "it was not driven by the need to get Scott preselected".

Towke accuses his opponents of fanning the rumours against him, and suggesting his Lebanese background made him unelectable in the heavily Anglo Shire. "What was done to

Towke was sickening to watch," says one of his supporters. "But Towke's numbers went to Morrison the second time around, that's the great irony."

Morrison – who flatly denies any knowledge of the deed – emerged the victor when, in an almost unprecedented event for the Liberal Party, the preselection was held a second time. (In October 2010, the party secretly refunded Towke $33,000 in legal costs associated with the Cook preselection.) Morrison angrily rejects any knowledge of muckraking or the race card being played against Towke. (Click here to read more)

News Limited's The Sydney Telegraph were the hitman that Scott Morrison and the Liberal Party used to destroy Michael Towke in 2007 so that Morrison could take the preselection for the federal seat of Cook. The SMH reported in 2009:

News Limited was willing to pay dearly for this story not to be published. It first offered a $110,000 payment, plus a private apology, to avoid going to court. But the price it demanded was that the matter be kept confidential. The company was told to take a jump. See you in court.

The Daily Telegraph had published four stories about Michael Towke which he believed had defamed him, destroyed his political career, and caused untold stress to his family. "These stories sent my mother to hospital," he told me. "They demonised me. I wanted to confront them in court." (Click here to read more)

It's only when putting the different stories together on Michael Towke and Scott Morrison does the full picture start to appear. What is says is that Morrison and his supporters in the Liberal Party will do and say anything for power so we should buckle up for one hell of a ride for the next 4 to 6 weeks until the federal election.

Chapter 41

Looks like PM Scott Morrison was sacked as Managing Director of Tourism Australia in 2006 because of fraud and theft

Looks like PM Scott Morrison was sacked as Managing Director of Tourism Australia in 2006 because of fraud and theft

BY SHANE DOWLING ON JUNE 8, 2019 • (43 COMMENTS)

Prime Minister Scott Morrison was sacked as Managing Director of Tourism Australia in 2006 and he has always refused to say why. One thing is for certain, it had to be massive wrongdoing by Morrison. Why? Because Scott Morrison, who was State Director of the New South Wales Liberal Party from 2000 to 2004, was sacked by a Liberal Party Minister in the Liberal Party John Howard government and they don't sack one of their own for a minor reason or even a major reason. Morrison's sacking had to be something, at the very least, bordering on criminal and more than likely actual criminal conduct.

Since 2006 Scott Morrison has refused to answer questions about his sacking and little has been known about the reasons for it until now. Journalist Karen Middleton published an article on Saturday (8/6/19) which she spent 6 months investigating and to me it makes it clear Morrison was likely sacked for deliberate lies and deception in relation to the awarding of government contracts worth $184 million.

Karen Middleton writes in The Saturday Paper:

Thirteen years after Scott Morrison was mysteriously sacked from a senior public sector job as managing director of Tourism Australia, a six-month investigation by The Saturday Paper has created the clearest picture yet of the events surrounding his dismissal.

Documents obtained by The Saturday Paper under freedom of information laws show Morrison received a pay rise less than a month before he was sacked, taking his annual base salary from $318,031 to $332,030, with discretion for his employer to add up to 2.5 percent on top.

Around the time of Morrison's dismissal, it was suggested he was paid out after having his contract terminated more than a year early. Sources have since confirmed this.

It was long speculated that the sacking was the result of a personality clash between Morrison and Bailey or differences over her plans to restructure the agency.

But late last year, The Saturday Paper uncovered an auditor-general's report from 2008 examining the handling of three major contracts, which had delivered a scathing assessment of Tourism Australia's management.

The report provided the first indication as to the real reason Morrison was removed.

The contracts were worth $184 million, and the auditor focused most on the two biggest – those with companies M&C Saatchi for global creative services or advertising campaigns, and Carat for media placement.

The audit report revealed that information had been kept from the board, procurement guidelines breached and private companies engaged before paperwork was signed and without appropriate value-for-money assessments.

Both before and since becoming prime minister in August last year, Scott Morrison has refused to answer questions about why the tourism minister took the unusual step in July 2006 of sacking him as head of the agency. He has also refused to answer questions about the handling of the contracts, which were signed the previous year. He did not respond to questions for this story before time of press. (Click here to read the full article)

It's starting to become more obvious by the day why Scott Morrison is so keen to crack down on whistleblowers because there are probably a few dozen people in government who know the real reasons for Morrison's sacking and if they have access to the documents, they could bring him down. Morrison has known he is in trouble for 6 months since Karen Middleton started her FOI requests for documents from government departments. That would be an added reason why the Morrison government have gone so hard after whistleblowers in the last few months.

It must be remembered that Scott Morrison has only been Prime Minister since the 24th of August 2018 and not much was known about his background before then so uncovering his history will heat up now with the article by Middleton. There won't be any turning back and journalists will continue to dig until the truth comes out and even more so since the Morrison government has gone on the attack against journalists with the AFP raids over the last week.

I published an article on the 5th of April titled "Prime Minister Scott Morrison and his dirty deal with the Labor Party and Sam Dastyari" in relation to Morrison's dirty tactics to be pre-selected for the Liberal Party in the seat of Cook in 2007 and the article helps fill in the pieces considering the new details of his sacking the year before from Tourism Australia. (Click here to read more)

It's interesting that on Thursday (6/6/19) the Government and AFP trotted out the acting commissioner of the Australian Federal Police, Neil Gaughan, to threaten journalists further and deny that the AFP held back the raids on the ABC and the News Corp journalist's home until after the federal election. One raid, maybe, but for 2 AFP raids on the media 3 weeks after the election, it is too much to believe it wasn't a political decision by the AFP not to upset the government. Mr Gaughan didn't do a very good job and was carved up by a Twitter user who specializes in body language as per below. (In the below tweet BL = body language)

Sara
@_sara_jade_

Following

Acting AFP commish & media questions. BL Discomfort, stress, excessive water intake dry mouth saliva reduction due to stress, tongue protrusion contempt. A smirk, arrogance , lip jut petulance . Lip compression holding back. Nose, face touching self pacifying -deception. #auspol

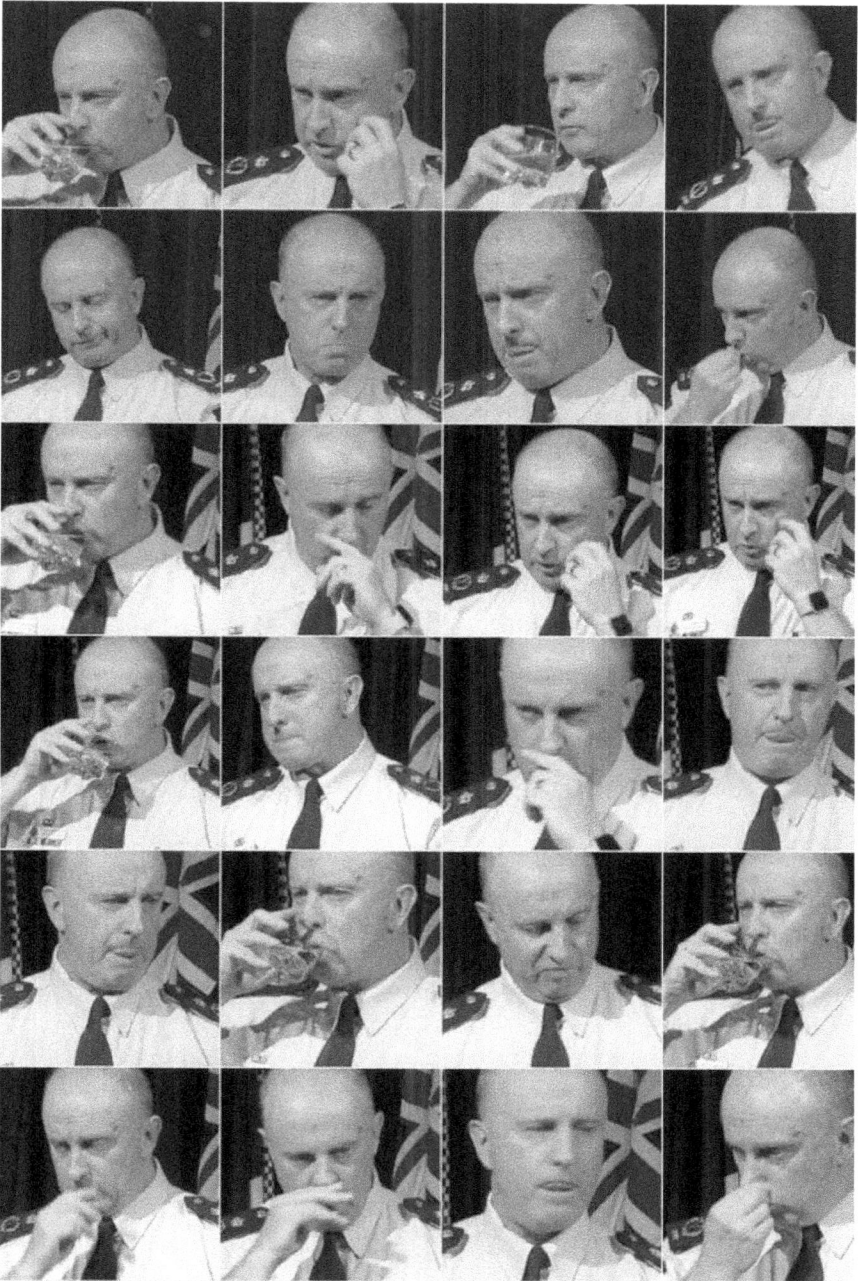

From the pictures, it was not too hard to work out that Neil Gaughan was lying like there was no tomorrow at the press conference which might explain why AFP Commissioner Andrew Colvin wasn't there and he sent out a patsy to take the heat.

Morrison's Wikipedia page says: "He lost his job in 2006, apparently due to conflict with tourism minister Fran Bailey over the government's plans to further integrate the agency into the Australian Public Service." (Click here to read more) That now needs updating given the new revelations.

This story is just starting and the pressure will keep building until something gives.

Chapter 42

NSW Police confirm PM Scott Morrison's mate Hillsong's Brian Houston still under investigation for concealing paedophile father

NSW Police confirm PM Scott Morrison's mate Hillsong's Brian Houston still under investigation for concealing paedophile father

BY SHANE DOWLING ON JULY 13, 2019 • (13 COMMENTS)

Prime Minister Scott Morrison and his wife were on stage leading prayers in front of 21,000 people on Tuesday night (9/7/19) with the Hillsong Church's Brian Houston who is still under investigation by the NSW police for concealing the sexual abuse of children by his father Frank Houston.

In 2014 while giving evidence at The Royal Commission into Institutional Responses to Child Sexual Abuse Brian Houston admitted he knew his father had abused children and he had failed to report it to the police so it is not a fact that is in dispute or a fact that Scott Morrison wouldn't know.

There are many reasons, which I outline below, why Scott Morrison should have never been on stage with paedophile protector Brian Houston who is under investigation by the NSW police.

I emailed questions to the Prime Minister as per below but he has refused to answer but the NSW police did respond to my email (as below) on Wednesday (10/7/19) and confirmed that they are still investigating Brian Houston which was first reported by the media in November 2018 by Channel 9. Why didn't Nine follow-up with the police as I did? Maybe it is because Nine's Chairman is former federal treasurer Peter Costello who is also a mentor to Scott Morrison and who has also led prayers at the Hillsong annual conference.

I sent the below email to the NSW Police Media unit on Wednesday at 5.04pm on Wednesday (10/7/19)

From: SHANE DOWLING
Sent: 10 July 2019 17:04
To: xxxx@police.nsw.gov.au
Subject: Media request: Brian Houston Hillsong Church

Dear Sir/Madam

I am a journalist and have a question in relation to Brian Houston who is the founder and a pastor at Hillsong Church.

Can you please confirm whether or not the NSW Police are still investigating Brian Houston from the Hillsong Church in relation to his handling of the sex crimes committed by his father Frank Houston or any other crimes?

Regards

Shane Dowling

Kangaroo Court of Australia

I received the below response from the NSW Police Media unit at 5.13pm on Wednesday (10/7/19)

From: xxxxx xxxxx <xxxxxxxx@police.nsw.gov.au> **On Behalf Of** #PMU
Sent: 10 July 2019 17:13
To: SHANE DOWLING
Subject: Re: Media request: Brian Houston Hillsong Church [DLM=For-Official-Use-Only]

Regarding your inquiry,

The matter continues to be investigated by officers attached to The Hills Police Area Command.

No further comment will be made while the investigation is ongoing

Regards,

Media Unit
NSW Police Force

Given it was widely reported in November 2018 that Brian Houston was under investigation by the NSW police why didn't any other media report that this week given Prime Minister Scott Morrison was on stage with Houston? All the other media could have done what I did and contacted the NSW police to see if Brian Houston was still being investigated.

There are many questions:

- What is an Australian Prime Minister doing on stage with someone under investigation for criminal offences?

- Why are the Australian Prime Minister and his wife Jenny normalising child sexual abuse by being on stage with Brian Houston and supporting him and his church?

- Is Prime Minister Scott Morrison interfering with a police investigation given he would have to know that his appearance with and support of Brian Houston would put pressure on the police not to charge Brian Houston?

- Why have no other media reported that Brian Houston is still under investigation by the NSW police? Are the media now too scared to upset the government given the government's threats to jail journalists?

Jenny Morrison, Scott Morrison and Brian Houston at Hillsong Church on Tuesday night (9/7/19)

Jeffrey Epstein

American billionaire and convicted paedophile Jeffrey Epstein was arrested in America on Saturday (6/7/19) and it has been all over the media since showing Epstein with his friends such as former President Bill Clinton and current President

Donald Trump. The point about Epstein is that he was arrested 4 days before Scott Morrison was on stage with Brian Houston and Morrison would have seen all the bad press for the politicians associated with Epstein. So, why did Morrison risk going on stage with Houston given he is under investigation by NSW police for concealing the sexual abuse of children by his father? It's worth noting that the Epstein matter also involves an alleged cover-up.

In the below video Scott Morrison answers questions from Brian Houston at the Hillsong Church conference on Tuesday (9/7/19).

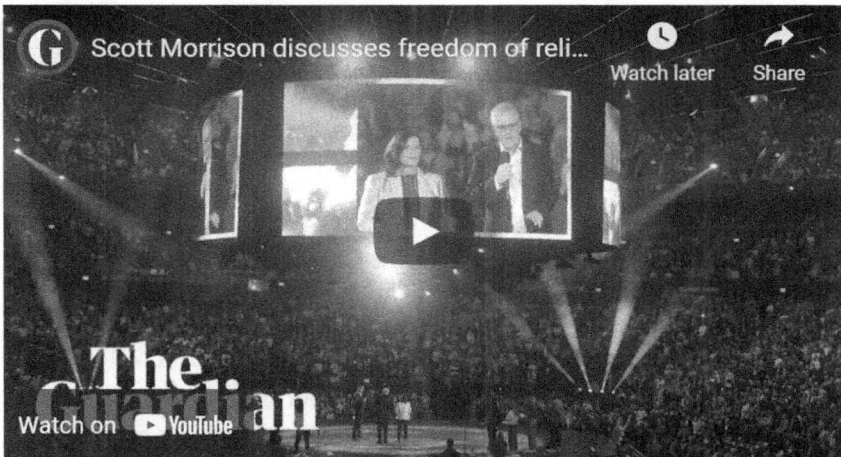

It costs $370 for a ticket to the annual Hillsong conference so supporting god isn't cheap.

Former federal treasurer and current Nine Entertainment Chairman Peter Costello at Hillsong Church in 2005. Nine Entertainment own Channel 9 and papers such as The SMH and The Age etc.

Many other politicians attended the Hillsong Church conference with Peter Costello in 2005: "NSW Premier Bob Carr and federal ministers Alexander Downer, Kevin Andrews and Peter Dutton, as well as NSW Christian Democrats MP Fred Nile, Liberal MP David Clarke and other state parliamentarians as they wanted the votes. (Click here to read more) Other than Scott Morrison I don't think as many politicians went this year with Brian Houston under investigation by the Police.

Hillsong Church – Brain Houston and the Frank Houston cover-up background

Brian Houston and his wife Bobbie started the Hillsong Church in 1983 and originally called it the Hills Christian Life Centre. It is like a franchise of the Assemblies of God. Brian's father Frank was also a pastor in New Zealand and Australia.

In 1999 the mother of a victim, referred to as AHA at the Royal Commission and who later outed himself on 60 Minutes as Brett Sengstock, made a complaint to the church. The church covered it up and the Child Abuse Royal Commission was critical of Brian Houston, his conduct in dealing with the abuse and failing to report it to the police.

Wikipedia says there were up to 9 victims and:

"Although Brian Houston was legally obligated to report the crime, he did not do so. The victim (Brett Sengstock) later testified to the Royal Commission into Institutional Responses to Child Sexual Abuse that Frank Houston offered him AU$10,000 as compensation at a McDonald's in the presence of Hillsong Church elder Nabi Saleh. During an internal church investigation, Frank Houston eventually confessed to the crime. The commission also heard that he was involved in the sexual abuse of other children in New Zealand."

"A further internal investigation by Assemblies of God in Australia, in conjunction with the Assemblies of God in New Zealand, found six additional child sexual abuse allegations, which were regarded as credible." (Click here to read more)

Brian Houston said in an interview in 2016 that he didn't know how many victims there were. Why hasn't he and Hillsong tried to find out?

Sixty Minutes reported in November 2018, as per the below video, that Brett Sengstock tried to sue the Assemblies of God for compensation but they refused to pay anything and claimed that they were not liable as Frank Houston never worked for them when Brett Sengstock was abused. That is the same routine the Catholic Church has used for decades to deny survivors compensation. Surely a god-fearing multi-millionaire like Brian Houston could have given Brett Sengstock some compensation.

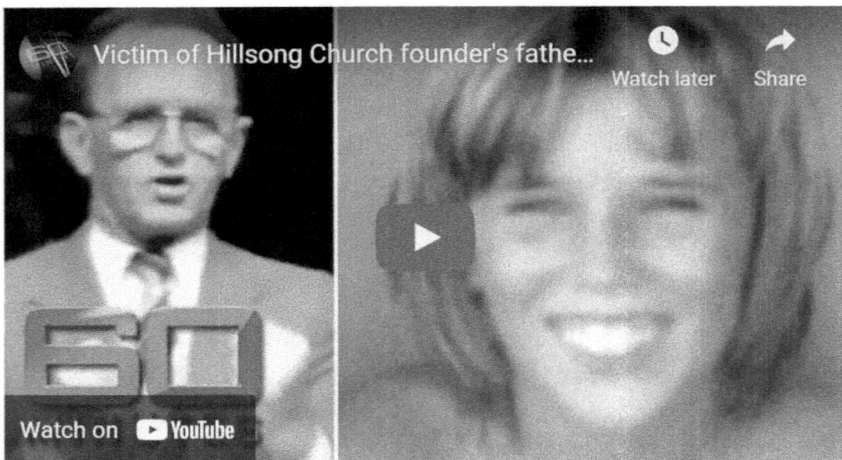

At the annual conference for Hillsong Church Scott Morrison said: "Australia needs more prayer and more love". What about the victims and survivors of Frank Houston's sexual abuse? Why didn't the Prime Minister mention them? (Click here to read more)

Scott Morrison would have been fully aware that the Australian media would report his attendance at the Hillsong Church conference and his support for the church and Brian Houston and what he said. So, Morrison was, in reality, preaching to all Australians and sending a powerful message to the police who are investigating Brian Houston not to charge him otherwise they will embarrass the Prime Minister.

I sent the below email to the Department of the Prime Minister and Cabinet on Friday (12/7/19) at 1.29pm and have not had a response at this time.

From: SHANE DOWLING
Sent: 12 July 2019 13:29
To: media@pmc.gov.au
Subject: Media request regarding Prime Minister Scott Morrison

Dear Sir/Madam

I am a journalist and have 8 questions in relation to Prime Minister Scott Morrison and his relationship with Brian Houston who is the founder and a pastor at Hillsong Church.

It was reported in the media that Prime Minister Scott Morrison and his wife were on stage with Brian Houston at the Hillsong Church conference on Tuesday the 9th of July 2019 and it has also been reported that Prime Minister Scott Morrison regards Brian Houston as a mentor.

The questions are:

1. Can you please confirm if Prime Minister Scott Morrison was aware that the NSW police are currently investigating Brian Houston for covering up the sexual abuse of children by his father Frank Houston?

2. Can you please confirm if Prime Minister Scott Morrison was aware that the Royal Commission into Institutional Responses to Child Sexual Abuse found that both the New South Wales executive and the national executive of the Assemblies of God failed to follow its complaints procedure when handling the allegations?

3. Can you please confirm if Prime Minister Scott Morrison was aware that the Royal Commission also found both executives failed to appoint a contact person for the victim (referred to as AHA), did not interview AHA about his allegations, did not interview Frank Houston, and did not record any of the steps it took?

4. Can you please confirm if Prime Minister Scott Morrison was aware that the royal commission also found neither the national executive nor Brian Houston referred the allegations to police, and the Royal Commission determined Houston "had a conflict of interest in assuming responsibility for dealing with AHA's allegations because he was both the National President of

the Assemblies of God in Australia and the son of Mr Frank Houston, the alleged perpetrator"?

5. Can you please confirm if Prime Minister Scott Morrison was aware that Brian Houston, who was then the national president of the Assemblies of God, confronted his father with the allegations in 1999 and the preacher confessed?

6. Can you please confirm if Prime Minister Scott Morrison was aware that Brian Houston called a meeting of the national executive, and relinquished the chair, but remained present during discussions on the allegations and disciplinary actions against his father?

7. Can you please confirm if Prime Minister Scott Morrison was aware that the Assemblies of God executive began investigations – later discovering a further eight alleged victims of Frank Houston – but did not make them public, telling its churches in a letter from Brian Houston there was "no reason" for it to be announced as others may use it to further their agendas?

8. Can you please confirm if Prime Minister Scott Morrison was aware that Brian Houston defended his failure to go to the police, despite having no doubt it was criminal conduct?

Can you please respond by 5pm today (Friday 12/7/19) in case I have further questions. My deadline for publication is 5pm Saturday the 13th of July 2019.

Regards

Shane Dowling

Kangaroo Court of Australia

The evidence against Brian Houston and the Hillsong Church of covering up paedophile Frank Houston's abuse of children has been around a long time and most of my questions to the Prime

Minister came from an article on the Royal Commission in 2015 (Click here to read). So, it's impossible for Prime Minister Scott Morrison to say he didn't know and explains why he refused to answer my questions.

Brian Houston and his family also gave an interview in 2016 on The Inside Story program and it is worth watching the part where they discuss Frank Houston because all they seem to care about is themselves and what impact it had on them. There was no discussion on what they would do for the victims and Brian Houston is caught out giving two different reasons why he didn't go to the police, one version for the show and another version when he was in the witness stand at the Royal Commission.

Why do Liberal Party Prime Minister's support paedophiles and their protectors such as former PM John Howard writing a letter of reference for convicted paedophile George Pell to use at his sentencing hearing and former PM Tony Abbott also publicly supporting George Pell after he was convicted? (Click here to read more) (Update: The High Court of Australia later overturned George Pell's conviction on a legal technicality. But there are many more allegations of George Pell sexually abusing numerous children which have been reported by the ABC and other media which have gone untested by a court.)

Is Scott Morrison interfering in a police investigation? Or trying to influence a police investigation like John Howard did with Gorge Pell?

In 2004 Frank Houston died and at his funeral service was the then Deputy Police Commissioner Andrew Scipione who later became Police Commissioner and is said to be friends with Brian Houston. Houston gave evidence in 2014 at the Royal Commission were he admitted failing to go to the police in relation to the sexual abuse of children by his father. Apparently, the police started looking at the issue given the evidence at the Royal Commission but did nothing because of lack of evidence but reopened the matter about the same time as the Sixty Minutes story went to air.

Sixty Minutes didn't have the same trouble the police did in getting plenty of evidence for their report in November 2018. It's worth noting that Andrew Scipione didn't retire as Police Commissioner until March 2017.

One of the saddest things about this issue is that thousands of survivors were promised compensation after The Royal Commission into Institutional Responses to Child Sexual Abuse ended in 2017 and the government set up the National Redress Scheme but after 12 months only 5% of applications have been processed. I think Scott Morrison should be focused on fixing that rather than helping Brian Houston promote himself and the Hillsong Church.

There is a tonne of evidence to charge Brian Houston with concealing a serious indictable offence, yet he hasn't been charged. Why? It makes you wonder if much will happen with the police investigation given the Prime Minister gave Brian Houston the green light on Tuesday at the Hillsong conference.

Make no mistake, Prime Minister Scott Morrison knew Brian Houston is still under investigation by the police and Morrison knew it was highly inappropriate for him to be at the Hillsong

Church on Tuesday night (9/7/19) helping promote it. But Morrison knows that he gets a lot of votes from the Hillsong Church and his local church which is linked to Hillsong so in a situation like this Morrison believes that votes count more than doing what is ethical and moral. I'll keep on following up on this story.

(Update: Brian Houston was charged by the police in late 2021 and will likely face trial in 2022)

Chapter 43

PM Scott Morrison, his mate Peter Costello, the $700,000 fundraising scam at Channel Nine and what the Old Media haven't reported

PM Scott Morrison, his mate Peter Costello, the $700,000 fundraising scam at Channel Nine and what the Old Media haven't reported

BY SHANE DOWLING ON SEPTEMBER 7, 2019 • (10 COMMENTS)

A major league scam went down on Monday night (2/9/19) where Nine Entertainment Chairman, known fraudster and former federal treasurer Peter Costello destroyed the media companies' reputation to raise $700,000 for his mate PM Scott Morrison and the Liberal Party.

The fundraiser, which cost $10,000 per person to attend, was held at the Channel Nine studios in Sydney and was attended by Prime Minister Scott Morrison, numerous federal ministers, mining executives, the bank's top lobbyist former Queensland Premier Anna Bligh and other business people. (Click here to read more)

I have been reporting for months about Peter Costello and his extremely close relationship with Prime Minister Scott Morrison and how that relationship is very profitable for Peter Costello and I suspect vice versa.

The media have been reporting the matter but almost all have refused to report anything about Peter Costello except to say he wasn't at the fundraiser and imply he had nothing to do with it which the reality is, it has his fingerprints all over it.

There were lobbyists from all areas of big business but what is not well-known or reported is that Peter Costello is also a lobbyist via his company ECG Financial Pty Ltd who has made $millions lobby the government through his Liberal Party contacts. Costello is certain to make $millions more from Liberal Party contacts given he has now helped them raise $700,000.

I wrote an article on the 24th of February 2019 titled "Prime Minister Scott Morrison and his puppet master Peter Costello" and I think the $700,000 Nine fundraiser has proven the title to be true. I started the article off saying:

Former Federal Treasurer Peter Costello has his fingerprints all over Prime Minister Scott Morrison as his puppet master, the $50 billion submarine contract scam and the federal government via his chairmanships of ECG Financial Pty Ltd, Nine and the $150 billion Future Fund. There is also documented evidence that Peter Costello has been deliberately hiding his lobbying activity from state and federal governments.

My investigation and ASIC company searches show that Peter Costello is a current financial owner of ECG Financial Pty Ltd and was previously a financial owner of the sister company ECG Advisory Solutions which I reported last week has made $millions from a dodgy deal to give advice in the $50 Billion submarine contract. There's also a prima facie case that Prime Minister Scott Morrison helped orchestrate the deal for ECG and his mates Costello and David Gazard who is a director and 50% shareholder of ECG Advisory via his company GPJT Pty Ltd.

There are clearly musical chairs being played by Peter Costello and others to hide the truth and the fraud and thefts. Specifically, what is being hidden is that Peter Costello makes a lot of money lobbying the government for large companies.

How it works:

There are 2 companies and one of them, ECG Advisory Solutions, is also a registered lobbying company and that seems to have become a problem as it was being widely published on the lobbyist registers that Peter Costello's private company was a shareholder in the company but he was not listed as one of the lobbyists. Yet he is the Chairman of the sister company ECG Financial.

Where this obviously became a problem for Costello is for example the $50 billion submarine deal where it was reported that Prime Minister Scott Morrison's mate David Gazard was appointed as an adviser. (Click here to read more) That is extremely concerning and needs investigating but it would have been a million times worse if the media had also reported that Peter Costello and/or his company had been appointed as an advisor. They must have realized a few years ago that having the Peter Costello link was a possible problem so he sold his shares is ECG Advisory but kept his shares in the sister company ECG Financial. (Click here to read the full article)

That article was a follow-up to the previous week when I published an article titled "Prime Minister Scott Morrison, his best mate David Gazard and the $50 billion submarine scam" on the 16th of February 2019 which started off:

Prime Minister Scott Morrison's best mate and closest political advisor, David Gazard, is profiting $millions from the $50 billion submarine contract Australia finalised this week with the French state-owned shipbuilder Naval Group. Naval Group is still under investigation for bribing Malaysia's former leader Najib Razak US$128 million.

What is becoming clear is that the $50 billion submarine contact is a money grab for numerous Liberal Party cronies which is disturbing given Naval Group was previously investigated by the Australian Senate in 2016 for bribery in Australia via one of their subsidiaries.

Firstly, we'll look at the bribery allegations against Naval group and Naval Group's former Australian operations CEO Sean Costello who was a former Liberal Party staffer and then David Gazard's relationship with Prime Minister Scott Morrison and Naval Group. (Click here to read the full article)

I went on to say in the article:

Scott Morrison and the David Gazard connection. And now add the Peter Costello connection

Scott Morrison and David Gazard

David Gazard is the man who Scott Morrison went to for advice during the leadership showdown between Tony Abbott and

Malcolm Turnbull in September 2015. The SMH reported in 2016 in an article titled "*Scott Morrison's relentless rise to power*":

"*On the evening of September 14, 2015 Tony Abbott's prime ministership was hanging by a thread. Abbott had made Morrison a last-minute offer to join him on a leadership ticket and to take over Joe Hockey's job as Treasurer. Hunkered down in his Parliament House office over a home-made curry, Morrison gamed his next move with his close friend David Gazard, a former Howard and Costello staffer, while Costello offered advice over the phone.*" (Click here to read more)

I wrote the above article's in February 2016 about Peter Costello, David Gazard and their lobbying companies but since then it has been reported that the lobbying firm ECG Advisory closed down on the 31st of July. Gazard has set up a new political advisory and government relations business DPG Advisory Solutions but doesn't seem to have a website yet.

Peter Costello, David Gazard and Jonathan Epstein launch their firm ECG in 2011.

It sounds like they closed down links to each other, doesn't it? Well no, they still have ECG Financial alive and well whose shareholders are Peter Costello, Jonathan Epstein and David Gazard who are the same three amigos who set up ECG Advisory. ECG Financial makes its money by advising "on mergers and acquisitions, foreign investment, competition and regulatory issues which affect business in Australia." such as the dodgy $50 billion submarine scam.

Scott Morrison's links to the same people should not surprise given he was likely sacked as Managing Director of Tourism Australia in 2006 because of fraud and theft. (Click here to read more)

Now back to looking at the $700,000 raised by Nine Entertainment, with the further details I have reported above, and it becomes even more disturbing that Peter Costello used Nine Entertainment to raise money for Scott Morrison and the Liberal Party. A question that no one has seemed to ask is if David Gazard was at the fundraiser?

The perceived bias, if not real bias, by Nine in raising the money was obvious to all including Channel 10 journalist Hugh Riminton who Tweeted:

Hugh Riminton ✔
@hughriminton

No shit, Sherlock...

Ben Cubby ✔ @bencubby · Sep 4
Nine boss Hugh Marks says it was a 'mistake' to host Liberal fundraiser
smh.com.au/business/compa... via @smh

5:02 PM · Sep 4, 2019 · Twitter for iPhone

379 Retweets   **2.4K** Likes

There are too many questions that the old media have refused to ask about the $700,000 fundraiser. Nine Entertainment who owns Channel Nine, The Sydney Morning Herald, The Age in Melbourne and The Australian Financial Review came under heavy criticism for holding the fundraiser as it made them look like nothing more than an extension of the Liberal Party.

Journalists working at Nine's papers published a letter to management critical on the fundraiser as it damages the credibility of the papers which said in part:

"raised the question of where the Nine newspapers' political loyalties lie".

"The former Fairfax mastheads have a long history of political independence," the journalists said.

"If this has changed and we are now associated with the Liberal Party, this should be conveyed to staff. A decision to host fundraisers for Labor or other political parties would be of equal concern.

"Our mastheads have done much to expose the corrupting influence of money on politics. It is vitally important that we remain independent of the political process." (Click here to read more)

How many of the Nine journalists who criticized management for the fundraiser have reported about their Chairman Peter Costello's involvement in lobbying? None, because they are obviously not allowed to.

Many voters have always had an issue with Nine Entertainment having former federal Treasurer and Liberal Party MP Peter Costello as Chairman but it became much worse with the $700,000 fundraiser. That needs to be added to the fact that the group executive editor of The Age and the Sydney Morning Herald, James Chessell, is a former media advisor to former federal treasurer Joe Hockey from Jul 2006 – Oct 2007 when he was the Minister for Employment and Workplace Relations.

Nine are now skating on thin ice when it comes to their credibility for unbiased news, and they need to sack Chairman Peter Costello to try and claw some credibility back.

Chapter 44

Scott Morrison and the Liberal Party caught stacking the courts with cronies to cover-up government corruption

Scott Morrison and the Liberal Party caught stacking the courts with cronies to cover-up government corruption

BY SHANE DOWLING ON SEPTEMBER 28, 2019 • (14 COMMENTS)

Scott Morrison and the Liberal Party have been caught out stacking the Administrative Appeals Tribunal (AAT), which is meant to keep the government accountable, with Liberal Party cronies. The AAT is a tribunal that reviews "a wide range of administrative decisions made by the Australian Government". It is where people go if they do not like a government decision against themselves and they want it overturned.

What is happening at the AAT is a good guide to what is happening with the appointment of judicial officers in all courts.

INQ reported on the 24/9/19:

"Over the past six years, dozens of people with ties to the Liberal Party have gotten plum gigs at the Administrative Appeals

Tribunal, despite many of them having no formal legal qualifications."

It's a glittering prize: a job as a member of the Administrative Appeals Tribunal, one of the plummest appointments within the gift of a federal government.

Tenure of up to seven years, renewable. Annual salary of up to $385,000 for senior members. Removal only by order of the governor-general after a vote from both houses of parliament. No compulsory retirement age. The prestige of effectively being a judge sitting atop a multi-pronged legal institution whose annual budget is nine times more than the cost of running the High Court. (Click here to read more)

On the 21st of February the government announced: "86 appointments to the Administrative Appeals Tribunal, comprising 34 new appointments and reappointments for 52 existing members. Most of the appointments have been made for five years with others being for a period of either three or seven years."

"I particularly thank The Hon. John Pascoe AC CVO for agreeing to take up the position of Deputy President. The Hon. John Pascoe retired as Chief Justice of the Family Court of Australia late last year." (Click here for the full list of people appointed to the AAT)

John Pascoe is one of the biggest crooks to ever call himself a judge and I'll detail that further on, but back to the AAT for a minute.

INQ followed up with an article titled "A who's who in the AAT zoo" and listed the appointments and their Liberal Party connections and pointed out the appointments who had no legal training in which there were many. Some are:

Name	State	Type of Connection
Gary Humphries	ACT	Former Liberal senator
John Sosso	QLD	Director-General, Justice Department (Newman government)
Robert Cameron	VIC	Liberal Chairman Kew State Electoral Council
Paul Clauson AM	QLD	Former attorney-general and minister under Liberal government
Michael Cooke*	NSW	Former adviser to Tony Abbott
Denis Dragovic*	VIC	Liberal preselection for the House of Representatives; Victorian Senate preselection
Ann Duffield*	QLD	Former chief of staff to Scott Morrison
Richard Ellis	WA	Former chief of staff to former premier Colin Barnett
Matthew Groom	VIC	Former Liberal Party member for Denison
James Lambie	QLD	Former policy adviser; senior adviser and chief of staff to George Brandis

Name	State	Type of Connection
Donald Morris*	VIC	Former senior adviser to Eric Abetz
Andew Nikolic AM CSC*	VIC	Former Liberal member of House of Representatives
Justin Owen	NSW	Lifetime member of the Sydney University Liberal Club; former treasurer of the Australian Liberal Students Federation
Jason Pennell	VIC	Liberal preselection for the House of Representatives
Belinda Pola	QLD	Former chief of staff to Mathias Cormann; former staffer to Joe Hockey
Christopher Puplick AM*	NSW	Former Liberal senator

*No known legal qualification, or has not been able to provide evidence of qualification when contacted. (Click here to see the full list on the INQ website)

"Appointments to the Administrative Appeals Tribunal were once subject to review via a separate council... until the Abbott government gutted it." (Click here to read more)

Predetermined judgments

The reason the Liberal Party is stacking the AAT so much is to make sure they get the decisions they want and to hide the corruption.

Another INQ article started off: "Members of the Administrative Appeals Tribunal are steadily losing their jobs and being replaced with people less qualified."

"Terry Carney lost his job as a member of the Administrative Appeals Tribunal (AAT) via a short, blunt email. It arrived five months after he delivered a tribunal decision which declared Centrelink's robo-debt scheme to be illegal — a finding that angered the federal government."

"I had one of those feelings in my bones," he remembers as the day approached for his contract to be renewed — or not. "I actually sort of paused and looked around in the hearing room when I completed what I knew might have been — proved to be — my last hearing." (Click here to read more)

All of those appointed to the AAT would be donating back to the Liberal Party so the appointment of cronies is also a good way to fundraise for the Liberal Party.

Attorney-General Christian Porter and Prime Minister Scott Morrison

An example – Scott Morrison FOI Whistleblower

A prime example of when someone could go to the AAT is if a journalist or an individual makes a claim under freedom of information laws for documents from a government department. If the government fails to hand over the documents and only give you limited documents or redacted documents you can complain to, the watchdog of FOI laws, the Australian Information Commissioner and Privacy Commissioner (OAIC). If you are not satisfied with the judgment of the OAIC you can then go to the AAT.

But let's look at it in practice. There was a recent report titled "Whistleblower hits out at PM's department over 'pervasive and toxic' disregard for law." The whistleblower "accused the government of flagrantly breaching laws to thwart the release of politically-sensitive documents" and the "whistleblower alleged the department breached FOI law in one of every two requests it received, particularly when the documents were embarrassing or sensitive." (Click here to read more)

If the government broke the law regarding your Freedom of Information request you would go to the OIAC but they are only a small department with limited powers.

Your next step would be going to the AAT. Who will decide your claim in the AAT? It's a good chance that it will be a Liberal Party crony and possibly even a former Liberal Party politician or Liberal Party staffer. Will they be unbiased? Of course not and that's why they were put there.

This is a judicial corruption website and has a role to help promote this type of corruption story and where I add value is my knowledge of the criminal history of newly appointed AAT Deputy President John Pascoe who I have reported on many times over the years. His handiwork of price-fixing and succumbing to blackmail shows up in a court judgment. John Pascoe even received his own chapter in my judicial corruption book "Love Letters from the Bar Table" that was published in 2009.

Well known fraudster and Liberal Party crony John Pascoe – Stacking the courts

John Pascoe started as Chief Federal Magistrate in 2004 when there was a Federal Magistrates Court before it changed its name to the Federal Circuit Court of Australia in 2013.

Prior to that John Pascoe was up to his neck in price-fixing, fraud and succumbing to blackmail in an attempt to conceal price-fixing as CEO and Chairman of George Weston Foods. Most of the details show up in a court judgment: Australian Competition & Consumer Commission v George Weston Foods Limited [2004] FCA 1093 (25 August 2004)

The judgment is a fascinating read because you can see the crimes of John Pascoe before he became Chief Federal Magistrate, then Chief Judge of the Federal Circuit Court of Australia, then Chief Justice of the Family Court and now Deputy President of the AAT.

I read the full judgment and dissected it in one of the first articles I wrote for this website in 2011 titled "The handiwork of Chief Federal Magistrate John Pascoe – witness bribing, price-fixing, succumbing to blackmail to conceal a crime and lying to shareholders etc. Is there anything this man cannot do?" (Click here to read the article)

An overview of the issues and John Pascoe's crimes I covered in the article are:

1. John Pascoe's time as CEO / Director and Chairman of George Weston Foods where there was mass price-fixing, witness bribing and John Pascoe succumbed to blackmail by Dick Honan (Chairman of Manildra) to conceal price-fixing.

2. John Pascoe's time as Director/Chairman of Aristocrat Leisure Limited where he was involved with making false and misleading

statements and breaching continuous disclosure laws. This led to a multi-million-dollar payout to the victims.

3. John Pascoe's attempt to conceal plagiarism by the former Federal Magistrate Jennifer Rimmer.

4. The fraud at the Federal Magistrates Court of Australia under his direction and management after auditors uncovered a $5 million blackhole.

5. Chief Federal Magistrate John Pascoe hearing a case where there was an alleged breach of the Trade Practices Act. The same Trade Practices Act that John Pascoe was breaching on an ongoing basis when he was CEO/Chairman at George Western Foods.

6. Is Chief Federal Magistrate John Pascoe permanently out to lunch? His lazy work ethics as Chief Federal Magistrate. In the 2011 article, I wrote: "I did a quick search of the judgments on the Federal Magistrates Court of Australia website and I could only find one judgment from John Pascoe in 2011 and 2 in 2010 and the previous years were not much better. If those numbers are right, I think Chief Federal Magistrate Pascoe has a lot to answer for. He has obviously been out to lunch plenty. And why did he need 2 offices?" (Click here to read more)

The ACCC V George Weston Foods judgment in 2004 was so damming of John Pascoe he was parachuted into the role of Chief Federal Magistrate a few months later by his good mate John Howard as Pascoe's career in the business world was over after the judgment. Now John Pascoe is in one of the most senior positions in the country meant to be keeping the government accountable.

How is the AAT going to keep the Liberal government accountable when it is stacked with Liberal Party cronies? The answer is simple, it won't and that is the way the corrupt government wants it.

Chapter 45

Scott Morrison left Tourism New Zealand in similar circumstances to his sacking by Tourism Australia. Why?

Scott Morrison left Tourism New Zealand in similar circumstances to his sacking by Tourism Australia. Why?

BY SHANE DOWLING ON NOVEMBER 2, 2019 • (6 COMMENTS)

Scott Morrison was sacked as the head of Tourism Australia in 2006 in mysterious circumstances which he has always refused to explain but he also left as the head of Tourism New Zealand in a hurry in 2000 with similar complaints about his performance and conduct. Scott Morrison has done a good job of concealing who he is from the Australian public, but more and more is starting to be revealed and it paints a disturbing picture and I think this article helps put one more piece of the jigsaw puzzle together.

Firstly, to re-cap what I have previously written about Morrison's sacking at Tourism Australia:

Morrison was sacked as Managing Director of Tourism Australia in 2006 and he has always refused to say why. One thing is for certain, it had to be massive wrongdoing by Morrison. Why?

Because Scott Morrison, who was State Director of the New South Wales Liberal Party from 2000 to 2004, was sacked by a Liberal Party Minister in the Liberal Party John Howard government and they don't sack one of their own for a minor reason or even a major reason. Morrison's sacking had to be something, at the very least, bordering on criminal and more than likely actual criminal conduct. (Click here to read more)

I quoted an article from The Saturday Paper which said:

It was long speculated that the sacking was the result of a personality clash between Morrison and Bailey or differences over her plans to restructure the agency.

But late last year, The Saturday Paper uncovered an auditor-general's report from 2008 examining the handling of three major contracts, which had delivered a scathing assessment of Tourism Australia's management.

The report provided the first indication as to the real reason Morrison was removed.

The contracts were worth $184 million, and the auditor focused most on the two biggest – those with companies M&C Saatchi for global creative services or advertising campaigns, and Carat for media placement.

The audit report revealed that information had been kept from the board, procurement guidelines breached and private companies engaged before paperwork was signed and without appropriate value-for-money assessments. (Click here to read the full article)

The 2008-2009 Auditor-Generals report on Tourism Australia – (Click here to read the full 2008-2009 Auditor-Generals report on Tourism Australia)

The 2008-2009 Auditor-Generals report on Tourism Australia covers the time Scott Morrison was Managing Director and the

$184 million of suspect contracts he was responsible for negotiating and says:

At paragraph 13 it says: The majority of Tourism Australia's marketing activities are delivered through its major global contracts for creative development and media placement services. Digital services, including the tourism online gateway australia.com, are also delivered under contract arrangements. **These three contracts consumed approximately thirty-five percent of Tourism Australia's total budget between 2004–05 and 2006–07**, underlining the importance of Tourism Australia having effective processes for selecting and managing its service providers

At paragraph 14 it says: "Tourism Australia's policies and guidelines provide a sound framework for undertaking complex procurements and managing its contracts. **However, relevant guidelines were not followed when procuring its global creative development and media placement services and, to a lesser extent, digital services.** In particular, procurement plans were not developed and the risks to the successful completion of these procurements were not assessed."

At paragraph 16 it says: The services provided under these major contracts, which to date are valued at in excess of $184 million, are fundamental to the success of Tourism Australia's marketing initiatives. The contracts accurately reflected the services to be provided. **However, the media placement and creative development contracts did not include performance information that would enable Tourism Australia to evaluate the effectiveness of the services provided even though, as part of a review of the draft contracts, this was recommended.**

Mr Unaccountable Scott Morrison was in full flight at Tourism Australia after a similar performance at Tourism New Zealand

Scott Morrison in 2005

Scott Morrison at Tourism New Zealand

"Mr Morrison, an Australian, helped set up the New Zealand Office of Tourism and Sport in the 1990s and "He left with a year to go on his contract in March 2000." (Click here to read more)

In June 2000 the NZ Herald reported:

The days of the Office of Tourism and Sport, a power-base of former Tourism Minister Murray McCully, may be numbered.

The Prime Minister has ordered a report from officials on the office, which was approved by cabinet, and on a body Mr McCully privately set up, the Tourism and Sport Ministerial Advisory Board.

The State Services Commission and Internal Affairs are looking at the office after criticisms in the Auditor-General's report on tourism last week.

And if Labour is part of the next government, it will abolish the office. Labour's sports and state services spokesman, Trevor

Mallard, says the Office of Tourism and Sport was set up last year "to push the political interests of McCully."

"It was designed to provide McCully with the advice McCully wanted and a method of sorting out organisations without McCully's hands getting dirty."

The office is a semi-autonomous body under the Department of Internal Affairs. The director, Scott Morrison, tenders advice to the Minister of Tourism and the Minister of Sport, Fitness and Leisure. The office also oversaw a damning consultants' report on the Tourism Board's performance for Mr McCully, without input from the Tourism Board.

Confusion over roles of the various bodies – the Tourism Board, the Office of Tourism and Sport, and the advisory board – contributed to the breakdown in relationship between the Tourism Board and Mr McCully, the Auditor-General, David Macdonald, said in his report.

Mr Mallard said the way the Office of Tourism and Sport operated was one of the reasons Mr McCully had got into trouble.

And a key reason for that was that it was run by Mr Morrison, an Australian who was seen as Mr McCully's "hard man."

Australian standards of public sector behaviour "are lower than ours," said Mr Mallard.

New Zealanders were much more traditional and had a Westminster-type approach. That meant more things on paper, more concern about process, and being less bombastic.

"My experience with Australian politicians is that rules and ethics are not as important to them as they are to New Zealanders."

Mr Morrison said he did not want to respond to Mr Mallard's personal comments. "I have no interest in New Zealand politics." (Click here to read the full article)

Given the above and the fact that he still had a year to go on his contract everything points to Scott Morrison being tapped on the shoulder by the New Zealand government and being told to resign or be sacked.

In March 2000 Scott Morrison left Tourism New Zealand and moved back to Australia where, after a brief stint at KPMG, he was appointed as the State Director of the New South Wales Liberal Party until 2004. In 2004 he was parachuted into the role of Managing Director of Tourism Australia in a blatantly political appointment until even the Liberal Party couldn't handle his dodgy conduct any further and they sacked him in 2006.

In 2007 Scott Morrison did his secret dirty deal with Sam Dastyari and stabbed Michael Towke in the back. Mr Towke was the pre-selected candidate for the seat of Cook and was in Morrison's way so false rumours were spread and the state executive of the Liberal Party refused to endorse Mr Towke's preselection after the rumours were published by News Corp. A second ballot was held, and Scott Morrison won. Mr Towke successfully sued News Corp.

Scott Morrison's time at Tourism New Zealand, Tourism Australia and his preselection to parliament all show unanswered allegations of abuse of processes, procedures and total unaccountability which is exactly how Scott Morrison is running the country and performing as Prime Minister.

When Scott Morrison stands in front of the media refusing to answer questions it should not surprise as he has a long history of refusing to be accountable but now, he is the Prime Minister and he owes it to the whole country to answer questions.

Chapter 46

NSW Police refuse to deny PM Scott Morrison has interfered in the investigation into paedophile protector Brian Houston

NSW Police refuse to deny PM Scott Morrison has interfered in the investigation into paedophile protector Brian Houston

BY SHANE DOWLING ON NOVEMBER 28, 2019 • (6 COMMENTS)

The NSW police are refusing to deny political interference by Prime Minister Scott Morrison in the police investigation of his good friend and mentor Brian Houston who is under investigation for concealing his father's sexual abuse of children.

The email I sent to the NSW Police yesterday (27/11/19) is below but I will quickly outline some of the background and a previous email I sent to the police which puts into context why it is important that the police answer the latest questions I have put to them.

Background

I have previously written about Brian Houston perjuring himself at the Child Sex Abuse Royal Commission when he was in the witness stand under oath in 2014 (Click here to read more) and I published the below video showing Brian Houston's lies which are also relevant to this article.

The NSW police have been investigating Brian Houston for a long time but still haven't charged him despite his open admissions as per the below video.

I emailed the NSW Police on the 10th of July 2019 and asked them if they were still investigating Brian Houston for covering up his father's sexual abuse of children which had been reported in November 2018. I sent the email and had a response 9 minutes later confirming they were still investigating Brian Houston as per below.

I sent the below email to the NSW Police Media unit on Wednesday at 5.04pm on Wednesday (10/7/19)

From: SHANE DOWLING
Sent: 10 July 2019 17:04
To: xxxx@police.nsw.gov.au
Subject: Media request: Brian Houston Hillsong Church

Dear Sir/Madam

I am a journalist and have a question in relation to Brian Houston who is the founder and a pastor at Hillsong Church.

Can you please confirm whether or not the NSW Police are still investigating Brian Houston from the Hillsong Church in relation to his handling of the sex crimes committed by his father Frank Houston or any other crimes?

Regards

Shane Dowling

Kangaroo Court of Australia

I received the below response from the NSW Police Media unit at 5.13pm on Wednesday (10/7/19)

From: xxxxx xxxxx <xxxxxxxx@police.nsw.gov.au> **On Behalf Of** #PMU
Sent: 10 July 2019 17:13
To: SHANE DOWLING
Subject: Re: Media request: Brian Houston Hillsong Church [DLM=For-Official-Use-Only]

Regarding your inquiry,

The matter continues to be investigated by officers attached to The Hills Police Area Command.

No further comment will be made while the investigation is ongoing

Regards,

Media Unit
NSW Police Force

This was a huge problem for Prime Minister Scott Morrison given the night before he was on stage in front of 22,000 people at the Hillsong conference with Brian Houston promoting the

Church. I published an article on the 13th of July titled "NSW Police confirm PM Scott Morrison's mate Hillsong's Brian Houston still under investigation for concealing paedophile father." (Click here to read more)

In September 2019 it was reported that Scott Morrison tried to take Brian Houston on his visit to the USA and Washington but the White House rejected Brian Houston. (Click here to read more)

On Tuesday (26/11/19) news broke that Prime Minister Scott Morrison had phoned the NSW Police Commissioner to ask about a police investigation into federal MP Angus Taylor which had only been announced a few hours earlier.

The police started "an investigation into the origins of an altered document used to attack the Sydney lord mayor, Clover Moore." (Click here to read more)

And a few hours later Scott Morrison was on the phone to the NSW Police Commissioner. The ABC reported:

"Federal Opposition Leader Anthony Albanese believes Mr Morrison crossed a line by calling Commissioner Mick Fuller after it was revealed police launched an investigation into an allegedly forged document used by Energy Minister Angus Taylor's office in a political attack against Sydney's Lord Mayor Clover Moore." (Click here to read more)

Scott Morrison and Police Commissioner Fuller previously claimed to be neighbours and friends but are now trying to downplay their friendship.

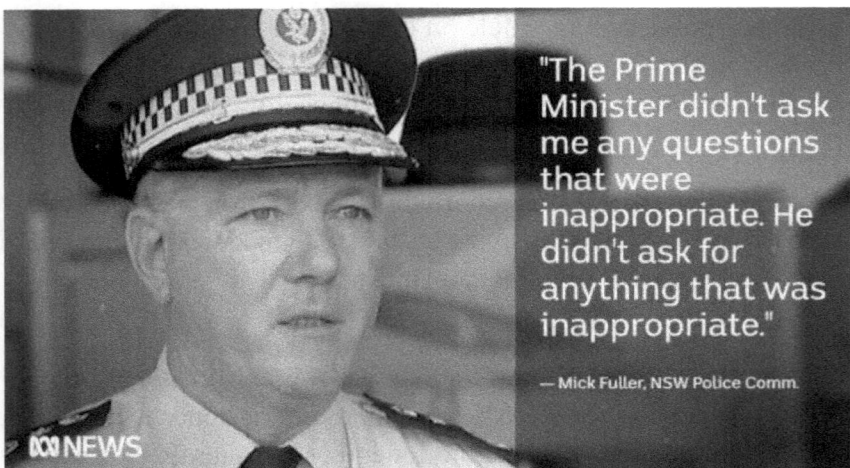

"The Prime Minister didn't ask me any questions that were inappropriate. He didn't ask for anything that was inappropriate."

— Mick Fuller, NSW Police Comm.

Putting two and two together it became obvious to me that if Prime Minister Scott Morrison phoned the NSW police to stick his nose into a police investigation into federal MP Angus Taylor then it is almost certain he would have also done the same for his good friend and mentor Brian Houston. So, I sent the below email to the NSW police media unit (27/11/19):

From: SHANE DOWLING
Sent: 27 November 2019 13:33
To: xxxxx@police.nsw.gov.au
Subject: Media request

Dear Sir/ Madam

Given Prime Minister Scott Morrison called NSW Police Commissioner Mick Fuller on Tuesday the 26th of November 2019 to discuss the police investigation into federal MP Angus Taylor only a few hours after the police investigation had been announced.

1. Has Scott Morrison at any stage also called Commissioner Fuller or any other police officer to discuss the police investigation into Hillsong Church Pastor Brian Houston?

2. Has anyone from Scott Morrison's office ever contacted anyone in the NSW police to discuss the police investigation into Hillsong Church Pastor Brian Houston?

Can you please respond by the close of business today so I can publish.

Regards

Shane Dowling

Kangaroo Court of Australia

At the time of writing this article, I haven't had a response from the police but they normally respond in a matter of minutes as the previous email shows, so it looks like the cover-up is in full swing. I'll follow-up in the near future.

Prime Minister Scott Morrison has always refused to answer questions about his attempt to take Brian Houston to the White House. But Scott Morrison had to have known at least since November 2018 that Brian Houston is under investigation by the NSW police, yet he still jumped on stage at the Hillsong Church in July 2019 with Brian Houston and also tried to take him to Washington in September 2019.

Scott Morrison just hopping on stage with Brian Houston and trying to take him to Washington would have put the investigating police in NSW under pressure to drop the charges against Brian Houston because they wouldn't want to embarrass the Prime Minister. That alone I think shows Scott Morrison is prepared to use his position as PM to interfere in a police investigation when it suits him for his own benefit.

Taking everything into account what is the chance that Scott Morrison has spoken to the NSW police either directly or indirectly via his staff to interfere in the Brian Houston police investigation? Almost certain I would say and the police wouldn't deny it when I emailed them.

Chapter 47

Circumstantial evidence that Scott Morrison directed the $100 million Sports Rorts fraud is being ignored by the media

Circumstantial evidence that Scott Morrison directed the $100 million Sports Rorts fraud is being ignored by the media

BY SHANE DOWLING ON FEBRUARY 1, 2020 • (13 COMMENTS)

Scott Morrison was sacked as CEO of Tourism Australia by the John Howard Liberal Party Government in 2006 for major financial fraud valued at $184 million which was almost identical to the current $100 million Sport Rorts fraud scandal. Both matters centre around abusing government processes and procedures to get money from the government. At Tourism Australia the tender process was abused and with Sports Rorts the process of allocating government grants was abused.

In both matters, Scott Morrison also refuses to answer questions or ducks and weaves to avoid giving direct answers. Although Morrison has denied he was a decision-maker in the Sports Rorts scandal but that lie is starting to unravel as the below video reports on the email trail linking Bridget McKenzie's fraudulent grants directly to Scott Morrison's office.

The Sports Rorts scandal is quite easy to understand. The government corruptly used $100 million in sports funding to try to buy votes in marginal seats or seats they were trying to win from other parties at the federal election in May 2019.

(The above video is from The Project on the 31/1/20)

Scott Morrison's history of government rorts by abusing processes and procedures

Some people try and throw doubt over why Morrison was sacked as CEO of Tourism Australia but I wrote an article in June 2019 titled "Looks like PM Scott Morrison was sacked as Managing Director of Tourism Australia in 2006 because of fraud and theft" and started off by saying:

"Prime Minister Scott Morrison was sacked as Managing Director of Tourism Australia in 2006 and he has always refused to say why. One thing is for certain, it had to be massive wrongdoing by Morrison. Why? Because Scott Morrison, who was State Director of the New South Wales Liberal Party from 2000 to 2004, was sacked by a Liberal Party Minister in the Liberal Party John Howard government and they don't sack one of their own for a minor reason or even a major reason. Morrison's sacking had to be something, at the very least,

bordering on criminal and more than likely actual criminal conduct. "

"Since 2006 Scott Morrison has refused to answer questions about his sacking and little has been known about the reasons for it until now. Journalist Karen Middleton published an article on Saturday (8/6/19) which she spent 6 months investigating and to me it makes it clear Morrison was likely sacked for deliberate lies and deception in relation to the awarding of government contracts worth $184 million." (Click here to read the full article)

Morrison has also "always refused to explain but he also left as the head of Tourism New Zealand in a hurry in 2000 with similar complaints about his performance and conduct." (Click here to read more)

Direct evidence versus circumstantial evidence in the Sports Rorts fraud

Direct evidence is starting to leak that Scott Morrison had direct input into the Sports Rorts fraud as the above video shows. But there is also plenty of circumstantial evidence showing Scott Morrison's history of abusing the system of government spending as per his 2006 sacking at Tourism Australia. It's an issue the old media in Canberra have failed to follow-up and they should have.

Scott Morrison was at the Canberra Press Club on Wednesday (29/1/20) giving a speech and the first few questions by the media hit hard on the Sports Rorts scandal but what Morrison did was fail to answer the questions or avoid giving any real answers. A legitimate question they should have asked would have been:

Q. Prime Minister Scott Morrison, given you were sacked as CEO of Tourism Australia by the John Howard Liberal Party government in 2006 for abusing the system in relation to a $184 million government tender why should anyone believe you weren't involved in the $100 Sports Rorts fraud scandal which is almost identical?

Chapter 48

Scott Morrison steals another $2 million to give to the Angus Taylor Cayman Island family trust

Scott Morrison steals another $2 million to give to the Angus Taylor Cayman Island family trust

BY SHANE DOWLING ON FEBRUARY 26, 2020 • (13 COMMENTS)

The Cayman Island company, Eastern Australia Agriculture, which was set up by federal MP Angus Taylor and corruptly given $80 million for water that didn't exist will get another $2 million for water that may or may not exist.

With the original $80 million purchase, the then agriculture minister Barnaby Joyce, had to rig it so he could pay well above market value so he got rid of the requirement for a tender process which is standard for government departments and then paid $millions more above market rates.

How many $millions will Scott Morrison and the government give to Eastern Australia Agriculture before the next election?

The chances of Barnaby Joyce having his own Cayman Island account, which ownership of are basically untraceable, would have to be red hot and the chances of some of the stolen funds being in it would be red hot as well.

When Barnaby was questioned on who the financial beneficiary of the original $80 million was, he refused to say for a long time but eventually said in one interview that it was a family trust. Given that Angus Taylor set up the company, but claims he no longer has an interest, one has to conclude the family trust is owned or controlled by Angus Taylor or one of his family members. If that's not the case Angus Taylor can correct the record by saying who the financial beneficiaries are which he would know but has refused to say.

One thing is for certain, both Angus Taylor and Barnaby Joyce know who is the financial beneficiary of the $80 million and who the true owners of Eastern Australia Agriculture are and given they won't say it is fair and reasonable they have a lot to hide. In those circumstances, it is also fair and reasonable for the public to use all available evidence to draw conclusions.

What the new $2 million fraud shows is that the Scott Morrison government doesn't care about being exposed acting corruptly. If they couldn't tell us who was ultimately getting the $80 million before why are they sending more money to the Cayman Islands?

Angus Taylor and Scott Morrison think stealing from taxpayers is all a big joke

What is also disturbing is that only one media outlet, The Guardian, has reported the new $2 million scam. And it has to be called a scam because we do not know who is getting the money and the government MP's who know, Joyce, Taylor, Littleproud and others won't say.

The Guardian report starts off:

The federal government is spending up to $2m buying water from Queensland agribusiness Eastern Australia Agriculture in a bid to keep an internationally significant wetlands from dying, despite paying $80m to the same company three years ago for water rights for the same purpose.

The $80m purchase of overland flows from Eastern Australia Agriculture has been controversial and is now under scrutiny by Australian National Audit Office.

The extremely large purchase was done without tender by the former agriculture minister Barnaby Joyce, who concluded that the opportunity was exceptional and that it warranted direct negotiations. (Click here to read more)

When Barnaby Joyce says he "concluded that the opportunity was exceptional and that it warranted direct negotiations" what he really meant was that it was an "exceptional" opportunity to rip off taxpayers $millions with his mate Angus Taylor.

Angus Taylor sent legal threats last year to journalists over his involvement in the fraud and theft but he has never backed it up and his lawyers refused to reply when I sent them questions last year. I take that as an admission by his lawyers that Angus Taylor was involved in the fraud and theft.

Federal Water Minister David Littleproud has to take responsibility for the scam

Water Minister David Littleproud has been crying about an article I published about him titled "Water Minister David Littleproud's family linked to $20 million Murray-Darling Basin fraud yet he is still Water Minister" as being false. He even used his appearance on the ABC's QandA program in October 2019 to attack social media and my article.

But Littleproud is now in a position where he can't duck responsibility because as Water Minister, he would at least have some say in water buybacks and would know, or could easily find out, who the financial beneficiaries of the new $2 million buyback are. That would also likely solve who the financial beneficiaries of the original $80 million Eastern Australia Agriculture fraud are.

Ultimately this is the same scam repeating itself and Scott Morrison has to take full responsibility because he has fostered the environment to allow it to happen and likely approved it himself given his previous form with rorts.

Chapter 49

Scott Morrison's lies start to unravel about his knowledge of the police investigation into paedophile protector Brian Houston

Scott Morrison's lies start to unravel about his knowledge of the police investigation into paedophile protector Brian Houston

BY SHANE DOWLING ON MARCH 7, 2020 • (9 COMMENTS)

Scott Morrison has admitted he lied about trying to take paedophile protector Brian Houston to the White House last September. Of course, Morrison doesn't call it a lie but what is a bigger lie that is impossible to dispute is Morrison also implying, on the recording below, that he didn't know Brian Houston was under investigation by the NSW Police for concealing his father's sexual abuse of children.

In September 2019 when it was reported that Brian Houston was rejected by the White House as a guest during Scott Morrison's visit all Morrison would say is that it was "gossip" when he was asked by the media if he had asked the White House to invite Houston. (Click here to read more)

Morrison told radio announcer Ben Fordham that in relation to Brian Houston being under investigation by the NSW police:

Prime Minister Scott Morrison: "So, I'm not quite sure what the accusation is about that"

Ben Fordham: "Well as I said it was relevant because as it turns out he was under police investigation and he still is according to NSW police. Would it be fair to say that you were not aware of that at the time?"

Prime Minister Scott Morrison: "No, these are not issues that I follow closely. All I know is that they are a very large and very well attended and well-supported organisation here in Australia"

What "issue" doesn't he "follow closely". That has to be admission he knew at least at some point that Brian Houston was under investigation by the police.

Below is the recording that lasts 1 minute and 22 seconds.

Scott Morrison also talks about the Hillsong Church and claims that Brian Houston was invited to the White House later as a guest and that President Donald Trump didn't have an issue with Brian Houston being at the White House because he was there a few months after Scott Morrison.

From what I understand is that Brian Houston was not at the White House as a guest but was there on a tour with other people from similar organisations in the US.

The lies of Scott Morrison in the Ben Fordham interview

Morrison says in relation to the scandal of trying to take Houston with him to the White House: "I'm not quite sure what the accusation is about that". It's been all over the media for months what the issue was and Morrison says he doesn't know what the accusation is. That's a blatant lie.

Morrison then says: "No, these are not issues that I follow closely".

Let's have a look at some of the facts.

1. Brian Houston's lies were exposed at the Child Sex Abuse Royal Commission in 2014 where he was caught covering up his father's sexual abuse of boys and which he perjured himself like no tomorrow in the witness stand under oath. (Click here to read more)

2. 60 Minutes did a story on one of Frank Houston's victims, Brett Sengstock, in November 2018 and also reported: "Brian Houston, the founder of the Hillsong Church, is under investigation by New South Wales police over his handling of the sex crimes committed by his father Frank Houston." A NSW police spokesman said the investigation has been reopened and is now "current and active". (Click here to read more)

3. On the 13th of July 2019, after I contacted the NSW police on the 10/7/19, I reported: "Prime Minister Scott Morrison and his wife were on stage leading prayers in front of 21,000 people on Tuesday night (9/7/19) with the Hillsong Church's Brian Houston who is still under investigation by the NSW police for concealing the sexual

abuse of children by his father Frank Houston." (Click here to read more)

4. After I reported that the NSW police were still investigating Brian Houston other media over the next few months also contacted the police and reported that they were still investigating Brian Houston. For example, The New Daily reported it in September 2019 and The Guardian also reported it in October 2019.

Royal Commission
into Institutional Responses
to Child Sexual Abuse

Brian Houston

Brian Houston at the Child Sex Abuse Royal Commission in 2014 giving perjured evidence

This story has been pumping all over social media for a year and especially since July 2019 when Morrison and his wife hopped on stage with Brian Houston to help him promote Hillsong. Yet Scott Morrison says "I'm not quite sure what the accusation is about that" and "No, these are not issues that I follow closely."

When Brian Houston was rejected by the White House it is almost certain it was because he was under investigation by the NSW police and Morrison would have been told, so again it's impossible for Morrison to now say he didn't know.

Brian Houston confessed he failed to go to the police when he knew his father had abused children which he also admitted on national TV as per the below video. Given Houston's admission, a powerful prima facie case has been made to charge Houston with concealing a crime and put those charges before a jury or judge to decide. So, why haven't the police charged Houston?

Brian Houston has refused to be interviewed by police but they don't need to interview him with his public confession.

The Police investigation started in 2015, stopped in 2017 and started again when 60 Minutes broadcast their story in 2018. All roads lead back to NSW Police Commissioner Mick Fuller who has been in the top job since March 2017 and the previous Commissioner Andrew Scipione. Scipione was, and possibly still is, a Hillsong Church member and he went to Frank Houston's funeral in 2004. There can be no doubt that it is a police cover-up. There can be no doubt that Commissioner Fuller, and Commissioner Scipione before him, have instructed police not to charge Houston.

Prime Minister Scott Morrison has advisors all over the place and he has a large team that follows the media as well as social media. And it must be remembered that Scott Morrison says Brian Houston is a close friend and mentor, yet he claims he knows nothing about the police investigation.

What really needs to be investigated is Scott Morrison's relationship with NSW Police Commissioner Mick Fuller especially after Morrison rang Fuller when it was announced that the police were investigating federal MP Angus Taylor. Are we to believe that Morrison would ring Commissioner Fuller on behalf of Angus Taylor but not ring Fuller in relation to his friend Brian Houston?

When I sent the NSW police media department questions asking if there was any interference by Scott Morrison in the Brian Houston matter they refused to answer. (Click here to read more)

Whatever the case Morrison has raised more questions then he answered. Probably the worst thing is that Morrison never apologized to the survivors when Ben Fordham made him aware that Brian Houston was still under investigation by the NSW police. And that would be because Scott Morrison already knew, and he didn't care.

One last point. Morrison said: "No, these are not issues that I follow closely. All I know is that they are a very large and very well attended and well-supported organisation here in Australia." Which could be translated to Morrison saying that survivors don't matter to him but a large organisation with lots of votes does count. And why does Morrison call it an organisation? I thought they claimed it was a Church.

Scott Morrison has a lot more questions to answer on this issue and he owes it to the survivors to tell the truth.

(Update: Brian Houston was charged by the police in late 2021 and will likely face trial in 2022)

Chapter 50

Has Scott Morrison's best mates David Gazard and Peter Costello again fraudulently profited from Australia's $90 billion Liberal Party / submarine slush fund?

Has Scott Morrison's best mates David Gazard and Peter Costello again fraudulently profited from Australia's $90 billion Liberal Party / submarine slush fund?

BY SHANE DOWLING ON MAY 9, 2020 • (6 COMMENTS)

Australia's $90 billion submarine contract was only finalised in 2019 after Scott Morrison's best mates David Gazard and Peter Costello were cut into the action by Morrison. That alone says there needs to be an open and public inquiry into the contract.

On Wednesday (6/5/20) further details were reported about suspect financial decisions regarding the deal.

The Australian defence force approved Australian taxpayer-funded pay rises and bonuses for the staff at the French-owned

Naval Group Australia even though "the project is already billions of dollars over budget and years behind schedule".

Defence has refused to reveal who in the department approved the remuneration changes and referred all questions on Naval Group's employment conditions and pay to the company.

South Australian crossbench Senator Rex Patrick labelled the pay rises and bonuses granted during the coronavirus pandemic "offensive". (Click here to read more) Someone somewhere in the government pulled strings to make it happen and who phoned them to make it happen? Was it David Gazard or Peter Costello?

When the contract was announced in 2016 it was valued at $50 billion. I published an article in April 2016 titled "Bribery allegations against Australia's $50 billion submarine contract winner".

Wind the clock forward to the 16th of February 2019 and I published an article titled "Prime Minister Scott Morrison, his best mate David Gazard and the $50 billion submarine scam"

As you can see from the previous articles there are numerous Liberal Party cronies, some who are friends with Prime Minister Scott Morrison, who are and/or have been profiting from the $90 billion submarine contract. That likely explains why in the middle of the Coronavirus crises, where millions are losing their jobs, Naval Group Australia was able to get the government to give their staff pay rises and bonuses even though they are behind schedule and over budget.

With so many Liberal Party cronies with their snouts in the trough with the $90 billion deal they want things to run smoothly so I suspect they have jumped on the phone to the government and made things happen. And given it was David Gazard's and Peter Costello's company that was paid to help negotiate the original deal were they paid to negotiate the pay deal with the government?

This week it was also reported that the federal government has spent almost two years trying to hide a critical report being made public regarding another $1.3 billion defence contract with French company Thales. Apparently, the report suggested Australia could have paid half the amount for a different vehicle through a United States military program. As I said above, Thales is well-known for bribing government officials which is a possible reason why the government is trying to hide the report. (Click here to read more)

So how did the contract go from $50 billion in 2016, and again confirmed in February 2019 as being worth $50 billion, to now being worth $90 billion? Whose pocket is the extra $40 billion in?

David Gazard and Peter Costello are not only Scott Morrison's friends but also his political advisors and the whole $90 billion submarine contract with Naval Group Australia absolutely reeks of fraud and theft by Liberal Party cronies.

. . . .

In 2021 Scott Morrison cancelled the submarine contract which raised more questions than it answered.

Two more articles that are a must read on the submarine scam are: *"France had Scott Morrison's mate David Gazard on their payroll for the $90 billion Submarine scam. Has Morrison pulled off one of the biggest stings ever?"* that was published on the 26th of September 2021 and:

"Malcolm Turnbull called President Emmanuel Macron to talk about the $90 billion cancelled Submarine deal. Why? What's in it for Turnbull?" that was published on the 3rd of October 2021 and reports that "former South African President Jacob Zuma is currently facing trial for allegedly taking a bribe for a $2 billion defence contract with the French" and former Malaysian Prime Minister Najib Razak allegedly taking a bribe from the French for a submarine contract.

Chapter 51

Scott Morrison uses the COVID-19 crises as cover for government corruption

Scott Morrison uses the COVID-19 crises as cover for government corruption

BY SHANE DOWLING ON JUNE 20, 2020 • (6 COMMENTS)

Scott Morrison tried to label Labor's Anthony Albanese with the corruption tag in Parliament on Thursday (18/6/20) and it backfired badly as The Speaker of the House pulled Morrison up and demanded a withdrawal as per the below video. It did make the news but only a small edited version and it is the full 1 minute and 45 seconds that tells the real story of Morrison not dealing with pressure and trying to bully.

Labor has had branch stacking corruption issues to deal with over the last week in Victoria and NSW but not at the federal level except for some foul-mouthed Tweets by one MP.

While on the other hand the number of corruption issues that Scott Morrison is covering-up grows by the day and includes, but is not limited to, Sports Rorts, Community Development Grants rorts, Robodebt, Water rights and the Hillsong cover-up etc. Cartoonist Alan Moir makes the point below:

Probably the 2 biggest scandals that Morrison has used the COVED-19 crisis to cover-up are the $2.5 billion regional grants scheme fraud and the Sports Rorts scandal with new email evidence showing that the Prime Minister's office was directing the Sports Rorts grants and not Bridgit McKenzie.

The Guardian reported on the 11th of May:

Just before we get to the new information, some quick background in case you've forgotten. Morrison has consistently minimised his role and the role of his office in this affair. He's consistently said the former sports minister Bridget McKenzie was the decision-maker for the grants, and his office just passed on feedback from MPs about meritorious projects.

With that backstory in your mind, let's get to the new information. Last Friday, the ANAO told the Senate in answers to questions on notice that Morrison's office asked McKenzie on 26 March to seek prime ministerial "authority" for intended recipients of $100m of sports grants, and to coordinate the announcement with Coalition campaign headquarters.

Assuming the ANAO is correct in this account, this suggests Morrison and his office were hands-on in the process, not spectators. Reminding the minister she needs authority to proceed is not being a glorified inbox forwarding service, it's establishing a chain of command.

The ANAO's tick-tock is particularly problematic, because before the Covid-19 crisis consumed everything, on 27 February, Morrison was asked a series of questions in parliament about his role. Morrison's answer to one of the questions in the House of Representatives was clear: "There was no authorisation provided by me as prime minister on the projects." (Click here to read more)

Morrison has still been using the COVID-19 crisis to refuse to answer questions about Sports Rorts and other corruption. You'll see him at press conferences belittling journalists that ask him about corruption issues.

In the last few weeks, the Community Development Grants program has been exposed as another pork-barrel slush fund for the federal coalition.

The New Daily reported in June:

I was wrong. The Community Development Grants program isn't the Coalition's hot $1.126 billion political rort – it's the Coalition's hot $2.5 billion-plus political rort.

It's not 11 times bigger than #sportsrorts, it's 25 times bigger and counting.

The government has a number of corrupt slush funds, but none more blatantly designed to buy votes with taxpayers' money than the CDG scheme purpose built in 2014.

As reported last week, analysis of the government's GrantConnect website showed Coalition seats "luckily" scored 75.5 per cent of last year's CDG money, while Labor seats managed just 19.9 per cent.

Of the 68 federal seats Labor now holds, 22 have never received a cent in CDGs while those that did score will tend to be of particular political interest or history. (Click here to read more)

If you haven't heard of the Community Development Grants program fraud you will as opposition Senators have gone fishing looking for information as The New Daily reported a few days ago:

The Senate passed a Greens motion on Monday ordering the Minister for Infrastructure, Regional Development and Cities to table documents by Wednesday relating to the government's $2.5 billion Community Development Grants rort.

The relevant minister, Deputy Prime Minister Michael McCormack, has prior form in not complying with a Senate Order for Production of Documents (OPD) when shedding light on rampant pork barrelling might prove embarrassing.

Senators Larissa Waters and Janet Rice won sufficient support for a motion seeking CDG documentation.

They may have more success than Labor did last year seeking documents on the government's rorted regional grants scheme.

The key difference is that the CDG racket was carefully crafted to avoid any embarrassing assessment of grant suitability by public servants, as happened with the regional grants and #sportsrorts. (Click here to read more)

The Community Development Grants rort is 25 times the size of the Sports Rorts scandal so at some time in the future, it will hit the government like a sledgehammer which might help explain why Scott Morrison was feeling the pressure in the above video trying to label Anthony Albanese as corrupt.

By Friday (19/6/20) the hashtag #LibSpill was trending on Twitter which is used when parties are having a leadership challenge. It was nothing more than wishful thinking as no one will challenge Morrison now but in 6 months time, it could be a different story.

Chapter 52

Scott Morrison and the Alex Hawke MP branch stacking scandal

Scott Morrison and the Alex Hawke MP branch stacking scandal

BY SHANE DOWLING ON JULY 11, 2020 • (13 COMMENTS)

A branch stacking scandal involving Scott Morrison's key ally, right-hand man in the federal parliament and Hillsong Church member Alex Hawke MP is finally going to be investigated after the Liberal Party have spent the last 2 years trying to sweep it under the carpet.

It was reported last Sunday (5/7/20) that a former NSW ICAC investigator has been appointed to lead an inquiry into allegations that Alex Hawke altered minutes of a branch meeting which should have shown that 10 new members, who were in a competing faction to Alex Hawke, were refused voting rights.

Mr Hawke is said to deny the allegations, but the inquiry was only set up after some of the 10 people who were denied their voting rights threatened legal action which is not a good look for the Liberal Party and Alex Hawke. (Click here to read more)

Branch stacking usually refers to adding false members to a political party but in this case, it was an attempt to block members joining the Liberal Party because they were in an opposing faction to Alex Hawke.

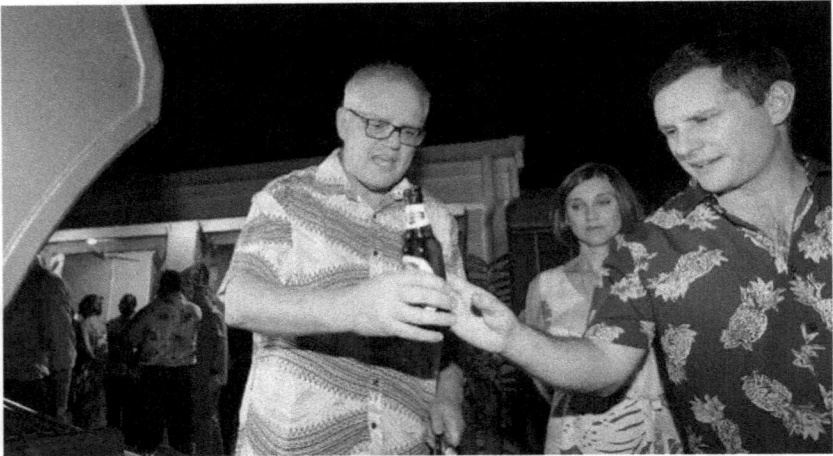

Scott Morrison and Alex Hawke

What is also disturbing about the inquiry is that Rupert Murdoch's The Sydney Telegraph and Sky News reported it had an "EXCLUSIVE" last Sunday the day after the by-election in Eden Monaro which was a close election with less than 1000 votes in it. How long had Murdoch's media been sitting on the story?

One of the key issues that the Liberal Party pushed in Eden Monaro was Labor Party corruption which they referenced the recent branch stacking scandal in Victoria as an example of Labor's corruption. While Scott Morrison and the Liberal's were promoting Labor Party branch stacking as a reason that Eden-Monaro voters should not vote for the Labor Party at the same time Scott Morrison and the Liberals, with the help of Murdoch's media, were concealing from voters their own branch stacking scandal.

Also last Sunday, the day after the election, the SMH published a story extremely damaging to Scott Morrison and the Liberal

Party titled "Morrison ditched Turnbull-era plans for greater transparency in political lobbying" which starts off:

"One of the Morrison government's first acts was to quietly kill off Malcolm Turnbull's plan for greater transparency about how lobbyists interact with the federal government, leaving in place a system widely regarded as ineffective and described as "light touch" by auditors." (Click here to read more)

The SMH is owned by Nine Entertainment whose chairman is former federal treasurer and Liberal Party member Peter Costello who also happens to be a close political advisor to Scott Morrison which might explain why they held the story until the day after the election.

It's also interesting that Nine Entertainment's Sixty Minutes and the SMH were happy to run a story two weeks before the Eden Monaro by-election on the Labor Party's branch stacking scandal in Victoria. Whenever a public interest story is ready to be published it should be, but Nine and the SMH received criticism from Labor Party supporters for publishing it 2 weeks before the election and then Nine clearly holds up the "Morrison ditched Turnbull-era plans for greater transparency in political lobbying" story until a day after the election.

Nine Entertainment is starting to look more and more like the Murdoch media.

The article I published last week titled "Rupert Murdoch and David McBride etc. What Australian media fail to report" dealt with public interest stories the old media were failing to report and as part of the article I raised two stories that should have been published before the Eden Monaro election. But the media manipulation was worse than I thought as the day after the election the above Liberal Party / Alex Hawke branch stacking storey appeared in the Murdoch media and the above Scott Morrison – lobbyist – lack of transparency article appeared in the SMH.

If both the Murdoch media and Nine Entertainment had of run the above stories before the Eden Monaro by-election like they should have it would have cost the Liberal Party a lot of votes and that is why they held the stories up until the day after the election. And the old media and their journalists wonder why they get bagged and ridiculed on social media. Next time you see an old media journalist having a whinge about how they don't get the respect they believe they deserve to get send them the link to this article.

The good news is the old media companies are all on the back foot in a major way and they won't survive because they no longer keep governments to account like they are meant to.

Chapter 53

Scott Morrison helps with the cover-up of the Barnaby Joyce run Watergate fraud which now totals at least $190 million

Scott Morrison helps with the cover-up of the Barnaby Joyce run Watergate fraud which now totals at least $190 million

BY SHANE DOWLING ON JULY 18, 2020 • (16 COMMENTS)

The estimated value of the fraud that Barnaby Joyce orchestrated when he was federal Water Minister has grown to at least $190 million with the Australian National Audit Office (ANAO) releasing a report on Thursday (16/7/20).

The report found that on Barnaby's watch the department only used a "limited tender" process which really means there was no real tender process and the whole system was corrupted.

It's well-known that Barnaby Joyce got rid of the requirement for tenders, at least for the $80 million Angus Taylor / Cayman Island fraud which was done without a tender.

The ANAO investigated $190 million of water buybacks which based on the report were done no better than the $80 million Angus Taylor / Cayman Island fraudulent water buyback so the whole $190 million spent on water buybacks likely involves fraud to some degree.

The blatant corruption is obvious in the ANAO report where at paragraph 16 it says "The department only negotiated price for one procurement". Why did they only negotiate on price for one purchase? That is one hell of a red flag pointing to government employees involved in fraud which we know was done on the direction of Barnaby Joyce and that's why he got rid of the tender process.

Calling it a "limited tender" process is a joke because it is really nothing more than a process deliberately designed to help facilitate fraud. The report goes on to say in paragraph 16:

"The department did not develop a framework designed to maximise the value for money of strategic water entitlements purchased through limited tender arrangements. Rather, the department relied on a methodology of valuations where gap-bridging water was required. The price the department paid for water entitlements was equal to or less than the maximum price determined by valuations. The department only negotiated price for one procurement." (Click here to read the report)

When the $80 million Angus Taylor / Cayman Island fraud was being exposed on social media in April 2019 just before the May 2019 federal election Angus threatened legal action against 2 journalists and I sent his lawyers the below email:

From: SHANE DOWLING
Sent: 22 April 2019 21:19
To: mark.obrien@markobrienlegal.com.au; paul.svilans@markobrienlegal.com.au
Cc: steven.lewis@markobrienlegal.com.au; monica.allen@markobrienlegal.com.au; tihana.mandic@markobrienlegal.com.au
Subject: Notice of intention to publish allegations regarding your client Angus Taylor – Criminal conduct by lawyer Paul Svilans

Dear Mr O'Brien and Mr Svilans

I will be publishing on my website in the near future a copy of the Tweet thread that was published on the 10th of April 2019 titled "Money For Nothing" (and your tricks for free)" published by Ms Ronni Salt @MsVeruca and & Jommy Tee – electric HiLux owner @jommy_tee which you threatened defamation proceedings against journalists Michael West and Margo Kingston for Retweeting as you claimed it defamed your client Federal MP Angus Taylor.

I have had time to have a look at the material and situation and it does not defame your client so I intend on publishing it on my website as it is in the public interest to do so especially given we have a federal election only weeks away. Even if it did defame your client, which it doesn't, it is protected as political communication which I am sure both of you are aware as per the High Court judgment Lange v Australian Broadcasting Corporation (1997) 189 CLR 520.

I should also bring to your attention that your conduct in making baseless threats to journalists could and would be construed by a court of law as an attempt to conceal the serious indictable offences that your client has been involved in. E.g the fraud and theft of taxpayers money by Angus Taylor and Barnaby Joyce in the #watergate scam. So, be careful of what you say and who you threaten otherwise you might find yourselves facing criminal charges.

I approached Barnaby Joyce (via Twitter) and asked him who are the lawyers he claims he is talking to in regards to #watergate but he has not responded. Are you also representing Barnaby Joyce?

If you would like to respond or make comment by 5pm Tuesday the 23rd of April 2019 I will be happy to add that as part of my article.

Regards

Shane Dowling

<u>Kangaroo Court of Australia</u>

End of email

Angus Taylor's lawyers never responded to the email nor did Angus Taylor sue the journalists.

The Angus Taylor – Barnaby Joyce $80 million #Watergate fraud involved a company associated with Angus Taylor, Eastern Australia Agriculture which is based in the Cayman Islands, receiving an $80 million windfall for selling water, that did not exist, to the federal government.

The Scott Morrison government gave Eastern Australia Agriculture another $2 million in February 2020 even after the first $80 million has been shown to be a blatant scam. I published an article titled "Scott Morrison steals another $2 million to give to the Angus Taylor Cayman Island family trust" on the 26/2/20 and said:

The Cayman Island company, Eastern Australia Agriculture, which was set up by federal MP Angus Taylor and corruptly given <u>$80 million for water that didn't exist</u> will get another $2 million for water that may or may not exist.

With <u>the original $80 million purchase</u>, the then agriculture minister Barnaby Joyce, had to rig it so he could pay well above market value so he got rid of the requirement for a tender process which is standard for government departments and then paid $millions more above market rates.

How many $millions will Scott Morrison and the government give to Eastern Australia Agriculture before the next election? (<u>Click here to read the full article</u>)

Former federal Liberal Party leader John Hewson wrote an article published in the SMH of Friday (17/7/20) which started off:

"Scott Morrison has stated he wants to govern in the "Howard tradition", but sadly that has also entailed adopting the worst of John Howard's strategies: to admit or explain as little as possible." (Click here to read more)

Right on cue Scott Morrison and the government announced today, Saturday (18/7/20), that the next fortnight sitting of Federal Parliament has been cancelled due to the coronavirus crisis. The SMH reported:

Parliament was going to sit for a fortnight from August 4 but the next sitting week, in which the government can pass legislation and the opposition can scrutinise its agenda, will now be from August 24.

Prime Minister Scott Morrison said he did not believe it would be right to exclude parliamentarians from one state – in a reference to Victoria, where new cases have hit successive records in recent days. (Click here to read more)

Scott Morrison has cancelled parliament for one reason and one reason only. He doesn't want the opposition politicians asking questions about government corruption like the Watergate fraud above which was exposed again last Thursday with the ANAO report.

And there are many other corruption scandals that Scott Morrison and the government don't want to answer questions about either. They are playing the old game of dragging it out as long as possible hoping people will forget.

The politicians in Victoria, and NSW if need be, can easily watch the parliament proceedings on TV or the internet because they are broadcast live and if there is an issue with that then Hansard, which is a transcript of parliament proceedings, is published on a daily basis as well.

The politicians in federal government are in a better position than almost everyone else in the country to do their job remotely because of the fact that parliament is broadcast live and transcribed.

Scott Morrison has already cancelled numerous sitting days for parliament this year and he wants everyone else to go to work and school children to go to school etc but he cancels parliament because he doesn't want to answer questions about all the government corruption scandals.

Like former federal Liberal Party leader John Hewson said, Morrison wants "to admit or explain as little as possible" and one of the best ways to do that is avoid being questioned in parliament which is exactly what he has done by cancelling parliament.

With the increased government spending during the Covid19 crisis, it leads to the increased possibility of fraud and that means there should be more scrutiny of government, not less.

Chapter 54

Scott Morrison says Woodside Energy bribing former foreign minister Alexander Downer $millions is OK

Scott Morrison says Woodside Energy bribing former foreign minister Alexander Downer $millions is OK

BY SHANE DOWLING ON JULY 26, 2020 • (15 COMMENTS)

In 2004 Australian gas and oil company Woodside Energy bribed then Foreign Affairs Minister Alexander Downer and the then head of the Department of Foreign Affairs Ashton Calvert to bug East Timor's (Timor-Leste) government offices. This was because Woodside had a huge financial interest in Australia's maritime border with East Timor which the two countries were negotiating at the time and the bugging was to give Australia an advantage in the negotiations.

East Timor had only had independence since 1999 and the Australian Government were trying to rip off a third world country on behalf of Woodside Energy who were headed up by Chairman Charles Goode "who sat on the boards of top Liberal Party fundraising vehicles that generated millions of dollars in political donations."

"The late Ashton Calvert, became a director of Woodside nine months after his retirement from Foreign Affairs, and very soon after the bugging." (Click here to read more) Alexander Downer jumped on the Woodside gravy train as a "consultant" not long after he left politics in 2008.

Woodside Energy currently has former Federal Resources and Energy Minister Ian Macfarlane (Liberal Party) as a Director.

In 2013 Australia's bugging of East Timor's government offices was exposed by Witness K and lawyer Bernard Collaery. When the bugging was exposed East Timor took Australia to the International Arbitration Tribunal to try and have the original deal made null and void and then to negotiate a better deal.

Witness K and Bernard Collaery were charged for exposing the Australian Government's criminal conduct and are currently before the court in the ACT. Witness K and Bernard Collaery were charged in June 2018 when Malcolm Turnbull was still PM but the court case now has Scott Morrison's fingerprints on it and he should withdraw the charges.

The story has been broadcast on Four Corners in 2014 and written about many times by various journalists and they always layout the facts that leave no one in doubt that Australian politicians and government officials were bribed by Woodside Energy to help Woodside's commercial interests. Yet the journalists never go that extra step and actually say it.

I'm happy to go the extra step and say that Woodside bribed Alexander Downer, Ashton Calvert and possibly others to bug East Timor's government offices and that should be investigated. Woodside should be made to reveal how much they paid Calvert and Downer.

In the video below, from the ABC in 2015, former NSW Director of Public Prosecutions, Nick Cowdery says Witness K and Bernard Collaery have committed no crimes.

Mr Cowdery also says there is a prima facie case to charge numerous Australian government officials with criminal charges for the bugging of East Timor's government offices. Mr Cowdery says if Alexander Downer directed the bugging, he could also face criminal charges.

In the above video, Bernard Collaery says there needs to be a Royal Commission and he is right. Anything less is a massive cover-up.

The above helps explain why the Scott Morrison government are throwing everything they can at trying to persecute Witness K and Bernard Collaery using the courts because they have exposed Liberal Party corruption at the highest level.

Some people might think that Alexander Downer is long gone from the Liberal Party government and they wouldn't run the court case against Witness K and Bernard Collaery to protect him.

Well, Alexander Downer still thinks he has influence with the government and he Tweeted on the 29th of June while he was watching the ABC's QandA program:

I'm going to advise the government not to participate in @QandA One minister and all the rest are political opponents. Better to leave it entirely as a @AustralianLabor @Greens show. The one @LiberalAus guest is only there to be denigrated.

10:49 PM · Jun 29, 2020 · Twitter for iPhone

And Alexander Downer's daughter Georgina Downer ran for the Liberal Party at the last federal election for Alexander's old seat of Mayo in South Australia which shows that Alexander still has some influence in the Party.

Alexander Downer and Georgina Downer

I plan on digging a lot further in this matter and you can help by emailing or tweeting the various government officials and asking them questions. Alexander Downer can be found here on

Twitter: @AlexanderDowner and the federal Attorney-General Christian Porter is at @cporterwa. The benefit of sending them questions on Twitter is that it is public, and everyone can see.

If Witness K and Bernard Collaery are jailed it won't help Scott Morrison and the government as it will escalate the problem tenfold by shining an even bigger torch on the issue.

Chapter 55

Scott Morrison's Hillsong mate Leigh Coleman who has allegations of fraud and bribery against him given $42 million in government grants

Scott Morrison's Hillsong mate Leigh Coleman who has allegations of fraud and bribery against him given $42 million in government grants

BY SHANE DOWLING ON SEPTEMBER 5, 2020 • (10 COMMENTS)

Leigh Coleman who is a former Hillsong Church executive and close friend of Prime Minister Scott Morrison has had numerous allegations of fraud made against him over the last 15 years including attempted bribery yet his company ServeGate Australia has still managed to be awarded $43 million in government contracts since 2015.

During the same period that ServeGate Australia was being awarded the $43 million in contracts due to the "strong business relations with decision-makers at very high levels including Ministers" as their website says, Scott Morrison was appointed

Treasurer in September 2015 and became Prime Minister in August 2018. So, was Scott Morrison involved in any way?

ServeGate Australia is now a registered tax-free charity and its operations are suspicious to say the least where they don't seem to do much work except take a percentage off the top and then sub-contract the real work out to other companies. This has been exposed in an article in The Guardian, but we'll get back to that in a minute because we should look at Leigh Coleman's past handiwork first, of fraud and bribery allegations, when he was at Hillsong Church and an organisation called Many Rivers which is also a registered tax-free charity.

Leigh Coleman's fraud and theft from Aborigines while working at Hillsong Church

In 2005 allegations were made that Leigh Armstrong and Hillsong Church tried a swifty to rip off the Riverstone Aboriginal Community Association but when caught out they tried to bribe them to keep quiet. The SMH reported:

THE Hillsong Church has denied it used an Aboriginal community to secure a federal grant and then tried to bribe the community to keep silent.

A Labor MP, Ian West, told the NSW Parliament last month the church's charitable arm, Hillsong Emerge, "misused" the Riverstone Aboriginal Community Association to apply for a $415,000 crime-prevention grant from the Federal Government.

Mr West said Hillsong used the community "to get taxpayers' money for its own purposes" and then "lamely tried to dole out some of the money in return for their co-option".

"Taxpayer funding which is needed for local disadvantaged communities is now being channelled directly into Hillsong's bank accounts," he said.

Mr West said Hillsong plagiarised funding proposals which were supposed to be made as part of a joint application with the Riverstone association.

In August, the Prime Minister, John Howard, announced the grant to Hillsong but did not mention the involvement of Riverstone or any other partners.

The head of Hillsong, Leigh Coleman, later wrote to the community offering to give it $280,000 from the grant.

Mr West said this was an attempt "to pay off the Riverstone Aboriginal Community Association in return for its silence".

Last week he told Parliament he had since been branded a "liar" during Hillsong services. (Click here to read more)

Mr West being "branded a "liar" during Hillsong services" suggests Brian Houston was involved at least to some degree.

In 2006 Leigh Coleman's operation at Hillsong Emerge – the evangelical group's former benevolent arm – had its funding discontinued after revelations the vast majority of taxpayer dollars went to employing staff. (Click here to read more)

It was also reported in 2006:

Indigenous development grants to Hillsong's benevolent arm have gone almost entirely to employing and providing offices for church staff, with only a trickle reaching Aborigines.

In one case, Hillsong Emerge spent $315,000 in federal funds employing seven of its own staff in Sydney to administer a "micro-credit" project that made only six loans to Aborigines worth an average of $2856 each.

Hillsong also failed to enable a single Aborigine to become self-employed under a $610,968 federal grant to encourage indigenous entrepreneurship. The $610,968 grant was approved in just three weeks, and Hillsong faced no competition since it was the only applicant.

The revelations are contained in answers from senator Eric Abetz, representing Employment Minister Kevin Andrews, to a detailed series of questions on notice from Labor's indigenous affairs spokesman, Chris Evans.

They show that far more funds are spent on Hillsong staffers and administration than actual service delivery. One federal grant paid $965,421 to Hillsong Emerge to administer $280,000 in loan funds. (Click here to read more)

No need to worry about Leigh Coleman: "In 2006 it was reported the Federal Government admitted he received $80,000 of federal indigenous development funds to top up his salary, despite having only indirect involvement in projects run by Hillsong Emerge. Mr Coleman declined to comment." (Click here to read more)

Leigh Coleman's fraud and theft from Aborigines while working at Many Rivers Microfinance

In 2011 News.com reported:

A CHRISTIAN charity which has so far spent more than $1.3 million to generate just $330,000 in loans for Indigenous Australians is being investigated.

Many Rivers Microfinance is run by a former Hillsong executive who has already come under parliamentary scrutiny over an earlier loans program that delivered only a trickle of funds to the Indigenous community.

In 2006 Leigh Coleman's operation at Hillsong Emerge – the evangelical group's former benevolent arm – had its funding discontinued after revelations the vast majority of taxpayer dollars went to employing staff.

Mr Coleman's current program at Many Rivers has since successfully raised millions of dollars from the Federal Government and some of the country's biggest companies including Rio Tinto, BHP Billiton and Westpac.

But since its inception in 2007 to the end of the 2010 financial year the latest available records show it has delivered just 74 microenterprise loans worth a total of $330,000.

While declining to provide evidence as to how the reported $1.375 million had been spent delivering them, the charity said that – like the discontinued Hillsong pilot – the bulk had gone on staff salaries and training.

Mr Coleman, who is chief executive officer, a director and also a company member of Many Rivers, declined requests to be interviewed. (Click here to read more)

Leigh Coleman speaking in support of a controversial Hillsong superchurch in Sydney where he identified himself as a "local resident". The proposed church failed to attract community support and was withdrawn. Vera Coleman is seated bottom left.

Leigh Coleman seems to be a serial fraudster who also uses charities to dog tax and avoid accountability.

Leigh Coleman and his new tax-free charity ServeGate Australia

The Guardian published an article on the 4/9/20 titled "The unconventional charity run by Scott Morrison's 'dear friend' Leigh Coleman" which starts off:

A company founded and run by a man the prime minister, Scott Morrison, describes as "a very dear friend" has received more than $43m in government contracts since 2015, mostly from defence, while being a registered charity helping Indigenous businesses with advice.

The company, ServeGate Australia, has as its founding CEO Leigh Coleman, who Morrison mentioned in his maiden speech as a key influence on his life. Its nominated charitable purposes are to increase Aboriginal employment and reduce welfare dependency.

The unconventional ServeGate model – described by Coleman as "unique" – involves contracting with the commonwealth government then subcontracting the work to conventional – almost all non-Indigenous – small and medium professional services companies.

Profits from the government work subsidise Coleman and other staff members' salaries while they provide advice to a small number of selected Indigenous businesses.

The company's website makes no mention of its charity status, and some companies that received subcontracted work through ServeGate have told Guardian Australia they were not aware it was a charity. (Click here to read more)

The Guardian article is well researched and left me in no doubt that Leigh Coleman is up to his old tricks as the company is very light on detail when asked basic questions and their answers are contradicted by others which suggest they are lying.

It's no surprise that friends of Scott Morrison are involved in government fraud. Scott Morrison's good mates David Gazard and Peter Costello have done very well out of Australia's $50 billion submarine contract because of their links to Morrison. (Click here to read more)

And Peter Costello returned the favour by using his position as Nine Entertainment Chairman and had a fundraiser at Channel Nine studios at Sydney to raise $700,000 for the Liberal Party. (Click here to read more)

It should be remembered that Scott Morrison was sacked by the Liberal Party in 2006 for likely fraud when he was Managing Director of Tourism Australia. I wrote an article on the matter which started off:

Prime Minister Scott Morrison was sacked as Managing Director of Tourism Australia in 2006 and he has always refused to say why. One thing is for certain, it had to be massive wrongdoing by Morrison. Why? Because Scott Morrison, who was State Director of the New South Wales Liberal Party from 2000 to 2004, was sacked by a Liberal Party Minister in the Liberal Party John Howard government and they don't sack one of their own for a minor reason or even a major reason. Morrison's sacking had to be something, at the very least, bordering on criminal and more than likely actual criminal conduct. (Click here to read more)

The question that Scott Morrison needs to answer is what involvement has he had helping Leigh Coleman and his so-called charity ServeGate Australia getting the $43 million in government contracts?

. . . .

Update: On the 13th of February 2022 I published an article titled "Scott Morrison's Hillsong mate Leigh Coleman, an alleged fraudster and crook, set to break $100 million in government contracts".

Closing arguments

What the book is about is highlighting documented corruption and alleged corruption that the old media haven't reported or rarely report. This has led to Australia being controlled by political parties that are nothing more than organised crime gangs who are systematically stealing $billions from the public via government "tenders" and "grants".

You won't hear the old media say this because the old media owners are involved with their snouts in the government trough. You only have to look at the grants, reduction in fees and the amount the old media companies made from Jobkeeper to see how much the old media companies have profited from a corrupt government they help protect.

Two other articles well worth reading which show how media companies have profited from the Morrison government are:

"How Billionaires Rupert Murdoch and Kerry Stokes will profit off the poor during the Coronavirus Crisis" published on the 1st of August 2020 and:

"Federal Treasurer Josh Frydenberg fraudulently gave his best mate, Seven's Ryan Stokes, at least $47 million of the taxpayer funded Jobkeeper" published on the 16th of November.

I think the only solution, until someone comes up with a better solution, is to vote as many independents into parliament as possible to give them the balance of power.

At the time of writing this book, February 2022, the federal election has to be held by May 2022 and Prime Minister Scott Morrison and his government has to go because all they are focused on is stealing as much money from the public as they can before they are booted out.

And if Morrison and his government go that means we will end up with a Labor Party government with Anthony Albanese as Prime Minister.

Irrespective of how honest Anthony Albanese may or may not be there are many people in the Labor Party who are waiting for their opportunity to commit the same level of fraud the current government and politicians are committing. And Australia can't afford that anymore so that is why we need independents in the lower house and Senate to try and make sure the fraud and theft of the public's money is stopped.

This book clearly does not cover all the corruption and alleged corruption of the 5 Prime Ministers because it would be over a million pages long if it covered it all.

References and videos

In the book, I have reprinted numerous articles from my website Kangaroo Court of Australia and the references used in the articles. The links to numerous articles, court judgments and transcripts etc. are in the articles on my website. So, please visit the website and search for the articles to use those links and watch the videos.